H. NORM/

Bestselling Author of Commu

2 in 1 collection

Bringing Out the Best

in Your

Marriage

Includes Two Books

Bringing Out the Best
in Your Husband

AND

Bringing Out the Best
in Your Wife

BETHANYHOUSE

a division of Baker Publishing Group
Minneapolis, Minnesota

Published by Bethany House Publishers
11400 Hampshire Avenue South
Bloomington, Minnesota 55438
www.bethanyhouse.com

Bethany House Publishers is a division of
Baker Publishing Group, Grand Rapids, Michigan

Bethany House edition published 2015
ISBN 978-0-7642-1642-8

Previously published by Regal Books.
This work is a compilation of the following titles:
  Bringing Out the Best in Your Husband © 2010 by H. Norman Wright
  Bringing Out the Best in Your Wife © 2010 by H. Norman Wright

Printed in the United States of America

Library of Congress Control Number: 2014956517

15   16   17   18   19   20   21   7   6   5   4   3   2   1

Contents

Book One

Includes Small-Group Study Questions

Bringing Out the Best in Your Husband

BETHANYHOUSE
a division of Baker Publishing Group
Minneapolis, Minnesota

You Are Called to Be an **Encourager**

"THANK YOU FOR BELIEVING IN ME." These are the words that say it all—words that make all the difference in a man's life! Whenever a husband responds in this way, his wife is fulfilling her calling.

When singer Kenny Rogers sang lyrics with the message, "She believes in me . . . yes, she believes in me," he gave credit where credit is due—to a wife who sought to bring out the best in her man.

When is the last time the man in your life turned to you and said, "Thank you for believing in me" or "Thank you for bringing out the best in me" or "It's your encouragement that makes my life different"? If you haven't heard similar words lately, read what these husbands say about how their wives bring out the best in them:

> My wife encourages me by making herself available to help me with details I miss when I am under pressure because of my urgent projects. She makes sure that her schedule allows her to be a part of my life. I am able to trust her in everything. She is committed to building up our marriage. She shows a genuine interest in what is important in my life, even if it isn't an interest of hers. What I desire from her is encouragement, and she's doing it.

H. NORMAN WRIGHT

She calls me several times a week at work to see how I am doing and to tell me that she has faith in me. That is so helpful, especially if I am struggling that day. She also calls to share her trials to give me a chance to encourage her. This in turn encourages me, because it makes me feel like she really cares about what I have to say. That makes me feel like she needs me. She's helped me become who I am today.

She understands my physical pain, supports me with her energy and does what she can to take over some of the things I do to make life easier for me. She supports decisions I've made and helps in implementing and carrying out the course of action we've chosen. She's there to talk to and voice her opinion. We can talk about most things in an analytical way.

My wife has been doing at least three things that I can think of to help me grow. Every time I do something that according to her was done very well, she speaks positive remarks regarding these things. For instance, when I preach, she tells me how well she thinks I presented the message. When I've not done well, she makes me remember that I can do it well. She helps me not to be discouraged by telling me she is sure that I will do better next time. To help celebrate my successes, she initiates a great night of lovemaking. That's a wonderful experience.

My wife encourages me by wanting to spend time with me and going places I like to go (art shows, ball games, movies, and so on). She stays busy on her own, doing something almost all the time (chores, time with kids). That's nice because I stay busy with other things or help with some of the same, and so the house runs smoothly without either of us being upset or critical of the other. She meets all my desires and needs in intimate ways. It's satisfying and something I look forward to. We talk 15 minutes to an hour every evening, and she has both a listening ear and affirming responses, as well as an open and honest way about her. She is complimentary, faithful, loyal, dependable and committed to making the marriage and family work. And our relationship is not a competition.

I've not always heard positive responses when I've asked men how their wives bring out the best in them. Some men lament a lack of encouragement from their wives:

At the present time, my wife doesn't do much in the way of encouragement. I don't know if she doesn't want to or maybe I am not letting her. We have each other, we are both newly saved, we do talk about the Bible, and that is encouraging. I guess I would like to hear her say she loves me. She only says it if I do. So I say it a lot more. When I have a bad day, I would like to relax. I just want to be supported in some of my dreams. She is the best part of my life. I just want to learn how to encourage her better too.

My wife does not encourage me with words. I am verbal and I do need that. I wish she would come and welcome me after I walk through the door at the end of the day.

I wish she would say she is proud of me and that I do a good job. I wish she would truly grant me forgiveness when I confess a wrong to her and ask for it. A hug or an unexpected kiss on the cheek from her would encourage me greatly. I have been frustrated with her words and actions in the past, and we cannot seem to overcome that. I have never been unfaithful, but I might as well have had an affair. We have been counseled. The advice has been to give it time; let her see God changing me; love her as Christ loved the church. I am trying to do that. I have come to the conclusion that I can do anything for her. I hope the Lord changes her heart this year.

There is no present encouragement. None! Her occasional praise for acceptably performed manual tasks is no encouragement whatsoever. I would be thrilled if she would simply acknowledge the legitimacy of my career and stop discouraging me from pursuing it. I would probably pass out from joy if she would go a step further and offer to seek ways in which I can pursue my calling with less impact on our family life.

Your husband's need for encouragement is a real need, and he desires to receive it from you. To a great extent, encouragement is the way to bring out the best in your husband. In a sense, it's like being his cheerleader.

ENCOURAGEMENT DEFINED

Through encouragement, every woman is given a power that can bring about change, growth and the fulfillment of potential in her husband. But it's difficult to be an encourager if you don't understand what encouragement really means.

To be an encourager, you need to have an attitude of optimism. The *American Heritage Dictionary* offers one of the better definitions of the word "optimist." It's a "tendency or disposition to expect the best possible outcome, or to dwell on the most hopeful aspect of a situation." When this is your attitude or perspective, you'll be able to encourage others. Encouragement is "to inspire; to continue on a chosen course; to impart courage or confidence."

Encouragement is sometimes thought of as praise and reinforcement, but it's also much more than that. Praise is limited; it's a verbal reward. It emphasizes competition, it has to be earned, and it is often given for being the best. Encouragement, however, is freely given. It can involve noticing what others take for granted and affirming something that others notice but may never think of mentioning. Bruce Larson shared this experience:

> Early one morning, I had to catch a plane from Newark, New Jersey, to Syracuse, New York, having returned late the previous night from leading one conference and on my way to another.
>
> I was tired. I had not budgeted my time wisely, and I was totally unprepared for the intense schedule before me. After rising early and hastily eating breakfast, I drove to the airport in a mood that was anything but positive. By the time the plane took off, I felt so sorry for myself.
>
> Sitting on the plane with an open notebook in my lap, I prayed, "O God, help me. Let me get some-

thing down here that will be useful to your people in Syracuse."

Nothing came. I jotted down phrases at random, feeling worse by the moment, and more and more guilty. Such a situation is a form of a temporary insanity. It denies all that we know about God Himself and His ability to redeem any situation.

About halfway through the brief flight, a stewardess came down the aisle, passing out coffee. All the passengers were men, as women have too much sense to fly at seven o'clock in the morning. As the stewardess approached my seat, I heard her exclaim, "Hey! Someone is wearing English Leather aftershave lotion. I can't resist a man who wears English Leather. Who is it?"

Eagerly I waved my hand and announced, "It's me."

The stewardess immediately came over and sniffed my cheek, while I sat basking in this sudden attention and appreciating the covetous glances from passengers nearby.

All through the remainder of the flight the stewardess and I maintained a cheerful banter each time she passed my seat. She would make some comment, and I would respond gaily. Twenty-five minutes later, when the plane prepared to land, I realized that my temporary insanity had vanished. Despite the fact that I had failed in every way—in budgeting my time, in preparation, in attitude—everything had changed. I was freshly aware that I loved God and that He loved me in spite of my failure.

What is more, I loved myself, the people around me and the people who were waiting for me in Syracuse. I was like the Gadarene demoniac after Jesus touched him: clothed in my right mind and seated at the feet of Jesus. I looked down at the notebook in my lap and found a page full of ideas that could prove useful throughout the weekend.

God, I mused, *how did this happen?* It was then that I realized that someone had entered my life and turned a key. It was just a small key, turned by a very unlikely person. But that simple act of affirmation, that undeserved and unexpected attention, had got me back into the stream.[1]

Encouragement is recognizing your husband as having worth and dignity even though he's imperfect. It means paying attention to him when he's sharing with you. It means listening to him in a way that lets him know he's being listened to. When a husband feels encouraged, he does his best.

THE ART OF LISTENING

The road to a person's heart is through the ear. Men and women today have few people who really listen to them. When someone else is talking, most of us are often more concerned about what we are going to say when the other person stops talking. This is a violation of Scripture. James tells us—men and women alike—to "be quick to listen" (Jas. 1:19). Proverbs 18:13 states, "He who answers a matter before he hears [the facts], it is folly and shame to him" (*NASB*).

While many of us have outgoing circuits, our incoming circuits are clogged. When one man was asked what his wife could do to bring out the best in him, he said, "Listen—listen without being judgmental or biased. Listen and be accepting. Listen just to understand me. Listen to me instead of criticizing me."

This requires listening not only with your ears but also with your eyes. My profoundly retarded son, Matthew, only had a few words in his vocabulary. My wife, Joyce, and I weren't sure if there was any meaning to those words. So we learned to listen to what he could not say by watching what he did and how he moved and for flickering eye movements that indicated the onset of a seizure. Matthew taught me to listen in a new way that helped me better minister to the people I counsel.

Not only do most of us need to learn how to listen to others, but we also need to keep in mind that how we listen needs to be tailored to the person speaking. Men and women have different listening styles, so it helps to understand what those differences are. Women tend to give more response and feedback while they are listening. These responses aren't necessarily agreement; they usually mean, "I'm with you" or "I understand" or "I'm connecting with you." Men, however, not only say less when they listen, but their feedback usually means, "I agree with you." Have you run into this difference in the way men and women give feedback when they listen? Most women have. They learn that when they are listening to a man, he may not need as much feedback from them as a woman would. When they listen quietly to a man, he may respond with words like, "Thanks for really listening to me. It helps me keep my mind on track when I'm not interrupted."

Poor listening skills have an impact on husbands more than many wives realize. One of the greatest longings of any person is to be listened to. Therefore, the gift of being a good listener is one of the most healing gifts we can give another person. For a man, what takes away from that gift of listening is when a woman gives unsolicited advice or thinks about what she is going to say while he is talking, and then interrupts or finishes his sentences for him. Other actions that take away from the gift of listening are squelching feelings with reassurances or taking the conversation off on a tangent, away from what he has said.

True encouragement combines the art of listening with validation that what your husband is doing or saying makes sense. It's letting him know, "You matter to me." When you encourage your husband, you respect him as well. You rephrase negatives to positives by discovering the constructive elements in situations, such as identifying his strengths and focusing on his efforts and contributions.[2]

This means that you find something of value to recognize when everybody else has despaired! Encouragement builds up your husband. It focuses on any resource that can be turned into an asset or strength.

Encouragement also means that you expect the best out of him. Consider what happened to this young man because his high school principal expected something more from him:

I remember vividly the day we had a school assembly. Three buddies and I went out behind the school auditorium. We all lit up. We knew we were safe: everyone else was in the assembly. And then, who should come around the corner but the principal. We were caught red-handed. My friends took off in three directions and left me just standing there. The principal collared me and dragged me down the hall in front of the auditorium just as the assembly was letting out. I thought I was going to die. Hundreds of kids saw me in this humiliating situation.

He took me into his office and chewed me out royally. It felt as if it lasted forever. Maybe it was only ten or fifteen minutes. I couldn't wait to get out of there. From that time on, I hated this guy. I waited for him to nail my buddies, but he never did. He knew who they were, but he did nothing. One day I saw him in the hall, and I asked why he hadn't gone after them. It wasn't fair that I was singled out.

Instead of giving me an answer there, he grabbed me by the collar and dragged me back into his office. He sat me down, but the chewing out didn't even last a minute this time. I'll never forget what he said. "I wish your friends the best. I don't know what's going to happen to them, but you could be somebody. I expect more of you than this. You're coasting through life. When are you going to do something with what you've got?" He turned around and walked out. I felt like I had been slapped across the face. He was right; I was coasting. And there is only one direction you can coast—down.

I was a junior at that time. I started working a little bit in my classes and made a new group of friends. My senior year I had an *A* average. I had been getting Cs and Ds before. I decided I wanted to go to college, but when I applied, I couldn't get in. My grades were too bad in a previous term. My principal wrote a letter of recommendation on my behalf, and in response the university agreed to admit me on a probationary status. I chose the field I did because of this man. He became like a mentor, like a second father to me.

Two years ago, I gave the eulogy at his funeral. I'll never forget him. I will always be different because of him. He gave me something to live up to.[3]

We live in a mistake-oriented culture. We've become skilled as flaw finders. In contrast, giving encouragement is not a deficit-oriented approach. To be an encourager you need to go counter to our culture and not be "conformed to this world." Would the man or men in your life say that you are more equipped to point out mistakes, weaknesses or liabilities rather than strengths? Your answer speaks volumes!

TRUE ENCOURAGEMENT SHOWS ACCEPTANCE

Encouragement and acceptance often go hand in hand. This story from the past dramatically illustrates what encouragement and acceptance can do for a man:

Peter Foster was a Royal Air Force pilot. These men [pilots] were the cream of the crop of England—the brightest, healthiest, most confident and dedicated, and often the most handsome men in the country. When they walked the streets in their decorated uniforms, the population treated them as gods. All eyes turned their way. Girls envied those who were fortunate enough to walk beside a man in Air Force blue.

However, the scene in London was far from romantic, for the Germans were attacking relentlessly. Fifty-seven consecutive nights they bombed London. In waves of 250, some 1,500 bombers would come each evening and pound the city.

The RAF Hurricanes and Spitfires that pilots like Foster flew looked like mosquitoes pestering the huge German bombers. The Hurricane was agile and effective, yet it had one fatal design flaw. The single propeller engine was mounted in front, a scant foot or so from the cockpit, and the fuel lines snaked alongside the cockpit toward the engine. In a direct hit, the cockpit would erupt into an inferno of flames. The pilot could eject, but in the one or two seconds it took him to find the lever, heat would melt off every feature of his face: his nose, his eyelids, his lips, often his cheeks.

These RAF heroes many times would undergo a series of 20 to 40 surgeries to refashion what once was their face. Plastic surgeons worked miracles, yet what remained of the face was essentially a scar.

Peter Foster became one of those "downed pilots." After numerous surgical procedures, what remained of his face was indescribable. The mirror he peered into daily couldn't hide the facts. As the day for his release from the hospital grew closer, so did Peter's anxiety about being accepted by his family and friends.

He knew that one group of airmen with similar injuries had returned home only to be rejected by their wives and girlfriends. Some of the men were divorced by wives who were unable to accept this new outer image of their husbands. Some men became recluses, refusing to leave their houses.

In contrast, there was another group who returned home to families who gave loving assurance of acceptance and continued worth. Many became executives and professionals, leaders in their communities.

Peter Foster was in this second group. His girlfriend assured him that nothing had changed except a few millimeters' thickness of skin. She loved him, not just his facial membrane, she assured him. The two were married just before Peter left the hospital.

"She became my mirror," Peter said of his wife. "She gave me a new image of myself. Even now, regardless of how I feel, when I look at her she gives me a warm, loving smile that tells me I am OK," he tells confidently.[4]

Time and time again we hear about the positive effect of an encouraging mother upon her son. I remember hearing an interview one day with Scott Hamilton, who has become a household name in professional ice-skating. During the 1992 Winter Olympics, Scott served as a commentator for the ice-skating events. During his time on TV, he shared about his special relationship with his mother, who died prior to his winning an Olympic gold medal. He said, "The first time I skated in the U.S. Nationals, I fell five times. My mother gave me a big hug and said, 'It's only your first National. It's no big deal.' My mother always let me be me. Three years later, I won my first National. She never said 'You can do better' or 'Shape up.' She just encouraged me."

Another man said, "My mom was a very supportive person. She believed in what I could do even when I didn't. Oh, she gave her opinion and lots of advice, but without being judgmental. And she cared about me as a person, not just about what I did or could do. In time, I felt that I could do anything I set out to tackle. But the best thing she ever gave me was her unconditional love."

Encouragement means showing faith in your husband and his potential. You encourage by believing in him without the evidence that he is believable.

Perhaps you have a dream for your husband. You're able to see things that he can't see, such as an untapped potential. Have you ever heard of the four-eyed fish? It's an odd-looking creature to say the least. It's a fish native to the equatorial waters of the Western Atlantic region. Anableps is the technical name of this fish. (Just don't name one of your children Anableps!) It means, "Those that look upward" because of their unusual eye structure. This unique creature has two-tiered eyes. The upper and lower halves of each eyeball operate independently and have separate corneas and irises. If you were to confront one in its natural habitat, you would see him with his upper eyes protruding above the surface of the water. This helps him search for food as well as identify enemies in the air.

Now remember, this fish also has lower eyes. These eyes stay focused in the water in the manner of most fish. On one hand, the fish navigates in the water like other fish. But the Anableps has the advantage of seeing what other fish can't see, because of its upper eyes. They see in both worlds. If you were like this, having four eyes, two for seeing what actually is and two for seeing what might be, you would be an unusual encourager indeed![5]

John Maxwell, in his book *Be a People Person*, says that we need to anticipate that others will do their best. "When working with people, I always try to look at them not as they are but as what they can be. By anticipating that the vision will become real, it's easy for me to encourage them as they stretch. Raise your anticipation level, and you raise their achievement level."[6]

Perhaps the best way to describe encouragement is through the example of gardening. I've raised flowers and vegetables for years. Some years were good, others I'd rather forget! At times I've raised tomatoes. There's a right way to raise tomatoes and a wrong way. The right way is to make sure you have good soil with plenty of nutrients. You need water, cultivation and fertilizers in the right amounts. You also need to stake the plant or use round wire cages for them to grow on. They need this support, or their branches break. Sometimes you need to put up a protective cover and, above all, watch out for insects, especially tomato worms.

After you've done all this you can take several weeks off to do nothing, right? No, you have to care for tomato plants consistently rather than sporadically, or you won't produce a crop.

Giving encouragement is like caring for tomato plants. It takes work—constant, consistent work—for it to be effective.[7] When you're an encourager, you're like a prospector or a deep-sea diver looking for hidden treasure. Every husband has pockets of underdeveloped resources within him. Your task is to search for those pockets, discover them and then expand them. As you discover the strengths in your husband, you'll begin to focus on them. You'll look at them and care about what you discover. At first, what you discover may be rough and imperfect. Talent scouts and scouts for professional sports teams do this all the time. They see undeveloped raw talent and ability, but they have the wisdom to see beyond that. They look into the future and see what could happen if all the potential were cultivated and developed. Is this the way you see your husband?

The following poem captures this idea in a unique way:

God, through the years
Of our married life,
You have been holding a crown
About ten feet above my husband's head.
He was simply too busy
Loving and serving to notice.
But I saw it.
Not only did I see it—
I watched him grow into it.[8]

Encouraging your husband means that you honor and respect him because you believe in him; many times your encouragement will help your husband live in such a way that he is worthy of being honored.

I entered sports late in life. I took up racquetball in my early forties. One of the reasons I kept at it was a young pastor who worked with me the first few months. At first, I was a bit discouraged, especially when I noticed the proficiency of some of the younger men. But Tom was patient, and he was excited whenever I did something right. He encouraged me; he believed in my ability; he saw me for what I could become, and that made so much difference. Almost 20 years later, I still played. I gained confidence, and some of those younger guys didn't beat me anymore!

BE A CATALYST FOR CHANGE

You are like the refiner's fire. What you notice and encourage can be refined in a positive way. Any movement that you see headed in a healthy, positive direction needs your attention and reinforcement.[9] You're saying, "Go for it. You can do it!"

One of the character qualities that enable a person to be an encourager is gentleness. This quality means that when you discover where another person is vulnerable or sensitive, you're not hard, harsh or forceful with him. When you discover a tender, sensitive place in your husband, you protect it rather then step on it. As you consider ways of encouraging your husband, ask yourself these questions:

- Am I gentle especially with those sensitive areas?
- Am I treating him the way that I would want to be treated?
- Am I building hope in his life?
- Does he feel safe around me with those sensitive areas?

Scottish poet Sir Walter Scott described the power of gentle words in his poem "Lord of the Isles":

O! Many a shaft at random sent
Finds mark the anchor never meant!
And many a word, at random spoken
May soothe, or wound, a heart that's broken!

A wife once shared with me how she helped her husband take some steps to move forward in his life. She said it would have been so easy to harp and criticize, which would have had a negative effect upon their relationship. She knew her husband had the ability to maintain his body in a healthy way, as well as do the work to complete his college degree, if she encouraged him in the right way. Here's how she did it.

> I worked hard to make good meals that were low in fat. I made only enough for two servings, so there weren't mounds of food sitting on the table begging to be eaten. I never bought junk food. My husband loves popcorn, and that became his snack food.
>
> Second, my husband is an excellent athlete who enjoys exercising when he has the time. He especially enjoys competitive sports. Although membership at a gym is expensive, I fully supported his doing this. Although he isn't fond of fast walking, I frequently asked him if he would walk with me. He called these "love walks."
>
> Last winter, he decided he wanted a Nordic Track. For months we looked through the paper trying to find a used one, but finally I encouraged him to buy a new one. I'm glad that we did it—he has gotten a lot of use out of it. Now his weight doesn't fluctuate twenty pounds every year, and he's in good physical condition.
>
> The next area of change was in my husband's education. My husband worked full-time during his college years, and it was impossible for him to finish his degree. Work always took priority over studies.
>
> After we had been married awhile, he was thinking about a job change but didn't feel confident that he was marketable without a college degree.

We looked into a college program especially designed for working people. It was an intensive and expensive program that guaranteed a degree in a little over a year. At first my husband didn't want to do it. The money, the time and the stress seemed overwhelming.

I had taught some college courses and assured him I would help him every step of the way. I explained that we could finance his education if we kept to a strict budget and put off having children for another year. I promised to do most of the household chores and other responsibilities so he would have time to study.

He entered the program. I typed papers, brainstormed projects with him, helped him do library research, quizzed him at test time, and cheered him on through the entire year.

He graduated summa cum laude! He has a degree and a good job. I don't believe he would have pursued this degree at this point in his life if we hadn't been married. My very presence in his life motivated him, because we were building a future together. I also think that my practical support eased the stress and struggle of that year. I'm thrilled to see his success.[10]

Perhaps you're like some wives I've talked to, or I should say, wives who have talked to me! They say:

"Why do I need to be the one doing all the encouraging? I need it as much as he does, and I'm starving for some."

"This sounds just like what I've been hearing for years. Women have to give, give and give. Some husbands we're nurturing, but some are spoiled. They're catered to all the time. And if I do more of this, he'll just expect more!"

"This sounds one-sided to me. Many of us women go through life starving for some need fulfillment. Why don't you work with husbands to get them to be more caring?"

These are good, honest questions. I have two responses.

First, this is *not* a book directed to men. It's written to encourage women to bring out the best in the men in their lives. If it were written to men, it would probably be even more direct! It's true that husbands have a great need to grow and develop as encouragers of their wives. In a marital relationship, a man often functions as a thermostat. He affects the temperature of the relationship. Most of us men grew up emotionally handicapped and relationally deficient, and I include myself in that description. We have much to learn! And we can and do learn. But there are other books and helps expressly written for men, including the companion to this book, *Bringing Out the Best in Your Wife*. But the book you are holding in your hands right now is basically for women only.

Second, as Christians, none of us really has a choice about whether we encourage others or not. It's not our decision to make. Scripture states that others will know that we are Christians by our love. One of the ways we reflect that love is by being an encourager to others. Look at what God's Word tells us to do.

In Acts 18:27, the word "encourage" means "to urge forward or persuade." In 1 Thessalonians 5:11, it means "to stimulate another person to the ordinary duties of life."

Consider the words found in 1 Thessalonians 5:14: "And we earnestly beseech you, brethren, admonish (warn and seriously advise) those who are out of line [the loafers, the disorderly, and the unruly]; encourage the timid and fainthearted, help and give your support to the weak souls, [and] be very patient with everybody [always keeping your temper]" (*AMP*).

Scripture uses a variety of words to describe both our involvement with others as well as the actual relationship. The word "urge" (*parakaleo*) means "to beseech or exhort." It is intended to create an environment of urgency to listen and respond to a directive. It is a mildly active verb. Paul used it in Romans 12:1 and in 1 Corinthians 1:4.

The word "encourage" (*paramutheomai*) means "to console, comfort and cheer up." This process includes elements of understanding, redirecting of thoughts and a general shifting of focus from the negative to the positive. In the context of the verse, it refers to the timid ("fainthearted" in the *KJV*) individual who is discouraged and ready to give up. It's a matter of loaning your faith and hope to the person until his own hope and faith develops.

The word "help" (*anechomai*) primarily contains the idea of "taking interest in, being devoted to, rendering assistance or holding up spiritually and emotionally." It is not so much an active involvement as a passive approach. It suggests the idea of coming alongside a person and supporting him. In the context of 1 Thessalonians 5:14, it seems to refer to those who are incapable of helping themselves.

First Thessalonians 5:11 states, "Therefore encourage one another and build each other up, just as in fact you are doing." Hebrews 3:13 states that we are to "encourage one another daily." In the setting of this verse, encouragement is associated with protecting the believer from callousness. Hebrews 10:25 says, "Let us not give up meeting together . . . but let us encourage one another." This time, the word means to keep someone on his feet who, if left to himself, would collapse. Your encouragement of others, and in the context of this book, your encouragement of your husband, serves like the concrete pilings of a structural support. One of my favorite verses is Proverbs 12:25: "Anxiety in a man's heart weighs it down, but a good word makes it glad" (*NASB*).

The Word of God is very clear about what you are to do. To be a consistent encourager to your husband, you will need to reflect the character qualities listed in 1 Corinthians 13. Here they are, amplified in a unique way:

- *Patient* (you are tolerant of frailties, imperfections and shortcomings of your husband)
- *Kind* (you are tender and thoughtful toward your husband)
- *Not jealous* (of genuine friendships with others or of the special gifts and talents of your husband)
- *Not boastful* (about personal appearance or achievements in an attempt to compete with your husband)
- *Not arrogant* (you are not disdainful of your mate's looks or his achievements; you do not belittle your husband)
- *Not rude* (you are not inconsiderate of your husband's needs or feelings)

- *Not insistent on your own way* (you are willing to compromise and consider your husband's needs and interests)
- *Not irritable* (you do not snap at your husband; you are approachable)
- *Not resentful* (you do not hold grudges; you are forgiving toward your husband)
- *Not rejoicing in wrong* (you do not delight in your husband's misfortunes; you do not keep score or tally perceived wrongs)
- *Rejoicing in right* (you are truthful; you do not try to conceal things from your husband)
- *Bearing all things* (you support your husband in his times of struggle)
- *Believing all things* (you have confidence in your husband)
- *Hoping in all things* (you do not wallow in pessimism about your relationship; you keep a positive attitude)
- *Enduring in all things* (you do not give in to the pressures of life; you are willing to stand by your husband when he's having personal struggles)[11]

One husband described why he felt encouraged by his wife. He said, "I was reading the Scriptures one day and found this passage. It summed it all up better than I could say it."

A good woman is hard to find, and worth far more than diamonds. Her husband treats her without reserve, and never has reason to regret it. Never spiteful, she treats him generously all her life long (Prov. 31:10-12, *THE MESSAGE*).

Hopefully, you are already a woman who is "worth far more than diamonds," a woman who consistently and persistently encourages her husband. But if you could do better, take heart in honestly reflecting on the questions found at the end of each chapter. They are offered as a catalyst to open the eyes and ears of your understanding and help you modify the way you communicate with your husband. If you do the work, the results will amaze you!

DISCOVER THE ENCOURAGER IN YOU

1. When was the last time (if ever) your husband thanked you for believing in him? What were the circumstances?

2. What is more typical of you—to tell your husband what he does wrong or what he does right? What behavior of his pushes your button the most?

3. Think back to conversations that have made a difference in your relationship with your husband, for better or for worse. What specific words or phrases came up repeatedly when you spoke to your husband in a negative way; spoke to him in a positive way?

4. Hypothetically speaking, if you deposited a dollar in a bank account for every time you've complained to your husband about his speech or actions, would you be able to pay for a new luxury car, a new wardrobe, or only a bag of groceries? What words or phrases, if banned from your speech, would bring that bank account to a zero balance?

5. Review the bulleted list of 15 character qualities that define love (from 1 Corinthians 13:4-7). Choose the characteristic most problematic in your relationship with your husband. If you don't already write in a prayer journal, buy an unlined journal book to keep handy in whatever place you like to sit and spend time with God. Using the journal, write a prayer, asking God to develop in you the 1 Corinthians 13 character quality you would most like to strengthen. Consider what kind of speech or actions would reflect that quality to your husband. (This will be a spiritual exercise to do over again and again as God shows you new ways to love and encourage your husband and empowers you to do it.)

The Discouraged Husband
(He's Not a Pretty Sight)

WHAT HAPPENS WHEN A HUSBAND DOES NOT RECEIVE ENCOUR-AGEMENT FROM HIS WIFE? He ends up feeling hopeless, helpless and handcuffed to his situation in life.

This husband sits in the chair in front of the TV. You can't tell from the expression on his face whether he's actually watching it or just staring into space. Is he awake? Is he in a daze? Is he even breathing? He's oblivious to the world around him. His body is in the chair, but that's about all. The rest of him seems to be elsewhere. He has things to do and many responsibilities. He used to be alert, creative, functional, productive and enjoyable to be around. Not now. Something has happened, and it can happen to any man.

For some, this state of being is occasional or periodic. For others it's a daily routine that can come and go. The condition? Discouragement. You know what I'm talking about. You've been there. We all have.

What happens when a husband is not encouraged? He feels stuck, immobilized and impotent. He can end up seeing himself as a loser, unable to solve problems or find solutions to the challenges of life. His confidence in his own abilities is off-site somewhere. Life is unfair, and the scales are constantly tipped against him. Entertaining such a pessimistic point of view can set him up for failure.

Anyone who is discouraged makes certain assumptions. Unfortunately, these assumptions are not favorable. A man who is discouraged assumes that he's inadequate, a failure and has very little worth. He believes others see him this way as well.

Some men live in a constant condition of discouragement. They want to be affirmed, validated, recognized, respected and have their accomplishments appreciated. They want to feel they've made a contribution to life. But when they don't feel this way, watch out. It's not a pretty sight! Discouraged husbands tend to start looking for ways to get all of the above, but their methods can be counterproductive. They can actually bring about more failure while they're pursuing the desired affirmation.

DIAGNOSIS: ACUTE DISCOURAGEMENT

A discouraged child or adult, who isn't being recognized and given sufficient attention, often becomes overbearing, loud and even obnoxious. Such behavior doesn't work; it just invites rejection. Intensified attention-getting efforts only bring more rejection.

It may be that the signs of discouragement are all around your husband, but you can't see them. You've labeled his behavior something else. Sure, there could be other reasons for these symptoms. There could even be some serious disorder; but for now, consider these as SOD—"signs of discouragement." Unfortunately, when you see these signs in your man, the last response you want to give is encouragement! You're turned off. But don't stay there!

Let's look at some behavioral symptoms of acute discouragement.

Obnoxious Behavior

It's true that some husbands need an audience—constantly. They have to be the center of attention. It doesn't matter whether it's positive or negative attention. They want all eyes focused on them. If there's no audience, there's no show. They need the attention of others to affirm themselves. Some of their actions could be bizarre, inappropriate or even shocking. That doesn't matter to them as long as they have your attention. Any reaction is better than none.

I've seen some husbands who as children were the class clowns. It didn't matter that others laughed at them or didn't think much of them. You may have been drawn to such a man because he made you laugh. But everyone who laughs reinforces the attention-getting behavior and keeps him focused on getting attention in unhealthy ways.

What do *you* tend to encourage in your husband by *your* attention? Healthy positive responses? Or unhealthy, inappropriate ones?

A Need to Control

Some husbands (and you may be thinking, *all men!*) have an excessive need for power and control. They seem to feel secure or reassured only when they're in the driver's seat. Being in control gives them a sense of encouragement they aren't receiving from others. After all, who feels like encouraging someone who overrides or dominates? The greater a man's need for power and control, the greater his hidden feelings of inadequacy and inferiority.

When such a husband is in the driver's seat, he feels important, even adequate, for a little while. He may have been pampered as a child. Weren't we all to some degree? But into his adulthood he carried with him the belief that everyone else will do unto him as his parents did. So he lives with constant frustration, because the world doesn't operate that way. He intensifies his efforts for attention, leaving little room for behavior that would bring the encouragement and positive responses he wants.

EXAGGERATION OR OUTRIGHT LIES

Sometimes husbands use dishonesty to get attention. It's repugnant to most of us, which causes us to focus on the behavior rather than the cause. We all hate to be lied to. It breaks our trust, and we feel violated. And yet, a discouraged man may lie for several reasons. His encouragement container is running on empty, so he resorts to dishonesty. It's an easy way to gain attention. His prevailing rationalization is that the truth isn't that important, and he won't get much response if he's truthful. Listen to Jim's experience:

> Even after I married, I felt a bit left out. Everyone else seemed to have a life that was more significant or important. When others talked, people responded; but when I shared anything, it seemed boring. So I began to embellish just about everything. It worked. I learned how to point out accomplishments that really meant very little. But I got praise and encouragement. One day I got caught in these lies . . . by my wife. It was hard telling her how insignificant I felt. She was shocked. She thought since I was so quiet and easygoing, I felt secure. Little did she know. But how could she? I never told her.

PERFECTIONISM

Most of us don't equate perfectionism with a feeling of discouragement. But perfectionism is the great cover-up. It's a way to camouflage a wide variety of self-perceived weaknesses. Perfectionists live with the fear of failure, so they take steps to try to ensure that failure will never happen. They live in a self-imposed prison and can become their own worst enemy.

Their expectations for themselves and for you are unobtainable. They've got to have a safe, secure and predictable environment. Often they either do not receive much encouragement because they are difficult to live with, or they do not believe the encouragement they do receive. They'll point out their own mistakes that you're not even aware of. These are people who need affirmation for who they are rather than for their endless striving. They need encouragement for any interaction that others perceive as relaxed and normal. Because blame probably helped create this condition, they certainly don't need to be blamed for the way they are.

CLOSED-MINDED

Have you interacted with a man who was closed-minded? You know, the kind who wouldn't consider any other possibility and had an opinion for everything? The more closed-minded a man is, the more discouraged he may be. It's his way of trying to create a predictable, safe world. He doesn't want to change because that would be an admission that what he did or thought may have been wrong. He doesn't want to be wrong, so this is his way of avoiding greater discouragement.

UNUSUALLY SELF-PROTECTIVE

Some discouraged people go into a protective cocoon. They retreat from both the challenges and the interactions of life. They create a safe environment and only allow safe people to join them. They're just the opposite of the attention seekers. If anyone wants to compete with them, they avoid the situation. If they're encouraged or pressured by their wives to try to get ahead at work, they ignore the request. They're very compliant, agreeing with anyone and everyone. It's hard to know what they believe and what they stand for. It's true that some men are this way because of their personality bent; but often, a discouraged man views competition as just another experience where he will lose and someone else will be affirmed. He thinks, *Why risk it? It's not worth it.*

One of the frustrations many women face is dealing with a husband who won't take responsibility. A lack of initiative, avoidance and passive-aggressive responses can be a pattern for numerous reasons. But think about it for a moment. If you were discouraged, would you really want to take on responsibility? It's just another possibility to have something go wrong and be criticized.

When a discouraged husband does make a mistake, he's very adept at placing the blame on others. Sometimes this person lives by a rulebook. It's safer when he doesn't stray from the guidelines. Usually he avoids making decisions or judgments. Too much could go wrong. In some ways he appears rigid, inept and irresponsible because he fails to take ownership. It's very easy to fall into a trap of letting such a person become dependent upon you.

It's not surprising that a discouraged husband has a lack of confidence. We need to remember that discouraged people have little courage. They've lost what they had in the first place. So why would we expect them to reach out and try? When you're discouraged, your perception of life changes. You're not motivated to be a risk taker. Your belief and faith in yourself is low, and your need for others to believe in you is higher than usual. When you're discouraged, you don't expect success. You don't expect the best; you expect failure.

A 40-year-old man summed it up when he said, "I've been discouraged for some time. I'm discouraged about my job, my kids, what I've done with my life. . . . I know I've acted in some dumb ways, but I just don't know any other way to act when I'm this discouraged. There's probably something else I could do that's better, but I can't think of what it is, and nobody else is showing me. And that discourages me even more."

When your husband is discouraged, his main concern is not how to break out of the discouragement pattern but how to look good and secure, and not appear weak and inadequate.[1]

FAULTFINDING DESTROYS

Whether a man finds fault with others, or whether he's on the receiving end, the result is feelings of discouragement. Faultfinding is a common form of criticism and a favorite pastime of the perfectionist. Do you know why faultfinding is so destructive in any relationship?

Faultfinding *deeply wounds a husband*. Constant verbal and nonverbal criticism sends the message, "I don't accept you for who you are at this time in your life. You don't measure up, and I can't accept you until you do." In more than 40 years of counseling, I have heard multitudes of people in my office cry out in pain, "My spouse's criticism ripped me apart. I was made to feel like dirt. I never felt accepted, and I'm still looking for someone who will tell me I'm all right." Faultfinding also wounds you. The wounded person becomes afraid or angry and retaliates through overt or covert withdrawal, resentment or aggression.

Faultfinding really *doesn't change the person on the receiving end*. Though he may appear to change his behavior in response to criticism, his heart rarely changes. He may simply learn to cover his rebellious attitude with external compliance.

Faultfinding is also *contagious*. A faultfinding person teaches intolerance to the other person by example. Thus, the person learns to be critical and unaccepting of self and others.

Finally, faultfinding *accentuates negative traits and behaviors*. When you pay undue attention to a person's mistakes or irresponsible behaviors, you tend to reinforce them instead of eliminate them.[2]

FAULTFINDING'S IDENTICAL TWIN

Criticism is usually destructive, but it's interesting to hear critics say they're just trying to remold their partner into a better person by offering some constructive criticism. But too often criticism does not construct, it demolishes. It doesn't nourish a relationship, it poisons. And often the presentation is like this description: "There is one who speaks rashly like the thrusts of a sword" (Prov. 12:18, *NASB*).

Criticism that is destructive accuses, produces guilt, intimidates and is often an outgrowth of personal resentment.

BEWARE THE ZINGER

Criticism comes in many shapes and sizes. You've heard of "zingers," those lethal, verbal guided missiles. A zinger comes at you with a sharp point and a dull barb that catches the flesh as it goes in. The power of these sharp, caustic statements is seen when you realize that one zinger can undo 20 acts of kindness. That's right, 20! And husbands don't handle zingers very well.

A zinger has the power to negate many positive acts. Once a zinger has landed, the effect is similar to a radioactive cloud that settles on an area of what used to be prime farmland. The land is so contaminated by the radioactivity that even though seeds are scattered and plants are planted they fail to take root. Subsequently, they die out or are washed away by the elements. It takes decades for the contamination to dissipate. Kind acts or loving words following the placement of a zinger find a similar hostile soil. It may take hours before there is a receptivity or positive response to your positive overtures.[3]

INVALIDATION

Another form of criticism is invalidation. When invalidation exists, it destroys the effect of validation. Sometimes people get along and maintain their relationships without sufficient validation, but they cannot handle continual invalidation. This is yet another example of one negative comment canceling 20 acts of kindness.[4]

Invalidation is like a slow, fatal disease that, once established in a relationship, spreads and destroys the positive feelings. As one husband said, "The so-called friend I married became my enemy with unexpected attacks. I felt demeaned, put-down, and my self-esteem slowly crumbled. I guess that's why our fights escalated so much. I had to fight to survive." To keep love alive, keep criticism out of it. God's Word has something to say about this (see Rom. 14:13; Matt. 7:3-4).

Instead of being critical when a problem occurs, perhaps you could respond like the pilot in this story as described in the magazine *Flight Operations*. Bob Hoover, a famous test pilot and frequent performer at air shows, was returning to his home in Los Angeles from an air show in San Diego. At 300 feet in the air, both engines suddenly stopped. By deft maneuvering he managed to land the plane, but it was badly damaged.

Hoover's first act after the emergency landing was to inspect the airplane's fuel. Just as he suspected, the World War II propeller plane had been fueled with jet fuel rather than gasoline.

Upon returning to the airport, he asked to see the mechanic who had serviced his plane. The young man was sick with agony of his mistake. Tears streamed down his face as Hoover approached. He had almost caused the loss of a very expensive plane and could have caused the loss of three lives as well.

You can imagine Hoover's anger. One could have anticipated the tongue-lashing that this proud and precise pilot would unleash for the carelessness. But Hoover didn't scold the mechanic; he didn't even criticize him. Instead, he put his big arm around the man's shoulder and said, "To show you I'm sure that you'll never do this again, I want you to service my F51 tomorrow."[5]

Can you think of a time when you've responded to your husband in a similar way?

You can be a passive as well as active discourager. Passive discouragement comes through the lack of encouraging your husband. It's like making him exist in a vacuum. Direct criticism is active discouragement. You may not be a critical person, but everyone has complaints at some time or another; that's normal.

Complaints can be voiced in a way that won't stir up defensiveness and can actually be encouraging. For example, instead of focusing on what bothers you, talk more about what you would appreciate him doing. He's much more likely to hear you and consider your request if you speak in a positive way. Talking about what you don't like just reinforces the possibility of the undesirable behavior continuing with an even greater intensity. The principle of pointing toward what you would appreciate also conveys your belief that he is capable of doing what you have requested. Doing this consistently, along with giving praise and gratitude when he complies, will encourage him and could bring about change.

THE POWER OF POSITIVE REINFORCEMENT

The power of praise cannot be underestimated. I've seen this in children as well as adults. I've also seen this principle work in raising our golden retriever, Sheffield (not that I'm comparing people to dogs). Sheffield was trained in basics by the time he was four months old and learned to bring in the paper, take items back and forth to Joyce and me, "answered" the phone and learned to bring it to me, and picked up items off the floor and put them in the trash. All it took was ignoring the times when he didn't do it right and giving praise and hugs when he came through. He learned that we believed in his ability to accomplish what he had been trained to do.

I don't think people are much different in this respect. Affirming and encouraging responses can literally change a person's life, because we all want someone to believe in our capabilities. An unusual example of this is found in the Babemba tribe in southern Africa. When one of the tribal members has acted irresponsibly, he or she is taken to the center of the village. Everyone in the village stops work and gathers in a large circle around the person. In turn, each person, regardless of age, speaks to the person and recounts the good things he has done in his lifetime. All the positive incidents in the person's life, plus his good attributes, strengths and kindnesses, are recalled with accuracy and detail. Not one word about his problem behavior is ever mentioned.

This ceremony, which sometimes lasts several days, isn't complete until every positive expression has been given by those assembled. The person is literally flooded by positives. When the people are finished, the erring person is welcomed back into the tribe. Can you imagine how all this makes him feel about himself? Can you imagine his desire to continue to reflect those positive qualities?

Has there been a time when you've done something similar with your husband?

ACTS THAT DESTROY SELF-ESTEEM

Criticism is the initial negative response that opens the door for other destructive responses to follow. Criticism is different from complaining because it attacks the other person's personality and character, usually with blame. Most criticisms are over-generalized ("you always . . .") and accusatory (the word "you" is central). A great deal of criticism comes in the form of blame, with the word "should" being included.

CAMOUFLAGED CRITICISM

Criticism can be hidden under the camouflage of joking and humor. And when confronted about it, the person will avoid responsibility by saying, "I was just joking." It reminds me of the passage in Proverbs that says, "Like a madman who throws firebrands, arrows and death, so is the man who deceives his neighbor, and says, 'Was I not joking?' " (Prov. 26:18-19, *NASB*).

Some husbands are very adept at discouraging themselves. In fact, some are masters at it. They have found ingenious ways to keep themselves crippled and stuck.

But often a man is discouraged because of responses from others—often from those closest to him. Most of the ways of discouraging others are quite subtle. I don't know of too many who make it a point to discourage others purposely. But it happens. *What every husband needs is an abundance of encouraging responses and an absence of discouraging ones.* I'm this way, and fortunately, Joyce was such an encourager.

SUBTLE DOMINATION

How might a wife discourage her husband? You can dominate him (or try to), but domination stifles growth. It deadens initiative. It takes away the opportunity for others to take on responsibility, and to grow and mature. We can dominate others by always being there and giving our "strength" to help them.

Continuous statements like, "Let me do that" or "This is the way that goes" or "Honey, don't try. I'll get someone who's an expert on that" could contain the subtle message, "You'll mess it up; let me do it." Redoing tasks that your husband has done has several possible outcomes. It could convey to him it's never good enough for you. He could end up thinking, *Why put forth a lot of effort? She'll just redo it anyway if I mess it up. After a while, she'll quit asking.* It's possible for any of us to end up letting another person get away with halfhearted attempts keyed by our responses.

True encouragement means that we believe in the other person's potential to learn to do something adequately (perhaps not perfectly or our way). It also means having the patience to work with a person as he or she learns, while showing we believe in them. If you're a parent, you know how long it can take for your child to learn and refine a task. Whether you're dealing with a child or an adult, you want to work yourself out of a job by letting the other person do things that you're already proficient in doing.

You need to have trust and confidence in the other person's abilities. You could be saying right now, "Yes, but you don't know the man I'm dealing with." You're right, I don't, but you don't want to limit him by a belief that he can never be different than he is now!

INSENSITIVITY

Sometimes a wife can discourage her husband by her insensitivity. He's excited about something, and you show no interest. He wants you to do something with him, but you're too preoccupied with your tasks. He asks you how his new shirt and tie look, and the look on your face speaks volumes. If your husband suggests that you have your devotions together, you respond with, "Finally, after 10 years you come around. Well, who suggested that to you?"

SILENCE

Another way we discourage is by our silence. I've heard women say, "When I affirm or compliment him, all I get back is a grunt, so I've stopped." "If I encourage him it will just go to his head. His ego is over-inflated as it is." "I would think the satisfaction that he gets from what he does at work from others would be enough." "I don't know why my husband is always asking me, 'How did I do?' or 'What do you think?' I always like what he does and think it's great. You'd think he'd remember what I said the time before!"

Silence can be loud. It has its own sounds, its own volume. It often says, "I don't care," "You're not important," "I can't be bothered." Silence can hurt more than words.

Your man won't know what you believe and feel about him unless you tell him.

Remember, one of the biggest discouragements for a husband is the feeling that he has failed in something, or is responsible for a problem his wife has. A husband tends to assume that when his wife talks to him about her problems, the reason she does is because he's the culprit. So he becomes defensive or rattles off numerous solutions. He needs to hear that he isn't the cause, and all he needs to do is listen to you.

When you want his opinion, a hug, a kiss or just his attention, let him know. One husband said, "I feel so comfortable and relaxed in my marriage. We both do a lot for the other, but one of the biggest helps my wife gives me is disarming me in advance. She lets me know what she wants or needs when she talks to me, and I've learned through this not to assume or be defensive. If she needs to confront me when I've blown it, I can handle it so much better now because of the relationship we've worked out over the years. I really feel supported by her."

We've just talked about some of the more subtle ways that a wife can wound and discourage her husband. Now let's go a bit deeper and consider where discouragement for a man might actually begin.

FIVE BASIC NEEDS

The genesis of marital discouragement for a man can sometimes be traced to one or more of five basic areas being unfulfilled, as identified by Dr. Willard Harley. Many men struggle with needs fulfillment in five basic areas that men expect their wives to fulfill. Often the failure to meet those needs is based on ignorance of the needs rather than a refusal to fulfill them. We may live in a country that has a high literacy level, but many of us are basically illiterate about relationships and the fine art of understanding our mates. But there is no valid reason for married couples not to be fulfilled today.

Although Dr. Harley also identified a woman's basic unfulfilled needs, for the purposes of this book, we will only discuss what he relates about a man's basic areas of needs fulfillment. You'll notice that a couple of these needs overlap with the 10 intimacy needs described in the next section.

The first need should come as no surprise: Men cannot do without sexual fulfillment. The second need, however, isn't as recognized: Husbands want their wives to spend recreational time with them. Recreational compatibility is very important to men, and it must be carefully cultivated, because tastes vary.

Men tend to enjoy activities that involve more risk and adventure than women do. Men often fear that if their wives join them, their activities will be limited. When a wife pressures her husband to spend his spare time with family, it can build resentment. What works best for most couples is actually having his and her recreational activities but putting an emphasis on shared activities. My wife and I enjoy fishing together, but many times she encouraged me to go fishing with my friends on the more intensive rugged outings.[6]

A third need, according to Dr. Harley, is for the wife to be attractive. This doesn't mean she has to be beautiful, but she should strive to maintain the level of attractiveness she had when they married. Of course, this should apply to men as well. I have seen as many men as women let themselves go after they marry.

A fourth need is for peace and quiet. Moms need time to recoup, recharge and rebound—but so do dads. Couples need to discuss how to accomplish this so both partners are satisfied.

Too often this becomes a source of tension and argument in a marriage and degenerates into a pursue/withdraw conflict.

The fifth area of need is admiration. One man shared his thoughts well on this subject:

> Because of men's high need to accomplish, they are in need of more positive encouragement than most women seem to understand. I have observed some wives withholding praise from their husbands because they either thought their husbands did not need more praise or that others were doing a sufficient job already. One of the best gifts from God is a spouse who acknowledges, encourages and supports her partner as a natural habit. One of the blessings from my wife that has a great impact on me is when she speaks well of me to others. This is particularly true when she doesn't think I'm listening, or when I find out indirectly what she has said to someone. We all want to be well thought of, and when our wives become our "public relations managers" we experience honor from them, which is truly humbling.[7]

Men thrive on honest admiration from women. They desperately need recognition and encouragement. Both husbands and wives need to specifically identify their unique needs and make a point of sharing them with their mates.

Top 10 Intimacy Needs in Marriage

If you're married, consider these top 10 intimacy needs in a marriage. When these needs are met, both husband and wife usually realize satisfaction.

1. ATTENTION

Attention means thinking about the other person, focusing on him by listening with your eyes and your ears in addition to showing interest, concern and support. It's a bit like entering into the other person's world. What Paul said about the Body of Christ—the Church—applies also to marriage: "That there should be no division in the body, but that its parts should have equal concern for each other" (1 Cor. 12:25).

If you share with your husband a request for attention, say what you need, what your husband's attention will do for you and how it will improve the overall relationship. This way of speaking can be a form of encouragement because it shows that you believe he can do it. Above all, when talking about needing his encouragement, don't attack, indict or blame.

2. ACCEPTANCE

The best description I have heard of the quality of acceptance in love is more than 30 years old. "Acceptance," this source said, is "an unconditional commitment to an imperfect person." The man in your life is imperfect. You obviously know that. True acceptance requires deliberate, positive and ready reception. As Paul said, "*Accept* one another, then, just as Christ accepted you, in order to bring praise to God" (Rom. 15:7, emphasis added). How can you show acceptance to the man in your life?

3. APPRECIATION AND PRAISE

Each of us needs appreciation and praise. Appreciation is gratefulness that is verbalized. In most marriages, however, the norm is for a wife to take her husband for granted.

Make a list of every helpful or positive thing you can remember that your husband does or has done. Then enumerate the times you have shared your appreciation to him for each one. Too often what we remember and are aware of is what our partner has not done. We have to look for the positives and reinforce them with praise if we want them to continue. Marriages that are satisfying are those in which there are five times as many positive exchanges as there are negative. Remember what the apostle Paul said in 1 Corinthians 11:2: "I praise you for remembering me in everything and for holding to the teachings, just as I passed them on to you."

4. ENCOURAGEMENT
We've already spent a good deal of time on this subject, but it's helpful for you to see that it makes any list of basic human relationship needs.

5. SUPPORT
The need for support in intimacy is described in the Bible as bearing one another's burdens. This doesn't mean doing what you think is best, but discovering exactly how your husband would like to be supported. It can also mean giving him a hug rather than a solution; putting dinner on hold so he can unwind for a half-hour; reflecting on and clarifying his responses rather than saying you are too tired to talk.

A counselee shared with me how his wife blessed him one day through her caring support and friendship. Phil, a man in his thirties, had been under intense pressure and stress for several weeks. His new job was a disaster because delays and unreasonable demands from his supervisor were wearing him down. Added to this, Phil and his wife had moved 2,000 miles away from home to take the job, and both sets of parents continued to express their displeasure about the move.

One particular day, everything was going wrong at work. In addition, Phil's parents called him at work to dump on him for abandoning them. As he was walking out the door at quitting time, his supervisor informed him he would have to work the following Saturday.

When Phil arrived home, he was totally dejected. His nonverbal signals screamed discouragement. He told me later, "I felt shattered, discouraged and unable to please anyone." He immediately headed for his chair and slumped into it in silence.

When Phil's wife entered the room, she could read his nonverbal signals and knew it had not been a good day. Phil explained what happened:

> Eileen just came over to me and stood behind me, gently stroking my hair and massaging my stooped shoulders. All she said was, "Would you like to talk about it or not?" Her sensitivity, her touch, her willingness to give me the freedom to talk or not talk encouraged me so much. I didn't feel all alone anymore. I knew I had someone who would stand by me even in my discouragement. I felt blessed. In fact, I know I am blessed in having such a wife.

Many of the responses in our surveys were from men requesting the kind of support found in Paul's letter to the Galatians: "Carry each other's burdens, and in this way you will fulfill the law of Christ" (Gal. 6:2).

6. Affection

Affection is a basic ingredient of marriage. It can mean anything from a sexual interchange to a nonsexual touch. Touch is communication.

Affectionate touching generates the sensation of warmth, security, and emotional satisfaction craved by every human being. Patting, stroking and caressing carry the nonverbal message of endearment and tenderness we all need beginning at birth. That physical need does not diminish when we grow into adulthood.

No amount of cultural restriction or stereotyping can eliminate the need for physical contact, although Americans tend to be less "touchy" in relationships than people from other cultures. Travel to Europe, Africa or Asia and you might be surprised to find how adults hug, hold hands and lean against each other.

Helen Colton cites in her book *The Gift of Touch* the observations of a social scientist who contrasted the touching habits of Americans with those of the French. Within an hour's time, French friends touched each other about one hundred times, while the Americans touched no more than three or four times. Touching is an expression of affection. How frequently does your husband need to be touched?

7. Approval

Every husband and wife looks for approval from a spouse. Romans 14:18 reminds us, "Because anyone who serves Christ in this way is pleasing to God and approved by men." Approval is giving positive affirmation, or thinking and speaking well of someone. It can be expressed in a word or a look. God models approval for us in His Word. What He said to Moses, He says to us: "I am pleased with you" (Exod. 33:17). God takes pleasure in you! He even rejoices over you in song (see Zeph. 3:17).

Married couples are to approve of each other. You have a choice: You can look for something to approve of, or you can look for something for which to disapprove. "Love," Paul wrote, "is ever ready to believe the best of every person" (1 Cor. 13:7, *AMP*).

8. SECURITY

Security involves trust. It means you can depend on the one in whom you trust. You can rely upon that person's word. You can count on that person to back you and praise you, not only in your presence but also when you are not there. You know that person is doing what is best for you. Psalm 15:4 speaks of people who inspire security and dependability: "[They] keep their promises even when it hurts" (*NLT*).

9. COMFORT AND EMPATHY

Having someone who understands us, identifies with us and can, therefore, comfort us is an important need. It is also an admonition from Scripture: "Therefore encourage each other with these words" (1 Thess. 4:18); "Rejoice with those who rejoice; mourn with those who mourn" (Rom. 12:15).

Comfort consoles in a way that touches the heart of the other person. Comfort can be different for each of us; therefore, we need to understand what brings comfort to our mate. Comfort can be expressed in words, silence, actions, sex, holding each other, and many other ways.

When a husband is hurting, his wife needs to be especially sensitive to his needs. It is important for a wife to determine whether her husband needs privacy or attention. It is equally important for her husband to tell his wife what he needs. Offering him unsolicited advice often makes matters worse. It sends the message that he can't or won't figure out the problems for himself. Being competent and being thought of as competent is so important to him that he tends to be touchy about it. He hears unsolicited advice as a criticism. Instead, his wife should ask him if he would like to hear her suggestions.

If you are trying to be comforting or empathetic, remember that men tend to handle their problems and struggles differently from the way women do. Exceptions do exist, but in general, the following statements are true of men:

- Men usually need to put the problem on the back burner, think about it and find a solution.
- Men do not readily have answers to their wives' questions or even their own problems when asked.
- Men tend not to want to say anything they might regret later. Silence (for a while) may be necessary.

10. RESPECT

Although both men and women need respect, men seem to need it more than women. When you respect people, you value them. You have a high regard for them and you honor them. "Love each other with brotherly affection and take delight in honoring each other" (Rom. 12:10, *TLB*).

When a wife respects, nurtures and affirms her husband, her love for him deepens. Haven't you found it to be true that when you don't regard something as valuable, and you neglect it, your feelings for it begin to wane? At the top of any man's list of needs is receiving respect from his mate; God created men that way. A man needs to be respected as much as he needs air to breathe. A man who doesn't receive respect from his wife is a man who begins to wither on the inside. But he's all right as long as no one is standing on the air hose running to the tank labeled Respect.[8]

God calls wives to respect their husbands (see Eph. 5:33). Some believe that respect is something that we all must earn.

However, just like love, respect from your spouse, and yours to him, must be unconditional. This is what Scripture teaches: "Show proper respect to everyone . . . not only to those who are good and considerate, but also to those who are harsh" (1 Pet. 2:17-18).

I've seen numerous instances in which a wife began to believe in her husband and showed him respect. The husband, in turn, began to change—both in his own thinking and beliefs and in how he treated and responded to his wife.

How can a wife show respect for her husband? Here are just a few examples:

- Express faith in his decisions and his ability.
- Leave him notes (men respond better to the written word) that tell him how much you value who he is as a person (and sometimes how you value his work).
- If he botches a task at home, don't sigh, roll your eyes and mutter at him; instead, thank him for trying.
- Make positive suggestions without demanding an immediate answer. Ask him to reflect on it for a while.
- Listen to his upsets and don't take his anger personally.
- Let him vent when he needs to.
- Encourage him in areas where he doesn't feel secure and let him know you stand behind him.
- When he makes a decision you're not in favor of, listen.
- Talk about his positive strengths in front of the children.
- Praise him at least once a day.
- Discover the uniqueness of his personality and learn to understand him and communicate better with him.
- Accept his maleness and celebrate the differences that come from this.

Here's a good example of a wife showing her husband the respect, admiration and love he needed from her. I greatly respected the late E. V. Hill, who served for many years as pastor of Mt. Zion Missionary Baptist Church in Los Angeles. When E. V. first began in the ministry, he was a hard worker who wanted to provide for his wife, but he was also a young preacher who struggled to make enough money just to pay for the necessities.

Pastor Hill's wife appreciated his efforts to protect and provide for her, even though some months there wasn't enough money to pay all the bills. One night, he came home and noticed immediately that the house was dark. When he opened the door, he saw that his wife, Jane, had prepared a candlelit dinner. He loved the idea, but when he went to the bathroom to wash up, he flipped the light switch and nothing happened. Then he went to the bedroom and tried the lights. Again, nothing. The entire house was dark.

He went back and asked his wife why the lights didn't work. Jane began to cry and said, "You work so hard, but it's rough. I didn't have enough money to pay the electric bill. I didn't want you to know about it, so I thought we would just eat by candlelight!"

Dr. Hill described this experience with deep emotion: "My wife could have said, 'I never had this happen in the home I was raised in.'" But she didn't berate or blame him. Instead she said, "Somehow we'll get these lights back on, but tonight let's eat by candlelight."

Showing our love and respect is a calling regardless of what the other person does. Belittling, correcting and giving too much unsolicited assistance diminish respect. Paul wrote:

However, let each man of you (without exception) love his wife as [being in a sense] his very own self; and let the wife see that she respects and reverences her husband (that she notices him, regards him, honors him, prefers him, venerates, and esteems him; and that she defers to him, praises him, and loves and admires him exceedingly) (Eph. 5:33, *AMP*).

A PORTRAIT OF RESPECT

It is important for a healthy marriage to continually grow. Love does not have to die. It wants to live. We kill it through neglect. One of the best ways to keep from falling into the trap of discouraging your mate is to live out God's Word in your own thoughts, words and actions. God has given instructions in His Word that will certainly point you in the right direction if you need a reminder of what He expects of all of us.

Let all bitterness and indignation and wrath (passion, rage, bad temper) and resentment (anger, animosity) and quarreling (brawling, clamor, contention) and slander (evil-speaking, abusive or blasphemous language) be banished from you, with all malice (spite, ill will, or baseness of any kind). And become useful and helpful and kind to one another, tenderhearted (compassionate, understanding, loving-hearted) forgiving one another [readily and freely] as God in Christ forgave you (Eph. 4:31-32, *AMP*).

Clothe yourself therefore, as God's own chosen ones [His own picked representatives], [who are] purified and holy and well-beloved [by God Himself, by putting on behavior marked by] tenderhearted pity and mercy, kind feeling, a lowly opinion of yourselves, gentle ways, [and] patience [which is tireless and long-suffering, and has the power to endure whatever comes, with good temper]. Be gentle and forbearing with one another and, if one has a difference [a grievance or complaint] against another, readily pardoning each other; even as the Lord has [freely] forgiven you, so must you also [forgive] (Col. 3:12-13, *AMP*).

What a wealth of instruction there is in God's Word! It's there for our good as well as for the good of those with whom we live. God's standard of love is not easy to achieve, but He is more than able to equip you to love and respect your husband when you ask Him to do the work through you. All it takes is a willing heart and prayer. God's ways are always best! I promise you will never regret putting away the kinds of words that can "kill" in favor of speaking words that bring life.

DISCOVER THE ENCOURAGER IN YOU

1. What symptoms described in the section "Diagnosis: Acute Discouragement" might you be seeing in your husband that you hadn't recognized as discouragement?

2. Often, your first concern when you are discouraged is to find a way to break out of that feeling; but your husband's main concern, at all costs, is to not appear weak

and inadequate. What might faultfinding, also sometimes referred to as "constructive criticism," cultivate in your husband?

3. Of your man's five basic needs, as identified by Dr. Willard Harley, which need gets the least amount of your attention? In what ways could you begin paying more attention to that need?

4. Which of the examples of how to show respect to your husband, found on p. 57, did you do this past month? If showing respect in these ways is difficult for you, or nonexistent, pick an example from the list and plan how you will put it into action *this week*. Later, record what you did and how your husband responded. (Don't be discouraged if he doesn't seem to notice at first; persistent encouragement through daily acts of respect will change your marriage for the good!)

5. What other acts of encouragement can you start practicing in the days, weeks and months ahead?

To Encourage Him, You Have to **Understand Him**

DIFFERENCES! They've been praised and cursed, glorified and condemned, identified as adding richness to relationships as well as blamed for the demise of many a marriage. Differences have always existed and they always will. Some differences are slight and some are extreme. Differences are not the problem in a relationship; identifying, understanding and accepting differences dissipate friction and misunderstanding. So, if you want to encourage a man, you need to understand him.

The book of Proverbs is filled with practical wisdom about life. One of its main themes is the value of understanding:

- "Incline your heart to understanding" (2:2, *NASB*).
- "Understanding will watch over you" (2:11, *NASB*).
- "Call understanding your intimate friend" (7:4, *NASB*).
- "Wisdom rests in the heart of one who has understanding" (14:33, *NASB*).
- "A man [or woman] of understanding walks straight" (15:21, *NASB*).
- "Understanding is a fountain of life to one who has it" (16:22, *NASB*).

Understanding is not an end in itself, but it's an important vehicle to give you wisdom and direction. Understanding your husband helps you feel for him and identify with his struggles and difficulties. It helps you know what to say and what not to say as well as when to say something and when not to say something, which is critical to developing a good relationship with your husband. Often the development of acceptance is tied into your level of understanding.[1]

Understanding seems to go hand in hand with another word, "empathy." When you understand and you are empathetic, you put yourself into the thinking, feeling and acting of another person and, in a sense, you structure your world as he does. It's as though you are in the driver's seat of the other person's vehicle, experiencing life as he does. It is viewing a situation through his eyes. Two biblical examples of this are found in Galatians 6:2 and Romans 12:15, which admonish us to bear one another's burdens, to rejoice with those who rejoice and weep with those who weep.

Not only is it difficult to separate understanding from empathy, but it's even more problematic to separate it from love.

I like the way the J. B. Phillips translation clarifies the meaning of the love we're to have for one another:

This love of which I speak is slow to lose patience—it looks for a way of being constructive. It is not possessive: it is neither anxious to impress nor does it cherish inflated ideas of its own importance. Love has good manners and does not pursue selfish advantage. It is not touchy. It does not keep account of evil or gloat over the wickedness of other people. On the contrary, it shares the joy of those who live by the truth. Love knows no limit to its endurance, no end to its trust, no fading of its hope; it can outlast anything. Love never fails (1 Cor. 13:4-8).

In more than 40 years of counseling, I have seen major misunderstandings in male/female relationships because of a lack of understanding and acceptance of differences. These differences exist because of gender, personality and learning styles. The longer I study and counsel, the more I'm convinced these three have an integral, blended relationship with each other. It's difficult to say that a man is a certain way just because he is male. He is that way because of gender, personality and learning style. When a man or woman understands these things about his or her spouse, the relationship can change and blend, and both the man and woman can be fulfilled.

In order to encourage a man, you need to understand his uniqueness so that your efforts at encouraging him can be designed to fit him.

I've heard many women say they understand men, but few actually do. They have beliefs about them, but many of those beliefs are based on stereotypes as well as cultural myths.

Listen to the words of one man:

> We believe women don't fully understand that men are different from women. They appear to realize they are different from us, but they don't understand how different we are from them—and that it is good that we are different. The difference is not a negative. Let's keep in mind that God created us differently for a purpose. And it is good. We don't want to be like women.

Take gender differences, for example. Often they're puzzling, baffling and one of the reasons for conflict. Instead of being an ally with that man in your life, you feel like an adversary.

Several years ago I had an experience that dramatically demonstrated gender differences in both thinking and communication style. Joyce and I were visiting historical Williamsburg, Virginia. It's a fascinating and charming setting that preserves and portrays colonial history.

One day, we decided to take the tour of the old governor's mansion. Our tour guide was male. As we entered the large entry hall, he began to give a factual description of the purpose of the room as well as the way it was furnished. He described in detail the various antique guns on the wall and pointed to the unique display of flintlock rifles arranged in a circle on the rounded ceiling. When he said there were 64 of them, some originals and other replicas, I immediately began counting them (a typical male response). Our guide was very knowledgeable, and he gave an excellent detailed description as we went from room to room. He seemed to be very structured and focused.

We had to leave before the tour was complete to meet some friends for lunch. Because we both enjoyed the presentation so much, we decided to return the next day and take the tour again. What a difference! Our guide was a woman. As we entered the same room we had entered the previous day, she said, "Now, you'll notice a few guns on the wall and the ceiling, but notice the covering on these chairs and the tapestry on the walls. They are . . ." And with that she launched into a detailed description of items that had either been ignored or just given a passing mention the day before. And on it went throughout the tour.

It didn't take much to figure out what was going on. It was a classic example of gender differences. Our first tour guide was speaking more to men and the second guide spoke more to women. Actually, we ended up with the best tour imaginable because we heard both perspectives. What a benefit it would be for the guides to incorporate both approaches into their presentation.[2]

This example of differences can be seen time after time. What you are going to read now I've written about in much more detail in my book *Communication: Key to Your Marriage.* You may have read about men from the perspective of other writers, but it's important to summarize some of the unique features of a man. This will help you know how to adapt your encouraging responses to your man's personality.

Make a list of the characteristics of the man in your life. How would you describe what he is like? Does he behave differently around other people? Look at your list again. This will be a road map that will provide you with the directions you need to encourage him.

HOW A MAN PROCESSES EMOTIONS

Let's hit the main issue right away: feelings and emotions. Recently, I came across a fascinating book by Michael Gurian, *The Wonder of Boys.* I wish every parent could grasp the information in this book. One section was titled, "How Boys Experience Their Feelings and Emotions." (Keep in mind that the reason for these male/female differences goes back to the presence of testosterone in men as well as the difference in the male brain structure.)

Boys have eight internal processing methods for experiencing feelings and emotions. You may see this in men as well. They have an *active-release approach.* They process and express their feelings through some sort of physical action, such as playing a game or engaging in another activity, or even by yelling. Have you ever noticed this?

Then there's the *suppression-delayed reaction method.* Whereas a woman may verbally process a problem aloud, men are basically wired for more of a delayed reaction. A man's brain is a problem-solving brain, so emotional reactions are delayed until the problem is solved. He could be irritable at this time but doesn't talk about the problem. Perhaps you've experienced this in your relationship with your husband or father or son.

Men also engage in the *displacement-objectification method*. Perhaps a boy or a man is angry. You want him to talk about it, but he won't. He might first talk about how someone else feels in a particular dilemma. Once he does that, he may then talk about how he feels.

Boys tend to make objects even of their feelings because that is safer. One boy saw a dog chained up and said, "Boy, what a life. He's tied down and stuck there. Can't go where he wants to and feels everybody is pulling his chain. Sometimes that's the way I feel when . . ."

He needs more time to deal with his feelings. That's how you can encourage him. He may need you to help him connect his feelings to the outside world. A wife realized that her husband had a difficult day at work because he was unusually quiet. Although his responses were unusually short, she discovered that he had had an overload of problems at work. So she said, "It sounds like you had an experience today like the red sports car I read about at the wild animal park."

"What are you talking about?"

"Well, it's that drive-through park where the animals roam around. A guy drove through in a really small red sports car and one of the elephants that had worked in a circus saw it. He came over and sat down on the car like he had been taught to do in the circus."

Her husband replied, "You couldn't have put it more aptly. Today I felt just like that car, except my elephant jumped up and down a bit!"

Yet another method of dealing with feelings is the *physical-expression method*, which boys use much more than girls. Exercise and games provide some of the outlets for their inner feelings. Again you can see how men use action rather than words.

You've probably heard the expression "going into the cave" approach. Several writers, including John Gray, the author of *Men Are from Mars, Women Are from Venus*, address the issue. On average, boys don't process their feelings as quickly as girls. Sometimes it takes them several hours to do so. (You may be thinking, *It's more like days!*) Men can become overwhelmed by a woman's feelings. They prefer isolation so they can sort out their feelings. They need to know it's okay to go into the cave, and it's okay to come out of the cave as well. Do you know a cave dweller? If so, do you try to drag him out of the cave or do you encourage him to enter it and stay there awhile?

There's another method men use called *talking about feelings*. It's often easier for a boy or a man to talk about his feelings after an event rather than during it. You need to remember that it is just physically more difficult for men to express feelings because of their brain structure. This isn't an excuse. It's the way God created males and females. It was His idea. You can encourage a man to talk about feelings, but what may come natural for you could feel awkward for him.

The *problem-solving method* is a process that often releases a boy's emotional energy. This is why you can expect the man in your life to move this direction as quickly as possible. You may talk it out, but he wants to solve. Seeing a problem creates feelings. When the problem is solved, he will feel much better.

The *crying method* feels unsafe to boys or men. Culture has helped to keep the tears pent up. Men do cry, but many of them can only cry on the inside. Only a few feel comfortable enough to express tears. The feeling of loss of control when this happens is an unpleasant exposure and vulnerability for most men.[3]

Men are very skilled at covering up their real feelings. They have numerous ways of hiding their emotions. For example, when a man is feeling sad, fearful, hurt or guilty, he may use anger to avoid the pain of those feelings. Expressing anger makes him feel more like he's in control. And because most people don't feel like getting close to someone who is angry, he is able to maintain a safe distance. When a man is truly angry, he may use discouragement or indifference as his Novocain to get away from the pain of those feelings.

When a man is feeling insecure, uncertain, ashamed or actually afraid, anger is useful to avoid facing those feelings as well. He may turn his anger into aggression to overcompensate for other feelings he can't safely express. One of the most frequent translations of one feeling for another is the exchange of anger for frustration.

One other factor to remember about men and anger:

A man's low self-image is usually the result of threats of an interpersonal nature, such as insults or undue criticism. Studies show that men with a high sense of self-worth are much less affected by criticism.

Insults and criticism are especially provocative of anger if the man already suffers from low self-esteem, instability relating to poor social adjustment, depression, anxiety and low life satisfaction. These men usually did not receive the affirmation they craved from their fathers during childhood, and they get angry when they are not affirmed and appreciated as adults. No matter how hard he tries, the man with low self-worth never quite measures up to the idealized vision of what he thinks others expect him to be. He may appear to be quite confident and secure, but in reality he is insecure and highly sensitive to the criticism of others, positive or negative.

A man's anger in response to his low self-worth serves a number of functions. It prompts him to express his displeasure at the affront he has suffered. It helps him defend himself against all his negative feelings. It encourages him to restore his wounded self-esteem and public self-image by going on the offensive. Yet in the process of trying to save his own skin, he may bring pain to others, especially to those closest to him.[4]

One of the best responses you can give a man about what he is experiencing or feeling is validation. Validation is the process or act of confirming or supporting the meaningfulness and relevance of what your man is feeling. It means listening to and understanding his perspective. It means walking with him emotionally without trying to change the direction he's going.[5]

Sometimes a wife makes the mistake of editing her own feelings because she believes her husband can't handle them. She tries to protect her husband (or any of the men in her life—father or son) from her own pain when she's upset. If you hold back your feelings because your man has difficulty handling them, you're not helping the relationship; you're creating emotional distance. It will leave you starving for emotional connection—from anyone! This is one of the reasons why some women stray from their husbands—to find emotional connection.

When you edit or block your feelings, you begin to lose your own identity. You may end up being unsure of whether you are the person who experienced that emotion or whether you're another person who is trying not to feel it. It's like asking, "Who am I?" "Who's the real me? The one who feels or the one who doesn't feel?"

The result is that some women don't encourage their men with positive affirmations because of the confusion they have over their feelings.[6]

GENDER DIFFERENCES IN BRAIN FUNCTION

There's another range of differences that has to do with personality. Let's look for a moment at Frank, who may be like a number of men (or women) you know.

Frank likes his life precise, structured and regulated. When he asks you a question he wants to hear a precise, definite response, not something vague or general. He tends to correct others when they tell a story because he's a stickler for details. He likes to see results in whatever he does. His attitude toward many situations in life is "If it ain't broke, don't fix it." Leave well enough alone.

He is bottom line in how he expresses himself, as well as being very linear in how he thinks. He breaks the problem down into pieces and goes through steps 1, 2, 3 and 4 to find a solution. Frank just loves structure. He likes to put things in order by regulating, organizing, enumerating and fitting things into rules and patterns.

Because of his gender-based brain uniqueness and personality, he can be ultra-focused. Perhaps this concept is new to you.

A male's brain is organized with a high level of lateralization. Men tend to shift farther left or right than women do. And there are some who make equal usage of both sides, since neither side is dominant.

Is there a generic right-brain/left-brain difference between men and women? Yes. This is part of the answer to why men and women are the way they are. A man's brain is more highly specialized. If I am a typical man, I will use the left side of my brain for verbal problems and the right side for spatial. This latter area tends to help men excel over women in a sport like baseball because a man can better perceive the relationship between ball and bat. If I am putting together a new barbeque grill that came in pieces, I use my right brain to visualize the end result. Thus I shift from one side to the other. I am seeing how it fits together in my mind. If I am discussing with a friend what restaurant to go to for dinner, I respond out of my left verbal side.

Personally, I feel that we men do not use all the abilities of the right side as much as we could; the emotional, intuitive side in men is often stunted, partly due to a lack of socialization training and encouragement and partly because of our tendency to use one side of the brain or the other at a time but not as much in conjunction.

A woman is different in the way she uses her brain. And it gives her an advantage over men! A woman's brain is not specialized. It operates holistically. A man shifts back and forth between the left and right sides of his brain. He can give more focused attention to what he is doing. But a woman uses both sides of her brain simultaneously to work on a problem; the two parts work in cooperation. Why? Because some of the left-brain abilities are duplicated in her right brain and some of the right-brain abilities are duplicated in the left side. Women have larger connectors between the two sides, even as infants, and can integrate information more skillfully.[7] In addition, women have from 30 percent to 40 percent more connectors between the left and the right sides of the brain.[8]

The way in which men use their brains is an exclusive mode. (Some women refer to it as tunnel vision!) It can exclude everything except what he is focusing on. It shuts out other possibilities. And men exert an abundance of energy to stay in this position. Most men like to know exactly where they are and what they are doing at a given point in time. It's a way to stay in control.

Life seems to revolve around some husbands. They like the sameness of their environment. When things stay the same they feel a sense of security and less of a drain on their energy. For example, if a husband walks into his living room and the furniture has been rearranged, his wife may be delighted, but he is bothered because he has to reorient himself. If he wasn't notified of the change in advance, he feels even more out of control. And he will work hard to get back in control.

So if your husband is at home and his attention is locked on the TV, the newspaper or fixing the car, he's in his exclusive mindset. If you talk to him, he experiences it as an interference or intrusion. And for him it's an energy leak. He hopes it will leave!

For most men, when they're working on a project or a task at home, it's not a fellowship time for them. When he does exert energy to shift from whatever he has been doing to concentrate on you, he's upset because of the energy expenditure. He has to change his focus and shift it elsewhere because he can't handle both at once. You may feel he's inconsiderate for not listening, but he feels you're inconsiderate because of the intrusion. Actually, neither person is being inconsiderate. You just don't understand the gender differences. If you did, you could each learn to respond differently.

Listen to what four different men said about this issue:

"Many of us would like to communicate with our wives as intimately as they communicate with their friends. But we find it difficult. Who will help us learn? We receive few offers, only complaints."

"Women say that we are single-minded. We are. Single-mindedness helps us reach our goals. We have difficulty listening when we are concentrating on something else. We are accused of being purposely inattentive and made to feel guilty, and even attacked for this. Why?"

"We want women to understand that we need more time to process what is said to us than women do. When we feel pressured to be different, we may use anger as our protection—to get others to back off."

"She expects me to have these reactions right at my fingertips and be able to call them up on the spot. Well, I can't do that. I don't operate that way; she does. I need a little more time to think things through. I don't want to say something I'm going to regret later on. Somehow she has the idea that wanting time to think is not being open and honest with her. That is ridiculous! I'm not trying to hide anything, I'm just trying to be sure in my own mind before I talk to her about it."[9]

Frank doesn't like to use his imagination very much or consider options. He likes the here and now. He's great at home when it comes to putting things together. He reads the instructions from front to back and then follows them step by step.

Shopping for him is a task! He doesn't go to enjoy the process. It's something to be conquered. Usually he'll call the store to see if they have the needed item. He prefers to go in, money in hand, pick it up, pay for it and walk out, never seeing any other items.

His philosophy of life is to work now and play later. Organized? That's his middle name. When he wakes up in the morning you wonder if he didn't plan his day while he slept. He knows what he will do that day. He has a schedule and follows it but comes unglued if things don't go the way he planned them. If a surprise or change comes into his life, watch out! He has a place for everything. And guess what? He's not satisfied until everything is in its place.

He likes order and special systems for keeping things in the garage, his fishing kit, hangers in the closet, shirts color-coded in order in the drawer, and his pens nearby arranged in order on the desk. His playtime is organized and so are his times of spontaneity! He might plan a week in advance to be spontaneous on a Saturday afternoon from 1:00 to 4:00. Not only is he decisive, but he is also bothered by those who can't seem to make up their minds.

So . . . does this sound like anyone you know? Or maybe your husband is just the opposite. But if this man sounds familiar to you, how would you go about encouraging him? What sort of things would you say or do on a regular basis?

Getting Fluent in a New Language

Let's consider how to communicate with a husband who is like Frank. You've probably figured out already that one of the ways to encourage this man's personality is not to frustrate him when you talk with him.

When you share with him, keep it brief, simple, focused, bottom line, result-oriented, task-oriented, linear, orderly, with not too many options and relatively free from change or surprises. Get the picture? You are probably thinking his life is sterile, boring! "That's not my personality!" you say. "That's not the way I live my life!" That may be true. But a husband who is like this and knows his wife is the opposite will be encouraged when he sees her making the effort to adapt and learn to speak his language. (Hang in here, wives. If this book were for men, I would be asking the man to adapt to your style when he speaks with you!) He is more likely to hear you and appreciate you. Even words of encouragement need to fit this adaptive pattern.

Listen to Ed, married several years to Sue, as he expresses his desire to be encouraged:

> I'd like to tell you about my outgoing wife. She's a real talker. She talks and talks. She even talks to herself. I'm just the opposite. I don't talk much at all. At first I was attracted to her talking. Then I was repulsed by it. My ears got exhausted.
>
> I couldn't understand why Sue had to think out loud so much. It's like she wanted the whole world to know about her wild ideas. And it's not just because she's a woman. I've seen men who are the same way. But it seemed like she would start talking before she engaged her brain. At times I felt like my space was invaded by her giving a running commentary on everything or saying the same things over and over or wanting an immediate response from me on a question I'd never had a chance to think about. That wore me out. I began to feel she didn't want to hear what I had to say.

There were even times when I'd go to the garage to putter around (and find some peace and quiet), and Sue would come out there, bring up a subject, ask my opinion, arrive at her own conclusion before I could think about it, thank me and walk out. I'd just stand there shaking my head and wonder, *Why even ask me?* I felt invaded and unimportant.

When we went to an activity, it was like she knew everyone there and wanted to stay forever. It seemed like she would never run down or get enough socializing. I've seen men like that too. I always wondered how they did it. It drains me but seems to give her a shot of adrenaline! I'd like to leave early, but she doesn't understand I'm exhausted by people.

Something else used to bother me—Sue is better about this now—she would interrupt me when we talked. It takes me longer to get things out and reach a conclusion. So, if I talked or thought too slowly, I either got interrupted or she finished my statement for me. We had a good discussion (argument) over that one. But she's much better now, and I don't avoid discussions with her. Sometimes I remind her that our speed of thinking and speaking is different, and that helps. That's when I'm encouraged about the relationship.

When we have a conflict, I think (or used to think) that there was just too much talking about the problem. Sue had the belief that if we just talked it through a bit more, everything could get resolved. Resolved! A few more words would be the last straw. We eventually learned to put some time limits on each segment of the conversation so I could have time to think. Then

I was ready to continue. I also worked on sharing my first reaction without having to do so much thinking and editing. When she's patient, it helps me work on myself.

Now and then I've said to her, "I want to resolve this, but since I'm getting worn down, why don't you write out what you're thinking or type your thoughts on the computer? Then I can read them over and be able to reason out my response." That's worked well for us. That way Sue doesn't get as loud either, since I really tend to withdraw when that happens. I used to tell her, "You're not going to get me to respond by shouting at me. It won't work." Now I say, "I want to hear you. I would appreciate it if you would say it softly and give me a chance to respond."

Sometimes I would ask her, "Why are you bringing that up again? We've already talked about it." Sue would say, "No, we haven't." And then we'd argue over whether we had or not. This went on for years until one day I heard her say, "Could it be that you rehearse conversations in your mind and then think we've already talked about it?" Bingo! That's exactly what I was doing, and when she said it, I realized she was right. Fortunately, we've learned to laugh about it. Sometimes I catch myself and say, "Yeah, I did talk to you about it . . . in my head."

What has really helped me (and us) is to realize that there's nothing wrong with Sue the way she is. That's just her. It's the way she's wired. I guess it's the way God created her. We're just different and are learning to adjust.

I've learned to appreciate the fact that she's encouraged me to be more social and involved with other people, and I've discovered I can be. It's become apparent that Sue needs more interaction and time with people that I do. Now I'm glad to provide it. It's all right for her to go places and gab, and I can stay home or get together with one of my male friends.

It's really helped me to understand that Sue needs to talk out loud to figure things out. And it doesn't mean that she's going to do what she's thinking out loud. She's just thinking. I've learned not to assume.

We're not perfect, but we are much more accepting. We've learned to be creative in the ways we approach each other. Being married to her has structured me. It's helped me to relate more to others. And I see her accepting who I am more and more.

Now let's hear what Sue has to say about her relationship with Frank:

I'm an ongoing, talkative person who for some strange reason was drawn to a quiet, reserved, thoughtful man. I loved him and wanted to be his helpmate. I knew we were different when we were dating, but I never realized just how much until we were married. When it really hit me was the evening I figured out that Frank seemed to be avoiding me. Even when I was talking to him it seemed like he couldn't wait until I quit talking. His responses became shorter and shorter. It was as though he thought if he said less I wouldn't have so much to respond to. I guess it was true, because eventually I'd get fed up and socialize on the phone. I actually felt rejected and hurt because I wasn't getting enough conversation out of Frank. I couldn't figure out why he was like that. At first I thought, *That's just the way men are.* But other men I had dated weren't always like that. In fact, I've known women who act like Frank. So I figured it's just the way he's wired.

I do enjoy getting together with others. I am energized by them. But it doesn't take long (at least it seems to me) for Frank to get worn out at a party and want to leave early. I've even seen him just sit off to one side by himself or go into another room for a while just to be alone. I used to think, *What is wrong with that man?* Then, I began to discover that Frank needs some quiet time and space to get his energy back. That's draining for me, but it perks him up. So I figured if this is who he is, let's work out some ways I can encourage him. Frank is friendly and communicates well, but he doesn't go out of his way to connect with people. I've had many friends, but he's satisfied with just two. There's the difference—just two! That wouldn't be enough for me. I need more people to talk with.

One of our biggest conflicts was in the area of communication. I like to get things resolved. That means talking through every part of an issue. But when we talked, or when I talked, the more he seemed to retreat. So I figured I'd just keep after him and he was bound to open up. No such luck! He'd retreat, clam up or say, "I don't know." I admit, I want answers right now. I used to say, "Frank, tell me right now. You don't need time. For Pete's sake, tell me!" And then nothing. Silence. It's like I just short-circuited his thinking ability. And later on I discovered I had! I wasn't letting him be who he really was!

I've discovered that Frank is more of what is called an inner person. Through some reading, I discovered he's the kind of person who likes to think things through in the quiet privacy of his mind without pressure—and then he's got a lot to say! I didn't know this at first. Now when I need his feedback or a discussion, I just go to him and say, "Frank, here's something I'd like you to think about. Put it on the back burner where it can simmer for a while, and when it's done, let's discuss it." He appreciates it, and we talk more. After I did this for a while, he told me, "Thanks for recognizing and respecting my need to think things through in the privacy of my mind." That felt good, because I like compliments.

I've had to learn he isn't comfortable thinking and responding quickly out loud. That's my world, not his. A few times we got into a conflict and I pressured him so much he just let fly with an outburst that seemed extreme. I learned not to push. It's better to let him think first.

I've also learned not to interrupt Frank with every thought that pops into my head. I'm finally learning to edit and pick times when I can have his attention. I know my thinking out loud used to bother him because he thought I meant every word of it. I just like to sort things out, and I don't care who knows it. So now I just warn him, "I'm just thinking out loud again. You can relax, because I'm not going to rearrange all the furniture in the house today."

You know, I used to think that Frank's quietness and withdrawal at times was a passive-aggressive way of getting back at me. But it wasn't. God made Frank and me as unique individuals. I just didn't understand it. Twice this last month he actually did some thinking out loud with me, which was wonderful.

I've also learned that when I encourage him to be who he is, I receive more of what I need to. That's a fringe benefit. The other day I knew he was frazzled, but I wanted to talk. Usually, I would have forced the discussion or tried to, but I remembered a couple of passages from Proverbs: "Don't talk so much. You keep putting your foot in your mouth. Be sensible and turn off the flow!" (10:19, *TLB*); and "Self-control means controlling the tongue! A quick retort can ruin everything" (13:3, *TLB*).

So I said, "You look like you need some recouping time. Why don't you go read or do whatever and maybe we could talk a bit later?" And we did talk—quite a bit. And I am learning to write him notes too.

Frank understands things that used to really get to me. He's better at communicating now, but I've learned that a few of his words mean a hundred of mine. When he gets a big smile on his face and doesn't say much, I say, "It looks like that smile is about five hundred of my words." And he says, "You've got that right. I just love good translators!"

So I've learned to give him time and space and not interrupt when he talks. And I don't assume anymore that he doesn't have opinions or want to talk. He's selective and more methodical. I use a scatter-shot approach.[10]

The stories you just read are true. The people, well, I've heard this conversation so many times I've lost count. In this case, the results were positive. We had an introvert husband and an extrovert wife learning about the uniqueness of one another and discovering that it is all right to be the way they are.

Keep in mind that most women tend to focus more on others and men focus more on themselves. This helps to explain why women tend to expand conversational topics, whereas men like to shrink-wrap their presentation. Men like to keep it short and to the point. They also like to hear others talk in this way.

Have you ever heard these phrases from a man? (If you haven't, something is wrong!)

"I'm doing okay."
"It's fine."
"No problem."
"No big deal."
"I can handle it."

What's the message behind these statements? Is it, "I'd love to talk more about this"? Not quite. It's just the opposite. It's his signal that he doesn't need or want to discuss this any further because he will handle, solve and take care of the situation.

Often a man has had a topic on the back burner that has simmered for a while; so when he's ready to communicate, it's cooked and ready to serve. This is especially true if he's an introvert like Frank. He speaks when he's ready. Discussing the issue inside his head helps him get ready to verbally communicate. But too often his wife may interpret this as not being interested or attentive, or as withdrawing from her. This may not be the case at all. You may want to ask if this is so and then encourage him to actually put it on the back burner to talk about later.

One wife left her husband a funny card that said, "Have I got a deal for you! Try and turn this one down. I like your conclusions, and I'd like them even more if you'd take a couple of minutes and tell me the process of how you arrive there. You know me. I'm just interested in how anything works. You can count on me to work on being more bottom-line when I'm talking with you. How about it?" It worked.

Most women enjoy sharing and expanding their topic out loud. When a man starts talking, he usually knows where he's going unless he's an extrovert and just thinks out loud. But when many women begin talking, it's a discovery process. They're not always sure where it's heading and where it may end up. But thinking out loud helps them decide. Most men don't operate that way.

One wife shared, "I asked my husband whether he wanted me to do my out-loud thinking in front of him or outside in the garage. He looked at me kind of strange and said, 'Of course, I don't want you to go outside. I'll work at getting used to it. That stuff we heard on gender differences has helped me make sense of it too.'"

Sometimes an introvert husband is not always ready to give more than a yes or no response. So some women "rescue" the uncomfortable silence by filling in with their own words. It's better to say, "I'm interested in what you have to say, but you may need to think about it for a while. That's fine with me; take your time. When you're ready to talk about it, let me know." Giving permission for silence will take the pressure off both of you. It's also an encouragement to him.

Or, "The look on your face tells me that you have something on your mind. I'd like to hear what it is." Or, "You may be concerned about how I will respond if you share what's on your mind. I think I'm ready to listen." Or, "It appears that you're having difficulty speaking right now. Can you tell me why?" Or, "Perhaps your silence reflects a concern about saying something correctly. You can say it any way you'd like."

One wife said, "Sometimes when I want to talk with you, you seem preoccupied or hesitant. I wonder if it's the topic or if there is something I do that makes it difficult for you to respond. Maybe you could think about it and let me know later." Then she stood up and began to leave the room. But her quiet husband said, "Let's talk now. I'm ready to comment on your last statement."[11]

I've already mentioned the idea of learning to speak the man's language. (Remember, I encourage men to do the same with a woman's language, so this isn't a one-sided arrangement.) Speaking your spouse's language includes not only vocabulary but also the person's packaging. Packaging refers to whether a person is an expander (sharing great volumes of details) or a condenser (sharing little more than the bottom line).

If he's an expander, go for it. If he's a condenser, keep it brief. Neither men nor women want to hear a monologue of the reasons why they need to fulfill a request. Expanders give a number of descriptive sentences as they talk, while condensers give one or two sentences. In approximately 70 percent of marriages, the man is the condenser, and the woman is the expander. Neither is a negative trait, but the expander wishes his or her partner would share more, while the condenser wishes his or her partner would share less. It is only when each of you adapts to the style of your partner that real communication occurs.

Always, always talk about what you want and present it in such a way that your man catches in your request the belief that he can do it. Nothing could be more encouraging!

DISCOVER THE ENCOURAGER IN YOU

1. Has there ever been a time when your husband reacted with a seemingly inappropriate or explosive response? What did you make of it?

2. What is one of your "Honey, I moved the furniture again . . ." stories that didn't end well?

3. After reading this chapter, what would you say are some of the causes of gender conflict?

4. How has your understanding of gender differences in brain function changed the way you interpret the times when your husband is distant or even highly reactive?

5. If you were to apply your new knowledge, what would be a loving thing you could do or say differently in everyday interactions with your husband?

Husbands
Speak Out

HAVE YOU EVER WANTED TO KNOW WHAT GOES ON IN THE MIND OF YOUR HUSBAND FOR A DAY?

Would it help you understand him? You're probably saying yes to both questions. I've listened to men for more than 40 years in the counseling office as well as conducted surveys nationally on various questions and issues. In conducting these surveys, I discovered that it was far easier to get women to respond!

In marriage conferences we've asked husbands to sit in small groups with their wives seated right behind them so they could listen to the men discuss assigned questions. After all the joking and wisecracks were over, it was amazing to hear the depth of the men's discussion. Their wives (who incidentally couldn't say anything) were also amazed at what they learned.

In one survey, each man was asked *indirectly* how he would like to be encouraged by his wife. The actual question was: "What one thing would you like your wife to do that would indicate to you that she understands and accepts what you deal with in your daily life?" (Some of these responses were shared in my book *What Men Want*.)

I would like my wife to appreciate and recognize the pressures we men go through and the responsibilities of being the provider and caretaker. Not only financially, but in the spiritual, emotional, social and mental areas as well. As a man, my concentration on the overall picture and goals. It's true that some of the attention to detail gets lost in the shuffle. But what I do is often misunderstood, and the appreciation for what I am doing gets lost.

I want to feel needed and know that I am important at home. I'm sensitive to not only what is said, but also how it's said. Criticism shuts me down. It would help if our wives who are full-time homemakers and haven't worked in the competitive, chaotic world outside of the home could understand that it is difficult and challenging for Christian men to interact and work under the constant influences of non-Christian attitudes all day.

Do women really understand how we feel about the responsibility for making ends meet? Their actions tell us they don't. We feel burdened to provide for the family whether our wives are employed or not. Many of us fear disappointing the family and failing in our roles of protector, provider, father, family leader and spiritual head. Our self-worth, our egos and our identities are linked to both work and home. It often appears that we are not as interested in what goes on at home as we are with what happens at work. That may not always be the case—we may just be exhausted from work. It is frustrating for us not to have more time to give of ourselves at home.

H. NORMAN WRIGHT

Robert Lewis and William Hendricks, in their book *Rocking the Roles*, suggest the following:

First, your husband needs your support for his work. How you feel about his work is vitally important. Work is one way he has of defining himself. So how you feel about his work translates in his mind into how you feel about him. If you encourage and back him in his work, your support stabilizes and energizes.

But suppose you care little about what he does for a living; suppose you make no effort to even understand it; suppose you're interested only in what kind of money he makes; suppose you choose not to understand the pressure he's under; suppose you resent his work, or maybe even compete with him through your own career. Through any of these attitudes, you'll knock the props out from under your husband and stir up his insecurity. You'll leave him feeling empty, resentful and confused.

In his mammoth work *Seasons of a Man's Life*, Daniel Levinson found that men choose women to marry who they think will "nourish their life's vision" and help them fulfill their identity in a life work.[1] They desire wives who are behind them, encouraging them, supporting them, and cheering for them. If, after marriage, a wife fails to share in her husband's vision or participate in it, or if she becomes apathetic toward his work, or even resentful of it, then that marriage will fall into deep trouble within a surprisingly short time.

For the record, I'm not saying that as a wife you should endorse your husband's workaholism. That's an unhealthy pattern, and I would never encourage a woman to enable that. But I want you to understand how important work is to the heart and soul of your man. How you stand behind his life's work is critical to his self-esteem.[2]

Right or wrong, good or bad, like it or not, a man uses his work to build his identity and to express who he is, just as a woman finds other ways to express who she is. Work also gives a man a purpose for his life; and for many, work is satisfying. In their book *Your Work Matters to God,* William Hendricks and Doug Sherman talk about biblical purposes for working: "Through work we serve people; through work we meet our own needs; through work we meet our families' needs; through work we earn money to give to others; through work we love God."[3]

Hopefully, these are the reasons your husband works! Listen carefully when he shares his concerns about work.

Suggestion: Encourage your husband to make a list of the various pressures he faces, or you make a list of potential work pressures and ask him to check off the main ones that apply to his job situation. Then ask how you can help. One wife asked to go to work with her husband for a day and just observe what he had to deal with. She told him beforehand that she wouldn't make suggestions or comments unless he asked her to do so. It may help sometime to turn on a tape recorder at home to record an interchange. This has helped many people discover if what they say is constructive and supportive.

One man said, "I long to be appreciated for who I am, especially at home. I want to experience unconditional love at home—not just performance-based love. I struggle with that all day long on a job. When I come home, I don't always want to hear how hard my wife worked. I need to hear some loving compliments, not just complaints! If I hear something uplifting first, I can problem-solve better."

Suggestion: One wife made a point of either verbalizing or writing a note stating how much she appreciates what the man in her life accomplishes. A grateful daughter took the time to write her father a letter expressing appreciation for all he had done for her. If you're a wife, you may want to practice the "Four-Minute Drill" at the end of the day when you first see your husband. During the initial four minutes, make it a point to touch, hug, affirm, and be friendly and positive. Save the complaints about "his kids" and the broken plumbing until after he's eaten dinner. Remember, what takes place during the first four minutes when you see each other at the end of the workday sets the tone for the rest of the evening. If it's positive, it tends to continue in that direction. If it's negative . . . well, need I say more?

One man said, "I would love my wife to give me a hug, a kiss (without having to ask for one or be the initiator) and ask me to share what's going on in my head. And, after I'm done unloading all my concerns and worries, not offer advice unless asked, but pray with me for God's guidance. This would help me release all my anxieties to God and provide a clean heart for my family."

Another said, "If she and I could sit down at the end of the day and review the highlights; to share what we really think without having her making judgments about the people I work with. It would be nice to have a sounding board, someone to just bounce ideas off of, without judging. I would value her honest opinion."

Suggestion: This man is looking for his wife to be a support. In a case like this, ask him how he wants you to pray for him in the morning before he goes to work, and then send him an email or text telling him that you're praying for him. Too often phone or other messages to a man at work are "I need your advice" or "Something needs fixing."

"SPEAK WELL OF ME"

A 40-year-old said, "I think I am still a big kid at heart. I would like my wife to give me more encouragement regarding my business life and my home life. Maybe more 'attaboys' or thank-yous or comments like 'Good job.' I am at a level in my company where I don't get it at the office. I do get some appreciation at home, but that kid in me needs more."

Suggestion: Have you ever asked who your husband's encouragers are at work? Or how he would like to be encouraged by others at work? Remember, too, if your husband is an extrovert, he's the kind who may think he's done a good job but won't really believe it until he's heard it from someone else. So, even if you've said it once that week, you may need to say it more. It may help to find out if he prefers to hear it privately or in front of others.

As one man put it: "I need continual affirmation that I am a good father/husband. I never had any training in being either one. I guess I need the acknowledgment that I am doing the best I can, even if I don't quite measure up to all desires and expectations. Please don't compare me to other fathers! I'm not them. We're all different and need some help. Give me physical affection and let me know you're glad you married me. Sometimes I worry about this."

Suggestion: It's easy to look around and compare what you don't have. It's very deflating to a man to be compared to others, even in a joking way. Men have to live with comparisons and competition all of their lives. They don't want this from their wives. It's a personal affront to them. You could encourage your man if he feels lacking in some areas by saying, "You know, we all do the best we can with the limited knowledge we have. I do appreciate that. Are you comfortable with what you know now or would you like to become even more proficient?"

"MAKE TIME FOR ME"

"The thing I want her to do the minute I walk in the door," said one man, "is not hit me with instantaneous decisions. But how would I feel if I had been with small children all day? Another possibility would be that she could give up some responsibilities to have more time for me. She often is still folding clothes through the ten o'clock news, after which we retire. Often I seem to be last on her list."

Suggestion: It's true! Many men feel they get the leftovers after the children. There are solutions though. Suggest these and give him a choice. Let him know you want alone time with him. This can happen if:

1. You hire a baby-sitter for an hour each evening.
2. You work out a plan together to simplify some of the tasks.
3. He could help with some of the tasks, which would give you some free time.

"I'm like many men," one man admits. "I love to create and build. Yes, I'm the one who watches *Home Improvement*. I like to work on the house, the barbeque grill, the boat and the lawn. I enjoy serving my wife in this way; but it sure would help if she would explain what she wants before I complete the project. It's disheartening and de-motivating to have to make changes once the job is finished. I hate to hear, 'Oh, I wish we had done this instead' after the work is done."

Suggestion: Be sure you've clarified and decided exactly what you want done before he gets involved. Once a man gets started on a project, he's single-minded. It throws him when changes occur, and if he hears after the fact that you would have preferred something else, he will interpret it as a personal criticism that he blew it. He feels his efforts were not appreciated. Two men shared both their disappointments and their desires in the area of receiving encouragement from their wives.

> Before my wife can do one thing to demonstrate understanding, encouragement or acceptance of my struggles, she needs to *make time* to talk in order to discover what they are. I know this is a priority that we must share together. However, I do feel like a lower priority in my wife's life (after the needs of the children, her church commitments and time spent with her friends) than she is in mine. I guess if I had to request only one thing, I would like my wife to change her tone that is critical, negative and belittling.

> I guess encouragement would be to work at taking the "log out of her own eye" so she could help me with mine. Then I could really trust her statements of understanding. I feel like I am working to get healthier, and as head of the family it should probably start with me— I'm glad it has anyway. I feel she has yet to really start, so it's harder for her to comprehend and understand. When I know myself better and when she's begun to understand me, then I feel her statements and support

will mean more, and I will be able to trust and receive them with more confidence. Too often now I feel that what I share comes back to "hit" me at a later date. Not having to worry about when I will get hit with this again would be a relief and be encouraging as well.

Suggestion: This is a common issue between husbands and wives. To reiterate an earlier point, we are not trying to let men off the hook at all. They share in these problems quite often by not being available, not sharing or by being defensive. But you can't wait for the other person to change before you respond in new ways.

"BE KIND TO ME"

Consider some scriptural guidelines for the way to interact with the men in your life. There is a right time to speak and a time to be quiet. Proverbs 10:19 emphasizes this: "In a multitude of words transgression is not lacking, but he who restrains his lips is prudent" (*NKJV*). *The Living Bible* is graphic in its rendering: "Don't talk so much. You keep putting your foot in your mouth. Be sensible and turn off the flow!"

"He who has knowledge spares his words, and a man of understanding has a cool spirit. Even a fool when he holds his peace is considered wise; when he closes his lips he is esteemed a man of understanding" (Prov. 17:27-28, *AMP*).

"Do you see a man who is hasty in his words? There is more hope for a [self-confident] fool than for him" (Prov. 29:20, *AMP*). Being hasty means blurting out what you are thinking without considering the effect it will have on others.

Romans 14:19 says, "So let us then definitely aim for and eagerly pursue what makes for harmony and for mutual upbuilding (edification and development) of one another" (*AMP*). The word "edify," which is part of helping, means to hold up or promote growth in Christian wisdom, grace, virtue and holiness.

A wife may correct what her husband says or does and tell him what to do and how to do something. But he probably won't respond well to her directions, especially if he does not feel admired. When a wife challenges, criticizes or corrects her husband's decisions or initiations (especially in front of others), he feels unloved, angry and humiliated. He wants to be encouraged to do things on his own. Instead, ask if he would like to hear an observation, and if he doesn't, let it go. When a wife shares her displeasure by asking questions that carry an accusatory tone, implying "You blew it," she can count on a defensive response.

Common defense-producing questions are "How could you?" or "Why in the world did you do that?" When questions are asked or statements made such as the following, a man will feel unaccepted, unapproved and unloved, and definitely not encouraged.

- "How can you think of buying that? You already have two and you rarely use them."
- "Those dishes are still wet. They'll dry streaked unless you redo them."
- "Your hair is getting kind of ragged, isn't it?"
- "There's a parking spot over there. Go over there and turn around quickly."
- "You shouldn't work so hard. None of the other men do."
- "Don't put that there. It will get lost."
- "You should call an electrician. He'll know what to do."
- "Why are we waiting for a table? Didn't you call ahead?"
- "You should spend more time with your sons. They miss you."

- "Your office is still a mess. How can you think in here? When are you going to clean it up?"
- "You forgot to bring it home again. Maybe you could write yourself a note."
- "You're driving too fast. Slow down."
- "Next time we should read the movie reviews; this wasn't good."
- "I didn't know what time to expect you. You should have called."
- "Somebody drank from the milk bottle again."
- "Don't eat with your fingers. You're setting a bad example for the kids."

These statements will elicit a response, but probably not the one you want.[4]

Share your concern in a calm voice, saying, "I am upset, and I don't want to be. Help me to understand what is happening. I need your perspective." This positive approach is more easily accepted than accusation.

"ACCEPT ME"

In a similar way, a man said the following: "The one thing I would like my wife to do is encourage me. To create for me a place in her arms or in my home that is a shelter from the things I am dealing with, not more demands, expectations or her personal suggestions on how I should deal with these things unless I solicit her opinion. Her encouragement would be in the form of words and actions. Words like: 'You're doing so well,' 'You can do it' and 'I know what you do will be the best.' And actions like finding ways to lighten my load; or just saying okay and doing something I suggest. Just agreeing would be a form of encouragement. Encouraging me to be myself would indicate to me that she accepts me, rather than always trying to change me. Wanting me to be different means not accepting who I am."

Suggestion: A wife often tries to improve her husband's responses or help him by offering unsolicited advice. And strange as it seems, when a woman offers unsolicited advice to a man, he tends not to see it as helpful but rather interprets it as her saying, "You don't know what to do, and you need my help." If the man came from a home in which he was criticized as a child, he will activate and transfer those leftover responses to his present relationship. Even if they're not experts, men like to think of themselves that way. It's the old desire to be proficient and in control. And if you suggest that he listen to the advice of an expert, he could really get upset.[5]

His response to you may be that he feels unloved because he feels you are not trusting him. You could say, "I've got a suggestion if you're interested. Let me know if you are."

Or a wife may try to change or control her husband's behavior by talking about how upset she is or letting him know her negative feelings. Again, his response is, "She doesn't love me because she doesn't accept me the way I am." Your requested change may be quite insightful, but it's not packaged in a way he can hear. Sharing the request in a positive way, pointing to the desired response and even expressing it in writing often works better.

"BELIEVE IN ME"

Do you find yourself noticing or acknowledging what your husband has done? Or instead do you comment on what has not been accomplished? That's discouraging and disheartening. Naturally, he feels unappreciated and taken for granted. Men and women want their efforts to be recognized and valued. Appreciation is the best way to see the desired behavior continue.

Men want to feel successful. They want to be successful in their male-female relationships. Too often they end up feeling like a failure, which is very discouraging. It's easy to give up and withdraw.

Here are some statements you can use to help a man communicate, to encourage him, but also to instruct him in a nonthreatening way.

- "I really feel safe when I share my feelings with you."
- "It really helps me solve problems and fix things when you listen to me."
- "I appreciate how you help me arrive at my own solutions to some of my problems!"
- "I really feel affirmed by you when you see my opinion as having validity. Sometimes I really need your perspective."
- "I like it when you let me problem-solve out loud and find a solution. I know you have some good ideas, and holding them back must be hard at times."
- "I want to take three minutes and tell you what happened. I think you'll find these details interesting and pertinent to this incident."

One of the statements *not* to make is, "You don't understand." Saying this not only discourages a man, but it also frustrates him. He then tends to tune out whatever your explanation is going to be. If he doesn't catch what you've said, you could say, "Let me put it in another way." Then be sure to put it in his language and keep it brief.[6]

Another man said he wished his wife would "defend me . . . not in a way that says I'm always right, but in a way that indicates she knows I'm really trying . . . there is a lot of criticism of men in today's society . . . I want to know my wife is on my side, not on the side that is critical. And I must say, I believe she is [on my side] and does [know I'm really trying]. For that I am grateful."

Suggestion: Making the statement "I believe in you" or putting an encouraging note with that message in your husband's pocket can be helpful. Watch the questions you ask, because a man may think you're being judgmental. Preface your questioning with, "I want to understand what you're experiencing. That's why I'm asking these questions."

"Desire Me"

"One of the ways I feel affirmed is sex," says one man. "I like sex and I need it. Sex is on men's minds a lot. Also, we are constantly barraged with sexual temptation in the media, from newspaper ads to films. They hit us at our weakest point. The guy who says he never notices is either lying or a walking cadaver."

Still other men say, "Our eyes are the problem. Men have innate visual scanners for anything that appeals sexually. Don't think we don't notice. The old adage that 'Women have to be in the mood, and men have to be in the room' is true. Resistance is a struggle for Christian men."

"There is also a strong connection between a man's sex drive and his ego. Women need to know how they impact us. We struggle constantly with keeping our sex life pure, especially when our wives are cold. Sometimes we don't want to be romantic—we just want to have sex. Other times we need to know we are desired, loved and accepted. We enjoy having our wives take the initiative."

Suggestion: Be as attractive as possible, and initiate and discuss what, how and when!

Three men in a small group were asked what their wives could do to encourage them. They were quite specific in what they said.

> I would love for my wife to ask questions that would lead to a greater understanding of who I am and what I have to deal with daily. I believe this would lead to a greater appreciation of me.

> Just to have her assure me that she will support and love me no matter what happens. Even if I lose my job or am uncertain about what to do next with my life. To affirm that God is in control and she is trusting Him to care for both of us.

> Women like to vent their feelings to a listening spouse without editorials or comments. I would like my wife to draw out my feelings about a situation but never editorialize or attempt to define what I mean. Next Tuesday evening after thinking about a specific situation, I may change my mind 180 degrees. I would like to be allowed to mull over things without being thought of as rude or disinterested.[7]

I asked this specific question of a group of men: "What could your wife do that would encourage you more?" Here are a few of the responses I received.

It would be nice if she would initiate lovemaking from time to time. However, the mitigating circumstances are three sons ages five, four and two. She has little energy left over most days.

I would love for her to be more consistent in assisting me with the everyday details that make up our days, such as dinner, laundry, housecleaning and paying bills. Through these helps, she encourages me that I'm not alone.

It would be encouraging to me if she would comment on the things that I do as favors because I am wanting to help out. She tends to see my efforts to help as obligations that I should be doing anyway. But I would like my wife to encourage me when I am down, distraught, overwhelmed and beaten. I don't need her advice or any sympathy. I just need to hear her gently say to me, "Honey, I know you are hurting. I may not be able to help you solve your problem, but tell me what is bothering you. And let's ask the Father to help you and to comfort you." And most of all, give me time to brew it over.

I want her to be more encouraging and truly desirous of giving encouragement rather than focusing on her own difficulties. And to be more encouraging in the sense that she's on my side rather than being adversarial, putting me on the defensive by saying, "Why didn't you say . . ." or "Why did you do that?" By avoiding reminding me that something should be obvious to me and why did I bring it up. By being more mindful of my need for touch or a hug, even if it's not obvious that I need it. By being more receptive and grateful for even the small things that I do to let her know I am thinking of her.

In a national survey that included more than 300 men of all ages, this is what the men said in response to the statement, "I would appreciate it if my partner would . . ." You may be surprised by some of the findings. The items that received the highest responses of "important" or "very important" were the following: Almost 100 percent of the men said listening to their ideas and being fun to be around were at the top of the list. Listening was a top priority: 80 percent to 90 percent wanted their wives to listen to their concerns, verbally say "I love you," show appreciation for what their husbands do for them, show independence and pursue their own interests.[8]

REAL MEN DO CRY

There is one last subject that is a source of tension, controversy and difference between men and women. Men have strong concerns about this issue—their feelings.

We're always taking hits about emotions, feelings or whatever you call them. There is confusion here for both men and women. We are emotional beings. We are not as insensitive as we are stereotyped to be, but we have difficulty moving from the logical/linear side of the mind to the emotional if we are left-brained males. Not all of us are left-brained either.

Stereotypes limit us. Women are convinced that all men think about is power and sex, or sex and power! So when we do open up emotionally, our response is automatically classified as one of these areas.

I would say many women don't understand the reality and depth of emotional pain men feel, especially when it is related to feelings of inadequacy imposed by society's markings of a real man—financial success, sexual potency, physical stature, competency, and so on. I wonder if the average wife knows how much her husband needs her support, admiration and affirmation.

My wife says things to me that hurt deeply. She says them in passing without much emotion or anger, just off the cuff. She seems to say them at times when discussion would be inappropriate (i.e., when other people are present). When we do get time to talk, the hurt is less severe or I just let it pass. This is probably more my problem than hers.

We struggle with emotions and stress. It seems that women, even those from the feminist groups, feel that they have all the stress. I don't know if they understand the gigantic responsibility we face being God's umbrella of protection for our families in a world that has such great negative influence and unhealthy attractions. It is hard to keep all your ducks in a straight line at times.[9]

WHEN A MAN SHARES HIS FEELINGS

Remember that when a man does share his feelings with you, it's often difficult for him. It's also a big step because most men haven't learned a feeling vocabulary, nor are they adept at giving word pictures. It would be helpful to him if you recognized his attempts and his progress.

JUST LISTEN

When feelings are shared he does not want to hear judgment or criticisms. Remember that the way he shares as well as the amount of sharing he does will probably not be the same way you share. That's all right. You're not to be his instructor at this time.

He may stop to think about what he wants to say. Don't fill in the silent times. In your heart and mind, give him all the time he needs to formulate what is occurring within him.

KEEP HIS CONFIDENCE

Since it is a step of vulnerability to share his feelings with you, keep what is said in confidence. Let him know you will do this. He doesn't want your mother, his mother or your friends to know.

DON'T INTERROGATE

When feelings are shared, he may be simply stating them, not offering them up for discussion. Either let him lead in this or ask if he wants you to just listen or respond. When you want to know what he is feeling, ask, "What's your reaction to this?" rather than, "What are you feeling?" He can respond best to the first question.

DON'T INTERRUPT

Never, but never, interrupt. I remember the first occasion I shared with my wife, Joyce, about the times when I had been depressed. I sat at the dining area table and Joyce stood 30 feet away with her back to me, washing the dishes. When I started sharing, she stopped what she was doing, came over, sat down and listened. Never once did she interrupt or make a value judgment on what I was sharing. I felt safe.

Interruptions cause men to retreat and think, *Why bother sharing?* Always remember, sharing feelings takes more effort, energy and concentration for men than it does for women. Men need to stay focused on one thing at a time. Interruptions throw them off course; and because they are goal conscious, they like to stay on course and complete the process.

Distractions make it difficult for a man to sort through the time-consuming process of interrupting his emotions. Many men are not emotionally articulate because they lack language skills in this area. When you are patient and accept this lack, it helps him talk more.

A wife shared with me a commitment note she gave her husband. She said it brought about the emotional interchange she had wanted for years. The note read, "Since sharing your emotions with me is such a cherished experience and so vital to a wonderful sexual relationship, I commit myself to you to respond in the following manner: When you share, you can count on me to listen, not expect you to describe your feelings exactly as I do, not interrupt, nor make value judgments. And finally, if we do enter into a discussion, I will limit my participation to fifteen minutes." Her husband was very encouraged!

Two days later she received a dozen roses and a note that said, "Thank you," and then, "My commitment when you share is 'ditto.' I won't try to solve the problem unless you ask me to!"

The Importance of Encouragement

You may look at the man in your life and see power, strength and determination. You may think, *Why does he need encouragement?*

He's got it all together. He's secure. You can't take everything at face value; there's always more to the picture.

Years ago, a handwritten note was passed from teacher to teacher. I think it describes all of us men:

> Don't be fooled by me. Don't be fooled by the mask I wear. For I wear a mask. I wear a thousand masks. Masks that I'm afraid to take off, and none of them are me. Pretending is an art that is second nature with me, but don't be fooled. I give the impression that I'm secure, that all is sunny and unruffled with me, that the waters are calm, and that I'm in command, and I need no one. But don't believe it. Please don't. My surface may seem smooth, but my surface is my mask. Beneath lays no smugness. Beneath dwells the real me, in confusion, in fear, in loneliness. But I hide this. I don't want anybody to know it.
>
> I panic at the thought of my weakness being exposed. That's why I create a mask to hide behind, to help me pretend. To shield me from the glance that knows. I'm afraid your glance will not be followed by love and acceptance, I'm afraid that you'll think less of me, that you'll laugh, and that your laugh will kill me. I'm afraid that deep down inside I'm nothing. That I'm just no good, and that you'll see and reject me.
>
> So I play my games, my desperate pretending games, with the façade of assurance on the outside and a trembling child within. And so my life becomes a front. I idly chatter with you in the suave tones of surface talk, I tell you everything that's really nothing. Nothing of what's crying within me. So when I'm going through my routine, don't be fooled by what I'm saying.

Please listen carefully, and try to hear what I am not saying, what I would like to be able to say. What for survival I need to say, but I can't say. I dislike the hiding. Honestly I do. I dislike the superficial phony games I'm playing. I'd really like to be genuine, spontaneous and me.

Can you help me? Help me by holding out your hand, even when that's the last thing I seem to want or need. Each time you're kind and gentle and encouraging, each time you try to understand because you really care, my heart begins to grow wings, very small wings, very feeble wings, but wings. With your sensitivity and sympathy, and your power of understanding, I can make it. You can breathe life into me. It will not be easy. A long conviction of worthlessness builds strong walls. But love is stronger than walls, and therein lies my hope.

Please try to take down those walls with firm hands, but with gentle hands. For a child is very sensitive, and I am a child. Who am I you may wonder? I am someone you know very well. I am every man you meet.[10]

DISCOVER THE ENCOURAGER IN YOU

1. What do you love and respect about your husband's personality?

2. How does your husband add purpose and meaning to your life?

3. Think of something you and your husband experienced or did together that gives your spirit a lift. In general, how does he make life more enjoyable?

4. Identify some of your husband's qualities, characteristics, skills or giftings that describe who he is and what he demonstrates daily through his work, his service to others or his relationship with you and your children. Record here what comes to mind.

5. Which of these qualities, characteristics, skills or giftings are you going to praise him for today?

What *Not* to Do

(or The Worst Mistakes You Could Make)

"ARE THERE LIMITS TO ENCOURAGEMENT? After all, you don't know my husband. Let me tell you about him. He's . . ."

"Does encouraging mean I sell out? Do I become a nothing trying to meet his needs all the time?"

These are good, honest questions. Hopefully, I can offer some answers!

Sometimes in an attempt to be an encourager, you end up crossing the line and become a pleaser. But that's not the only line to avoid crossing. In this chapter, we'll look at problem behaviors that plague many marriages. Space does not permit discussing the background and reasons for those behaviors. Instead, we'll focus on suggestions that will help you avoid doing the things that can harm your marriage relationship.

SERVING ONE ANOTHER

It's easy to fall into thinking you either have to control or be controlled. But God never advocates domination of one marriage partner over the other. Sometimes, however, one partner ends up being smothered by the other. Allowing this to happen is no way to encourage someone! If you end up letting the other person control you, the result is that you end up feeling unnecessary. Total dependence on another is not the way Christ has called us to live. Jesus has called us to equality, not domination.

Jesus has called us to willingly serve one another, not just one to serve the other.

From the passage in Ephesians 5:22-31, and from the creation account, it's possible to discover what a husband needs from his wife. As we look at the early chapters of Genesis, we see that a man needs a woman of strength, a helper who will respond to his leadership as he sets out to subdue and populate the earth. Nancy Groom, in her book *Married Without Masks,* states:

> Adam (even after the Fall) would have been disappointed if Eve had refused to engage with him as his partner in the work God had called both of them to do. He did not need a slave; he needed a woman who knew who she was and was confident in her gifts. An alive, vibrant woman gives zest and excitement to her husband's life. He needs that.[1]

Remember this fact: One of the main causes for the death of love is when one partner controls and dominates. Look at what God's Word says: "For all of you who were baptized into Christ have clothed yourselves with Christ. There is neither Jew nor Greek, there is neither slave nor free man, there is neither male nor female; for you are all one in Christ Jesus" (Gal. 3:27-28, *NASB*).

What our world sees as a leadership model goes counter to what Jesus said: "But Jesus called them to Himself and said, 'You know that the rulers of the Gentiles lord it over them, and their great men exercise authority over them. It is not this way among you, and whoever wishes to be first among you shall be your slave; just as the Son of Man did not come to be served, but to serve, and to give His life a ransom for many" (Matt. 20:25-28, *NASB*).

Servanthood is the model of leadership Jesus is teaching. Remember that the only healthy way you can really encourage another person is to be sure that you encourage yourself. You can do this because you know who you are in Jesus Christ.

The best way to be healthy as well as to be an encourager in a marriage relationship is to be healthily independent or *interdependent*. The person whose identity is found through others often ends up in an addictive relationship.

We are all called to be dependent on God, but dependency in human relationships is not a Christian calling.

Neither is independence. An *independent* woman thrives on individuality, few restrictions and self-gratification. She finds her identity through herself.

There is a third option called *interdependence*. The interdependent woman has a strong sense of personhood and bases this upon being affirmed by God. She knows she has been given gifts and is willing to use them, but she can also rely upon others. This woman views others as her equal and also values herself. Are you a dependent, independent or interdependent woman?

In her book *Free to Be God's Woman*, Jan Congo gives three options in which to view ourselves and others. A *dependent* woman says, "I am nothing and you are nothing," or "I am nothing but you are a person of worth and dignity." The *independent* woman says, "I am a person of worth and dignity, but you are expendable." The *interdependent* woman says, "I am a person of worth and dignity, and you are a person of worth and dignity."

In this last option, competition does not exist. Competition between women, and between men and women, is a reflection of insecurity.

The interdependent woman allows herself and others the freedom to grow and be in process. She is comfortable with role flexibility. She is relying on God's expectations for herself rather than others' expectations.

This style of living does not knowingly intimidate and does not feel intimidating. The interdependent woman does not try to prove she is superior to others; nor does she attempt to live the way the world values people.

One final thought: An interdependent woman demonstrates balance in her relationships. She enters into relationships with others; she does not restrict them nor is she responsible for them. She discovers the value of commitment.[2]

This idea of what it means to be interdependent is well summarized by Jan Congo:

Now we, as Christ's followers, find ourselves growing through healthy relationships. In 1 John 4:12 (*NASB*) it says, "No one has seen God at any time; if we love one another, God abides in us, and His love is perfected in us." The Christian life was not meant to be lived in a vacuum. We are encouraged to be involved in relationships.

As we rub shoulders with each other we see the need to be committed to one another. Only in commitment to imperfect human beings can we follow in our Master's footsteps.

The very word "commitment" grinds on many eardrums today in this independent, self-centered society of ours. Yet it is only after we have committed ourselves to the God of love that we can commit ourselves to care for others and identify with them in their various stages of growth. We refuse to make others either our projects or our heroes. Instead we choose to walk, as much as is humanly possible, be available to them, to be as gentle with them as Jesus Christ is with us and to be vulnerable to them, demonstrated by our willingness to speak the truth in love about ourselves when we are with them. I choose to back up my words with an authentic lifestyle. In relationships I am willing not only to give but also to express my needs honestly and receive from others.

We are one of the best means of getting God's life and love to others. Jesus is our source of strength, so never do we purposely choose to have others become dependent on us. In all of our relating, we must remember that the purpose is for Christ to be formed in you and in me (see Gal. 4:19). If we find ourselves imitating anyone but Christ or presenting someone else to imitate us, then we need to confess and readjust. We need to honestly share, with no inhibitions, what we see happening, and together we need to get our friendship back to its original purpose—that Christ will be formed in both of us.

Love is the evidence that I am Christ's woman. Only through dependence on Christ alone will I find myself freed to be a most courageous lover who will not lose her identity through loving but will find her God-given purpose in loving.[3]

Encouraging your husband does *not* mean that you become so absorbed in him that your identity and value come from him. *It doesn't mean* becoming a doormat with no ideas, opinions or voice; nor does it mean becoming an appeasing woman. Encouragement is not manipulation. It's not done for the purpose of reshaping him for your own dreams, desires or wishes. Absorption, appeasement and manipulation are actually forms of control.

A Balanced Control

Did you realize that if you cooperate with a controller you're encouraging him? That's right, you're encouraging him to continue to control! If you happen to be in this situation, here are some phrases you can use that will encourage him to respond in a healthier way. Remember that your tone of voice and nonverbals have much to say as well.

- "When you remind me to put the magazines in the rack when I leave the room, I really feel bothered and hovered over. Please wait until I'm through reading for that time period and I will put them away. I do understand how important this is to you."

- "When you tell me how much lipstick to wear, I don't feel accepted. I feel like you're trying to make me over so I won't embarrass you. I would like you to let me be me and decide how I would like to groom myself. If you do this I will feel more positive toward you. And I think you will like the result."

- "When you continue to check the way I'm cooking the meal, I feel like a child. I feel like my abilities are being evaluated by someone who is not an expert, and it irritates me. Please let me do my job the way I do it. Then if you don't like the end result, we can discuss it to see what can be done."

Notice the formula in these three examples: You share your feelings, identify the unacceptable behavior, follow with a request and then share what your husband will gain by responding to what you've said. It may help to identify the consequences if your request is unheeded. Some consequences will be obvious, but it may help to clarify the natural consequences. And you need to be willing to follow through.

How does expressing your thoughts and feelings like this encourage your spouse? It promotes a balanced relationship, and you no longer participate in the control issue.

UNHELPFUL REMINDERS

Avoid mothering the man in your life. Let me say it another way. Never, but never, mother a man. When you act like a mother with your spouse, you can't encourage him. Treating an adult like a child is demeaning and makes you a controller! If you mother him, he will continue to act in a way that makes you continue to want to mother him, and on and on and on it goes.

How do mothers sound? They remind. They actually make the other person (child or adult) rely on them to bail them out. Why would a person remember to do something when he has someone who will remind him? Have you ever made statements like these?

- "Honey, be sure you've got your wallet."
- "Don't forget to stop and pick up some milk and butter on the way home."
- "Jim, don't you ever look at the gas gauge? You know how many times you've run out!"
- "Be sure to take a coat with you; you usually get cold."
- "John, if I've asked you once I've asked you a hundred times . . ."
- "You didn't call for the plane tickets. I'll do it for you . . . again."

You may be thinking, *What's wrong with those statements and questions? Aren't they just helpful reminders?* Perhaps—if you remind so that he learns to remember by himself and you won't have to remind him anymore! Reminding once in a while may be helpful, but if you have to repeat again and again, it's obvious the reminders are not working. They're what I call bailout responses. They take the responsibility away from the other person. These statements say, "You're a child; you can't remember anything. I'll do it for you."

ABORT THE RESCUE EFFORTS

Similar to reminding is another approach: It's called rescuing. Years ago there was a song out with the title "Rescue Me." If a man in your life sings this song, don't listen.

How do you know if someone is playing the role of a rescuee? Would that man be incapable of functioning in his daily life without your help? If so, don't rescue. Encourage growth.

Do you tend to be stronger than him? If so, don't reinforce his weaknesses and foster dependency. Find his potential and encourage growth.

Does he tend to be unhappy unless you're doing something for him? If so, don't play this game. Encourage by showing you believe in his capability to do it himself.

Does he make excuses for himself or do you make excuses for him? Remember that excuses cripple and perpetuate helplessness.

But aren't you to love your husband by helping and serving him? Yes, but it can become rescuing when you believe that it's your responsibility to solve his problems or protect him from the results of what he's done.

Rescuing doesn't work. It doesn't promote growth or change. It doesn't help your man grow.

Sometimes women gain fulfillment by being a rescuer. It makes them feel good and look good in the eyes of others. The downside is that you could end up angry, resentful, feeling exhausted or even demeaned.

Why do some women get caught up in being a rescuer? Rescuing puts you in a position of control or power. It keeps others from focusing on your mistakes or problems. After all, who are they to talk!

Rescuing is a great diversion. You don't have to deal with your own issues if you're busy saving others.

It also doesn't make for much of an equal relationship or mutual submission, as Scripture asks of us (see Eph. 5).

WHEN RESCUE ISN'T CALLED FOR

Rescuing is another word for fixing. In contrast, loving encouragement means support, being available, being cooperative and sympathetic.[4]

You may be guilty of mothering, or rescuing your husband if you continually do things for him that he could and should do for himself. It keeps him responding as a child.

Do you find yourself caught up in playing Twenty Questions with him, trying to find out what he wants, doesn't want, is or isn't thinking? Guessing games to get information are just that—games. They belong with kids, not adults.

Mothering involves making assumptions that your man is going to commit the worst of all sins—forget or be absentminded. Mothering reinforces his tendency to do what you don't want!

It's also a violation of the love chapter—1 Corinthians 13. Love gives the other person the benefit of the doubt.

Close to this behavior is taking charge of events or activities that you think he's going to mess up. It lets him off the hook and helps him continue to be irresponsible.

By the way, you will get results with these approaches. He will probably show some anger, which will breed resentment and could even turn into passive resistance or out-and-out rebellion. Anger is just one possibility. I know you don't want that to happen!

When you continually rescue your husband, he's not going to feel so good about himself because he's going to feel less than competent. And he may blame you, which is a big turnoff for him. The end result is that his romantic interest in you could diminish greatly. When resentment exists, it's difficult for romance to stay around. Over time, his original love feelings could disappear as well.

STOP PERPETUATING DEPENDENT BEHAVIOR

What options do you have? Actually, you have several options, and they're positive for both of you. When you follow through with these you're sending the message, "I believe in you. I believe in your capabilities to be responsible, mature and act like an adult!"

The solutions are quite obvious. You will need to change your way of responding regardless of how you feel, what you've been through with him and how you've responded to him. First, ask yourself, *Has what I've been doing worked? Do I have much to lose with a new response?* If you answered no both times, then go for it!

First, don't do anything more for your man that he should be (meaning, that he is capable of) doing for himself. If he asks you for something, and you're used to getting it for him, let him get it for himself. Don't make suggestions. Don't pick up after him. Don't bail him out of experiencing the consequences of his lack of action. Yes, it probably means that your life could be a bit more frustrating for a while. But you need to stick to your commitment. If you hear complaints, let him know that you know he's capable of assuming the responsibility himself. You may be the first person in his life to show a belief that he can be different. Treat him as though he is reliable. I've seen so many women who end up being the clock, calendar, key finder, garbage enforcer and appointment regulator. Don't rescue! Don't bail him out!

I've dealt with husbands like this in counseling situations. As we discussed together the situation, the dialogue often went something like this:

Norm: John, you have a fairly responsible job, don't you?

John: Yes, I do. I've been there three years now.

Norm: And you've received a couple of promotions, haven't you?

John: Yes, one just recently.

Norm: John, when you're at work, who is it that reminds you of what to do, when to do it and how to do your job?

John: Well, no one. I can handle all that myself. I don't need reminders.

Norm: So you don't need any kind of reminders or support like that at work?

John: No.

Norm: I guess my question is, what's the difference?

John: What's the difference?

Norm: Yes, why are you so different at work? You're competent, reliable and functional, and you follow through. At home you're just the opposite. It appears that you're making a choice. You have the

capability, and you choose to be that way at
work. At home you have the same capability, but
you choose not to use it at home. I wonder what
kind of message you're sending to your wife?

If a man is functional at work and not at home, there's
some kind of game-playing going on that needs to be exposed
and stopped.[5] Read the story of Eric and James as told by James
Walker in his book *Husbands Who Won't Lead and Wives Who
Won't Follow:*

For a wife who has grown accustomed to it, refusing to
"mother" can be painful. Some women may be faced
with the disturbing thought that perhaps this role was
exactly what they wanted in marriage. They saw the es-
capist's irresponsible tendencies, and they felt right at
home with the prospect. The challenge of taking someone and remaking him might have been an equally com-
pelling reason. Whatever the rationale, the notion of now
opposing this lifestyle by doing nothing goes against all
of her natural instincts, including her maternal desires.

Eric's habit patterns included giving no help around
the house. To Jane it was a constant source of irritation.
He sat watching TV while she asked, "Could you take
out the garbage?" Her second, third, and fourth requests
were always fended off with his desire to wait for a com-
mercial, to finish the article he was reading, or the excuse that he had to wait till morning when he could see.

When she'd finally had enough, Jane agreed to begin some passive resistance. She asked Eric the familiar question, "Would you take out the garbage?" She

asked only once. Thereafter, she began filling paper sacks beside the overflowing garbage can. The children noticed their shrinking kitchen, but it took Eric five days and walking into the pile on his way to the refrigerator between commercials to bring up the subject.

Jane's reaction was a calm one: "I asked you to take that out the other day. I knew you'd get to it whenever you were able." It was a polite but firm reply that communicated esteem for Eric and a new line that she would not cross. There are easier ways to handle a garbage problem. But Eric and Jane's problem was not garbage; it was irresponsibility.

Jane found pleasure in controlling her emotions by refusing to become angry. She also noticed a new delight in not allowing her emotions to be dictated by her husband. Her confidence grew to the point that she told Eric, "Sweetheart, you can notice when the garbage is full. From now on, I'll just let you decide when to take it out." Basically, Jane had to decide what she could live with—an overflowing trash can or a growing anger and resentment toward her husband.

The difficult area for Jane was the checkbook. When they both agreed on a budget, it was decided that Eric would pay the bills. She got a check each week for groceries and her areas of management, i.e., clothes for her and the kids, school supplies and household expenses.

Jane knew it was only a matter of time before things would bog down financially.

Several months later, as Eric looked for socks among the discards scattered on the top of his desk, he noticed and dug through the overdue bills piled around the

"IN" box—just where he and Jane had agreed they would be placed. Frantically, he ripped them open to survey the damage. Each one was more devastating than the last. They were like cold buckets of water on a groggy morning. As he came down the stairs to find Jane, he felt angry and inwardly frightened.

Jane tried not to blink as he screamed into her face. She calmly looked into his eyes and said, "You agreed to be in charge of our finances, sweetheart. I did put the bills where you told me."

"Why didn't you open them and tell me about them?" he shouted.

"I just thought of them as your mail and I had confidence in you that you'd take care of them," she responded.

Later, as a much calmer Eric talked to me, he reassembled his thoughts. "I knew that all my life I just tried to get by. I didn't think of myself as lazy, but I suppose I was. I know I wasn't God's prize husband. Jane deserved better. But that day it hit me. Things weren't going to get any better if I didn't change."

What Jane had been trying to get across to Eric for twelve years, the garbage can and the bill collectors had managed to turn around in three months![6]

Sometimes a husband may not act capable because of other reasons, such as the fear of failure.

When a husband fails in one area, he will take on only "safe" tasks. Why should he attempt something that carried with it the uncertainty of risk? Therefore, some husbands will pull back from activities over which they don't maintain a high degree of control or in which they aren't certain of success.

This happened with Tom when he lost his job. Though he did not admit it at first, it was a terrible defeat.

Tom was also a good auto mechanic. He had an aged car he tinkered with as a hobby. With a cavalier attitude, he told Cindy, his wife, "Now I've got the chance to put that old convertible on the road. I'll look for a job when I'm ready. So don't bug me about it."

Tom told his friends he had enough money saved so that he could take his time to pick the job he wanted. He even bragged that he might make so much money on the sale of that old car that he could start working for himself. In point of fact, he was spending more cash for parts than their situation allowed, and he knew he was only staying busy enough to allow himself the luxury of not thinking.

Only later did Tom admit he was really afraid of being turned down for a new job. He deeply feared that his own incompetence or personality had cost him his former position, and he had no desire to suffer through a series of job-interview rejections.

The more Cindy expressed fears for their future, the more Tom heard one theme loud and clear: "You're not providing for us, and you're a failure." Cindy never said it, but Tom heard it. When Cindy initiated prayer, urged Tom in Bible reading or some area of spiritual leadership, he only saw her dissatisfaction with him. Whenever he entered the house and heard Cindy talking on the phone to a friend from church, he could tell by the hushed tone of her voice that he was the subject of conversation. He dreaded the glances of her friends at church and was embarrassed when the pastor inquired if they needed help. Therefore, he continued to lose himself in car grease, matinee movies and Monday Night Football.

To compound his inner doubts, Tom began to see that his circumstances were putting him in the same place as his own father, a man who had never held a steady job for long. That notion horrified and angered him. He had no desire to live a life where he lacked respect. Tom became suspended between the fear of being a second-class citizen in his own home and his need to avoid the risk of further failure.

It was only after Cindy began the process of expressing her trust in Tom again and the belief that he would do the right thing that he began to see his home as a place where he could be safe. Home for Tom became a location where he could be understood and an avenue where he could risk failure and still not be devastated.

Each day Cindy's smile told him she believed in him and simply chose to ignore his failures. With that encouragement, Tom's inner motivation grew. Cindy's attitude toward her husband was not one that came from a downtrodden self-image but one that was a deliberate choice on her part. Again it was encouragement that made the difference.[7]

A wife shared with me how she was able to help and encourage her husband.

My husband had no conception of organization. He's a perfectionist, and if something couldn't be done perfectly then he wouldn't do it at all, or he'd leave a job half complete. Needless to say, we had a lot of half-finished projects, a lot of mess and a lot of tasks never started.

I'm not a nag and I didn't pester him about the unfinished projects, but I did pick up the tools and materials left lying around and put them in big piles. I also have a drawer (big drawer) in the kitchen that I called his tool drawer. Anything I found lying around I put into that drawer. That way if anything was missing, he could find it either in a pile or in the drawer.

This caused a lot of arguments because he said it was his house, too, and he should be able to have his items wherever he wanted. (My husband is a carpenter and some of those items included big boards on which he would write notes or phone numbers or lists of materials needed. I started burning the boards in the fireplace.) All this was after many requests for him to write on tablets and put things away.

I started buying him organizational tools—a small handheld computer and tablets—and we worked on writing lists on things he needed to accomplish in a day. He prioritized the list. If he didn't have the materials needed to start a job, then it went to the bottom of the list.

I showed him it was okay to do a job as good as you could; it didn't have to be perfect, and it didn't have to be better than anyone else could do it. He began to feel good about starting something, completing it and crossing it off his list.

I praised him when he began a job, during the job and, of course, after it was complete he got lots of praise.

Most of the time the finished project was better than anyone else could have done it.

Praise was very important to him and I found he needed to hear me praise him to other people. I would tell the person what his next project was going to be and how excited I was about his plans. I guess he just needed a system to get him organized. He could see that if he didn't get organized his stuff was going to get burned or he was going to have a pile in the backyard as big as the house. He needed to know his projects were appreciated and we didn't expect perfection.

ENCOURAGEMENT CUTS BOTH WAYS

In any kind of encouragement directed toward your husband, be sure you don't fall into the trap of giving up your ministries, hobbies or interests because they're not important to your man. Sometimes these changes occur so gradually, you're not even aware that you've made them. This wouldn't be healthy for you or for him. What's important to you doesn't have to have the same level of importance to him. You both need to encourage each other's uniqueness. The more you give up who you are, the less you care about yourself. This will tend to build up anger or resentment and you will be less likely to want to encourage your mate.

I'd like to come back to another concern that's mentioned elsewhere in this book. If you don't feel good about yourself or you don't encourage yourself, you will have difficulty honestly and genuinely encouraging the significant man in your life. How do you see yourself? How are you feeling about yourself?

Another trap that may sound scriptural is, "I must decrease so he can increase." That's not what the Bible says. But some highly gifted and competent women feel that in order to build up and encourage a man they need to hold back their abilities and giftedness because if they expressed who they really are their man would feel insecure. I hope my response to that doesn't sound too harsh but, if he does, it's not your fault. It's his problem.

You may say, "I don't hold back or cover up." But sometimes women do and they aren't even aware of it. For example, do you put yourself down, make derogatory comments about yourself or call attention to any mistakes you make in front of your husband? Do you brush aside his compliments or argue about them to prove he shouldn't have a positive opinion of you? Do you put a lid on your abilities so that the attention usually is directed to him?

All of these are telltale signs.[8]

This is not the way you were called to live. Your strengths and giftedness are from God. They're not meant to be thwarted by anyone.

DISCOVER THE ENCOURAGER IN YOU

1. What is the difference between relational dependence and interdependence?

2. How would you describe your relationship with your husband—as dependent, independent or interdependent? Give some examples.

3. What kinds of tasks or actions do you remind your husband to do or not do? How often do you remind him? How does he respond when you remind him?

4. Based on the content of this chapter, would you say that you "mother" your husband? Might you be guilty of perpetuating irresponsible behaviors in him? What are they?

5. Try an experiment this week: No matter how difficult it is for you to remain silent, stop reminding your husband to do what he can and should do. Let him experience the consequences of his choices. If he gets upset, calmly tell him that you have every confidence he is able to take care of those details. After one week, record what you are feeling. Also record what changes have come about in your husband. (Don't get discouraged if one week is too early to turn things around.)

Sex and Romance—

Yes! It Does Bring Out the Best

"**ENCOURAGE HIM SEXUALLY?** What man needs any encouragement there? His 'on' button is never 'off'!"

"I don't think that's an area I can do much about. The sex is there, but romance is what's needed. I'm not sure how to encourage him romantically."

Is sex all men ever think about? Well, they do think about it . . . a lot. Sexual thoughts flit in and out of a man's mind all day long. Men think about, dream about and daydream about sex far more than you probably ever realized. Even though men slow down in their thoughts about sex when they're in their forties and fifties, they still think about it several times a day. Men tend to dream about sex three times as often as women do. Their performance orientation to life flows into the sexual area as well, and their greatest fear is the "I" word—impotence. Archibald Hart describes it well:

Sure, the average man thinks of other things, like football and politics, but eventually all mental roads lead back to this one central fixation. Sex. There are times when the obsession fades and even vanishes. Give him a golf bag or a fishing trip. He'll forget about sex for a while. But sooner or later, like a smoldering fire, it will flare up again. Strong, urgent, forceful and impatient, the sex drive dominates the mind and body of every healthy male. Like it or not, that's the way it is.[1]

Men want sex for a number of reasons, including physical release; giving or receiving comfort, affection and encouragement; love; proving one's popularity, masculinity or sexual ability; and expressing tenderness. The average man sees sex as the main way to be close to his wife.

One husband said, "I guess sex means many things to me. Sometimes I'm romantic, and that's the reason. I want to be close. Other times I'm down, and sex is comforting. Sometimes I just want a quick release."

The sexual relationship could be the primary means a husband uses to feel connected to his wife. It can be a time of special closeness for them both.

We live in a sexually oriented society. We talk a lot about sex but we really don't talk about sex. Contradictory? No. You probably know what I mean. Most couples don't have serious in-depth talks about sex and romance. It just happens. They do it. It may be fulfilling, and then again, it may not. But it's a vital part of married life and can be so enriching for both husband and wife.

Let's face it. Sex is at the top of the list for men. They struggle with it. Too often they think of just their own needs. Men won't like this statement, but most men are not as knowledgeable about sex as they think they are! We as men have a lot to learn about lovemaking. And believe it or not, women can help their men learn about sex and romance. But you need to understand a man's sexual needs.

Husbands do want more from sex than just sex! They want a *complete* relationship. Complete—meaning intimate—sexually, emotionally, spiritually and relationally. They hunger for intimacy, despite the fact that many substitute sex for sharing emotion. Some, however, are able to connect with both.

Husbands who tend to confuse emotional needs for sexual needs and view intimacy as sex become frustrated, grumpy and upset when they don't have a sexual outlet. Sex is usually their only source of closeness.

Although husbands want sex, they are often unsure of what they really want and how to obtain it. The problem is not insurmountable. Both husband and wife need to talk, listen and discuss their sexual needs. Many men feel more comfortable discussing sex in the darkness of the bedroom because the risk of intimate sharing is diminished there.

Dr. Archibald Hart conducted a national survey with men and the subject of male sexuality. Approximately 150 men who participated in the Hart report were asked the question, "Do you feel that women understand men's sex drive?" The "no" response was a strong 83 percent, which probably indicated a lack of sufficient sex in a relationship.[2]

What do men want their wives to understand about their sexuality? That they are normal when it comes to sex; that an understanding of one another's needs must be recognized and both partners must work toward mutual satisfaction.

Husbands want their wives to understand and accept the strength of their biological drive. The male sex drive is not a fault, nor is it a mistake. God is the author of sex. Husbands want their wives to know that looking at other women does not mean they don't love their wives. A look of admiration is not a sign of straying.

They also want their wives to initiate lovemaking—at least part of the time. They get weary of being the pursuer, and they do appreciate some novelty.

At times husbands do not want sex, but they do want closeness. Often wives interpret every physical overture as a prelude to ending up in bed—sometimes for good reason. No one is a mind reader. It simplifies everything when the man verbalizes his intent and desire.[3]

As you reach out to encourage your husband with sex and romance there can be two side benefits. He will learn more, and you will be more satisfied.

LANGUAGE STYLE AND SEX

There is a relationship between sex and your language style.

A VISUAL MAN'S SEX LANGUAGE

The visual person takes his tendency into the bedroom as well as every other room. The visual husband (and remember that most men tend to be highly visual) is aroused by what he sees, and he appreciates visual detail. The décor of the bedroom as well as what a spouse wears (or doesn't wear) is part of the process of creating romance. All visual people are not responsive to the same sights. It is important for the visual spouse to share with his mate the kinds of stimuli he appreciates. If you have a visual spouse, ask him what sights are pleasing to him and allow time for him to look at you.

Attention to visual details is important at all stages of a romantic evening that leads to sexual expression. A restaurant that captures a romantic atmosphere with lighting, warm colors and comfortable furniture is part of the foreplay that leads to a fulfilling sexual encounter.

AN AUDITORY MAN'S SEX LANGUAGE

An auditory husband may take for granted all your efforts to look good, but he will enjoy romantic music on the stereo. This is usually the time for soft, soothing music rather than a Sousa march or a rap song! And don't forget to disengage the telephone, fax, beeper and other distractions when it's time for lovemaking. The auditory partner is especially distracted by annoying sounds and interruptions.

Also, verbal expressions may be more important to this person, even during lovemaking. But be sure your auditory partner wants your verbal expression at this time. The bottom line of romance is always doing those things that your spouse wants and avoiding those things your spouse dislikes.

A TACTILE MAN'S SEX LANGUAGE

A feelings-oriented man will respond best to the feel of various fabrics, the touch of the skin and fragrances such as perfume and massage oils. Whereas a visual person may respond to the subdued atmosphere of dim candlelight, the feelings person likes the fragrance of the candle. Room temperature is also very important to the feelings-oriented individual.

Did you ever think of quietness being an enhancement to the romance or sexual life of your marriage? Most men greatly appreciate times of being quiet together, especially if you're the talkative one and he's the quiet person. A woman might be surprised by the answer when she asks her husband the question, "How much do you value your quiet time or our quiet time together?" Usually the answer indicates it's very much valued. So, what can you do? You could practice being quiet with your husband. If he tends to be quiet, give him some quiet time. Perhaps he's relaxing in a room reading or watching TV. You could go in and sit next to him without saying anything. You could read or watch TV with him. You could invite him for a walk around the block and enforce a gag rule on yourself. Don't bring up anything unless he does and then only talk about his topics.

We all enjoy most forms of stimulation to some degree, but each of us finds some things more romantic than others. What does your husband prefer? What do you prefer? Have you really identified your specific sexual needs in this way and shared them with your spouse? Have you asked him about specific preferences? If not, why not do it soon? You may be pleased and delighted with the information you receive![4]

Now let's get to some specific suggestions.

Saying "I love you" is a message that needs to be conveyed to your spouse every day. But creativity helps you convey the message in many ways that show you really mean it. So here are some wild and different ways to get your message across. You may feel a little silly or embarrassed at first when trying some of these, but the response is well worth the effort. Some of these suggestions could really connect with your husband.

THIRTY WAYS TO HOLD ON TO ROMANCE

1. Find books on other languages in the library or a bookstore and copy "I love you" in several languages. Either write out the message or learn how to pronounce the message properly.
2. Write the words "I love you" backwards and place the message in your husband's shoe.
3. When you steam up the bathroom, write "I love you" on the mirror and ask him to come in while it's still readable. (You might also consider taking a shower together!)
4. Put a balloon in the car with the words "I love you" on it or in it.

5. Spell "I love you" with candies on your husband's pillow, desk or favorite chair.

6. Make a huge "I love you" banner and tape it to the ceiling over your bed.

7. Carve "I love you" in wood and float your message in the fish tank, orange juice container, or even the toilet!

8. Paint "I love you" on a household object (refrigerator, mirror, garage door, and so on) with removable paint.

9. Buy an inexpensive glider and soar it toward your husband, pulling a tiny "I love you" banner (or paint "I love you" on the wings).

10. Take him kite flying. Make sure your kite says "I love you" in some creative way. (The new kites are great! My wife and I tried this.)

11. Bake the message on or inside a pastry (cake, fortune cookie). Or put a written "I love you" message inside the Thanksgiving or Christmas turkey. Imagine your husband's reaction as he unfolds the message in front of your guests!

12. If you have a talking bird (parrot, mynah, cockatiel), see if the bird can be taught to say "I love you" adding your husband's name. (Be sure the bird doesn't have an obscene vocabulary as well!)

13. For a special occasion, write "I love you" on your eyelids so the message shows when you close your eyes.

14. If you have a telephone answering machine, leave an "I love you" message on it for him.

15. Bury or hide the message and give him a treasure map to find it. It is also nice to have a small gift with the message when the searching entails some time and effort.

16. Say "I love you" in sign language. Simply raise your right hand palm forward, lifting thumb, index finger and pinkie while keeping the two middle fingers folded down.

17. If you have a swimming pool, write "I love you" on the bottom of the pool with different objects.

18. Write "I love you" on the kitchen counter with sugar or flour.

19. If your husband keeps a daily calendar, write "I love you" messages on several of the dates.

20. Write "I love you" very small and fasten it inside his glasses or sunglasses with clear tape.

21. Tie the message to one of your pets in such a way that your husband will have to take it off the pet to read it.

22. Record "I love you" messages on videocassette or audiotape and mail it to your husband. Write a wild title on the tape's label. Be sure to put "personal" on the envelope if you're sending it to an office.

23. Give your husband an "I love you" ornament for Christmas.

24. Purchase a dozen Valentine's cards in February and send one to your husband each month of the year.

25. Buy a package of candy and open it carefully at one of the seams. Put several love messages inside with your husband's name on them, then reseal the package. Make sure he's the one to open the candy—not the kids!

26. Purchase a book of blank pages at a stationery store. Write a love message inside using one word per page. (Be creative. The book may contain 50-100 pages.) Take the book to your public library, tell the librarian your plan and ask him/her to keep the book until

your husband comes to claim it. Send him a card (perhaps a reserve book card purchased from the library) with a message that the library is holding a special book reserved for him.

27. Get ideas for handmade love-message cards from stationery or card stores. Be creative with size, color and design.

28. Place an "I love you" message in the "personals" column of the local newspaper. Send him an anonymous message to read the personals every day that week until the message is discovered.

29. Write each word from the message "I love you" on three separate sheets of paper and put each in an envelope. Ask three different friends to drop off one envelope to your husband during the week.

30. Your turn to come up with some ideas. List four other ways to say "I love you" that might be special for the man in your life.[5]

Do men need to hear the words "I love you" in order to feel loved? Yes; but more than that he needs to hear that his wife appreciates him and what he does. He wants to know that his hard work and attention to detail around the house is highly valued. Someone has said that when your relationship with your man is full of gratitude and not just actions, you'll receive feelings. Gratitude also enhances the romance and sexual relationship.

A TIME-TESTED WAY TO A MAN'S HEART

One of the ways to romance the man in your life is through food. That's right—good old basic food. The average husband finds that it's romantic when his wife makes a special meal for him. For some, mealtime is a time to connect. Going out to dinner at a nice, quiet restaurant is a wonderful setting for romance. Find out what foods are really special for the man in your life. Then be creative!

When your husband is in a relaxed mood or when the two of you are out to dinner, say, "I need 10 minutes of your time to conduct an interview with you. I can't tell you yet what it's about, but you will eventually know more about it." Then ask him the following questions:

1. When you used to date in high school or college, what were your favorite types of dates? Why?
2. During those years, did you dream about an outstanding date that you always wanted to have but never did? (I don't mean with a certain movie star!)
3. What are your favorite colors?
4. What is your favorite type of movie?
5. What are your favorite travel spots to visit?
6. What are your favorite foods?
7. What type of restaurant do you like best?
8. What are your three favorite desserts?
9. What are your favorite flowers?
10. What is your favorite cologne/perfume?
11. What are your favorite types of books?
12. What shows or plays do you enjoy the most, and why?
13. What three types of activities would you like to try, given a chance to do so?

The result of the interviews should give you ample ideas for numerous dates, either simple or extravagant, that incorporate many of your partner's favorites.

COMMUNICATION BY TOUCH

Sexual touching is a vital part of a husband-wife relationship. But as with other forms of marital communication, meaningful touch takes time and effort to develop. The intense drive for physical contact that precedes the wedding and lasts for a while afterward often becomes a rut: "Well, it's Thursday night. I guess it's time to have sex again."

Each of you will differ in your desire for the expression of physical love. One of you may enjoy a great amount of bodily contact while the other is satisfied with much less. Your specific tastes for touch may also be different. One may enjoy passionate embraces, caresses and massages while the other prefers more relaxed contact such as resting his head on his partner's lap. One may like holding hands for an hour; the other for two minutes.

In order to increase the enjoyment of physical touch in your marriage, evaluate your present experience with touch. After each of you has completed the following statements, share your responses:

- Some of the ways I like to be touched are . . .
- Some of the ways I do not like to be touched are . . .
- I think you like to be touched by . . .
- The times I like to be touched are . . .
- The times I prefer not to be touched are . . .
- I think we touch each other _____ times a day.
- Who does the most touching in our relationship?
- Who prefers to do the touching in our relationship?
- When I am touched it makes me feel . . .
- When you are touched you feel . . .
- The way we could improve our touching would be to . . .[6]

Cliff and Joyce Penner have developed the following discussion tool for couples so that couples can increase their understanding and enjoyment of their sexual relationship.

COMMON DIFFERENCES TO BE NEGOTIATED

Check the statements that pertain to you on a separate piece of paper. Ask your husband to do the same.

I like to initiate
I like making love in the morning
Direct initiation is the most positive for me
I like to have sex several times per week
Regarding kisses, I like them long and wet
I like to do a lot of talking:
    Before making love
    During making love
    After making love
I like noisy lovemaking
Explicit sexual talk is arousing for me
I like to talk about it afterward
I like to get and give lots of touching
Direct stimulation is most positive for me
I like to make love with the lights on
I like my partner to have eyes open when lovemaking
I like oral sex when it is the woman stimulating the man
I like oral sex when it is the man stimulating the woman
I like our lovemaking experiences to be different every time
I look forward to a lot of excitement and creativity
For me there is a strong connection between my sexuality
    and my spirituality

I like my spouse to initiate

I like making love at night

I like subtle initiation

Having sex once every week or two is fine for me

I like kisses to be short and dry

I have little need for talking:

    Before making love

    During making love

    After making love

I like quiet sex

I like subtle and indirect sexual talk

I have no need to talk about it later

I don't have much need to give or get much touching

I like very indirect stimulation

I like the lights off

I don't like oral sex when it is the woman stimulating the man

I don't like oral sex when it is the man stimulating the woman

I like our lovemaking experiences to be pretty much the same
    every time

I like predictability

I am not aware of much connection between my sexuality and
    my spirituality

Each of you should note any of your unique differences that need to be discussed and negotiated.[7]

GUIDELINES FOR ROMANTIC GETAWAYS

Here are several practical tips for those special occasions when you would like to get him alone and away from the house for a few hours or a few days.

1. *Plan Ahead Together.* When planning a getaway, look on the Internet for information about various hotels or resorts in the area. Look over the information together and fantasize about your getaway, even if you will only be gone for one night. Plan your itinerary and schedule together. The planning, dreaming and anticipating will boost your enjoyment of the event. If the getaway is a surprise for your husband, the anticipation is yours, but the enjoyment will be mutually shared.

2. *Use Discount Books.* One way to save money on getaways is to use discount books. For example, I'd order an Entertainment book for Orange County of Southern California. Since Joyce and I enjoyed eating out on many of our dates, the Entertainment book was a money saver. The book contains coupons offering two meals for the price of one at from 75 to 100 different restaurants. It was through the Entertainment book that we discovered a very romantic restaurant located only three miles from our home. We frequented that restaurant for several years. There were also coupons for 50 percent discounts at many hotels. This is just one of many discount plans. One word of warning however: Don't scrimp too much on a romantic getaway. You are investing in your marriage!

3. *Communicate Your Preferences.* If your getaway will take you to a resort, hotel or motel that is new to you, be sure to let the staff know of your special

needs and wants, likes and dislikes. Do you want a room with a view, a quiet room or a nonsmoking room? Would you enjoy a fireplace, Jacuzzi or hot tub? Do you prefer a king-size bed, a waterbed or twin beds? Attention to these details will make your getaway even more special.

4. *Cover Details at Home.* Think through and plan for all the details of baby-sitting, pet care and mail and newspaper pickup before you leave so you don't need to think about them while you are gone. Make a list of what needs to be done beforehand as well as important tasks that will need your attention when you return. Some couples even use a preplanned getaway checklist. If one of you is Mr. or Mrs. Super-checker-upper, write yourself a note assuring that you have checked up on everything at least twice! When our children were out of the home, Joyce and I no longer needed a baby-sitter when we got away. But we did need a combination house-sitter and pet-sitter to care for two golden retrievers, 200 tropical fish and the yard.

5. *Establish Ground Rules.* These are some things that should be excluded from a romantic getaway. A list of mutually agreed-upon ground rules may help set the stage for the romantic atmosphere you're getting away for. No talking about work or the children. No talking about conflicts, in-laws, bills or other irritating topics. Don't worry about staying on diets. Do not take briefcases or make phone calls

to the office. Take along recreational reading only. Make a commitment to unplug the TV while you are there. Yes, you heard me correctly. Unplug the television even if major sports events are on!

6. *Don't Overplan*. Allow gaps in your getaway schedule to relax and loaf and talk and love. Practice spontaneity.

7. *Emergencies Only*. If you are going away for several days, tell your friends and relatives that you don't want to hear from them unless an emergency arises. And be sure to define what you mean by an emergency.

8. *Spread the Word*. Tell everyone you meet on your outing—hotel clerks, waiters, bellhops—that this is one of your romantic getaways. You'll be surprised how many people will do their best to help you enjoy your special event.

9. *Pray Together*. Set aside special times for prayer, perhaps focusing your prayer on thankfulness for your sexual relationship as suggested in chapter 9. Read portions of the Song of Solomon aloud to each other for your devotions.

10. *Share Love Words*. Tell each other how much you love one another, using many thoughtful and creative approaches. Share your romantic memories together—a favorite getaway in the past, a memorable card or letter, an outstanding lovemaking interlude

you recall. Also plan what you are going to share with friends and family when they ask you where you went on your getaway and what you did. Again, be creative.[8]

One of the best steps you can take for your husband, yourself and for your marriage is to become experts about the sexual relationship. Even today in our sexually oriented society, most men and women are still quite uninformed about the sexual process. Ask the typical man if he's ever read a book on sex and his answer is, "I don't need to read any book. I know all about it. I'm a great lover!" That's a myth! Perhaps in his dreams.

That's why one of the best steps you can take to encourage your husband is to purchase the following books and suggest you read the first one mentioned out loud to one another.

A Celebration of Sex by Doug Rosenau would be my recommendation. The book *52 Ways to Have Fun, Fantastic Sex* by Cliff and Joyce Penner would give you some creative ideas; and then a book that you might want to give your husband as a gift is *Men and Sex* by Cliff and Joyce Penner.

By the time you finish these resources you will be knowledgeable. You never know where you will find practical, enlightening information. Now consider these suggestions.

1. *Laugh.* God had quite a sense of humor when He designed sex. Think of getting your bodies together and doing what you do in a sexual experience. When you sit back and think about the uniqueness of the sex act, it's actually hilarious. And to think of the incredibly great feeling that happens in your bodies by doing such rollicking acts is awesome.

2. *Experiment.* To experiment is to test or try how something works or discover something new. You cannot fail when you experiment because there is no predetermined outcome.

3. *Surprise.* If surprises are not negative for the other spouse, a little surprising action or gesture can clearly send the message of thoughtfulness. For the spouse who prefers predictability, plan your surprises together. Sexual surprises will add a lot of fun for the two of you.

4. *Shock.* A little shock, a slight shake-up, or a new burst of interest, excitement or adrenaline is a source of energy to get you connected with each other and bring passion.

5. *Treat.* Treats are endless resources of sexual fun. Treats can fall into these main categories: purchases, accoutrements, preparation, attention and activities.

6. *Pleasure.* You can never go wrong if you focus on pleasure. If both of you are taking responsibility for doing what feels good to you and respecting what feels good to the other, the giving and receiving of pleasure is guaranteed not to fail. Pleasure or pleasing refers to skin-to-skin touch that has no demand for arousal or orgasm or any response or action. It is just for the sake of touching or being touched. No demand means exactly that. There is no expectation;

your and his responses to the touch can be pleasant, warm, comfortable, enjoyable, arousing or neutral. The pleasuring can be an end in itself, or it can
lead to an erotic lovemaking experience.

The woman best serves the man by allowing herself to be
aware of her sexuality and to share it openly with him. Remember, nothing turns a man on more than a turned-on woman.
And as you are able to discover and know yourself, and share
yourself freely and openly with him, he will feel served.

Sex is about the process of enjoying pleasure, not about
your pleasing him or his pleasing you. Mutual pleasure is the refrain of sexual fulfillment. Ultimately, your husband will be
pleased only when you are pleased, and you will be pleased only
when you respond to your natural instincts of extending and
enjoying pleasure. When you listen to and pursue your need for
pleasure, you will be totally satisfied. Then he, too, will be satisfied. Hence, you serve him most by pursuing your sexuality
and making sure you are pleased.

Sexual expertise is learned. We hope the two of you can become authorities on yourselves and communicate your awareness of your likes and dislikes to each other. You can become sex
experts with each other. Your husband can't know your sexual
hungers unless you tell him. Because you are likely to change in
your preferences from one time to another, telling him once is
not enough.[9]

DISCOVER THE ENCOURAGER IN YOU

1. How do you know when your husband wants more out of sex than just sex?

2. What does intimacy mean to you? What does it mean to your husband? How do you blend the two to get both of your intimacy needs met?

3. What is your husband's sex language? Can you speak it? What more could you do to show him that you are fluent in his language?

4. What are some of the most romantic things you've ever done for your husband, using his sex language? Describe the effect on your relationship in other areas.

5. How does your physical relationship with your husband promote wholeness in the emotional, mental and spiritual aspects of your life?

Women Who Encourage Their Husbands **Speak Out**

MANY WOMEN, AND WIVES IN PARTICULAR, ARE INVOLVED IN THE PROCESS OF ENCOURAGING THE MEN IN THEIR LIVES. The comments in this chapter come directly from women who responded to our survey. They are honest and direct accounts. As you read them, you may wonder, *Would I be willing to do that?* After you finish the chapter, you may discover some new ways to respond to your husband, or you may even end up feeling like you're doing a pretty good job already.

Consider the following slice-of-life comments from women who encourage their men . . .

> I encourage my husband by being attentive to his words, actions and desires. I know that he wants to honor the Lord, cherish me and protect me. (Sometimes I choose to believe this.)

> Finances are a key area where I have to work the most. The strings of the purse seem to be the strings to his heart. Watching expenditures and keeping good records are key.

> Discipline of our children has been a struggle. Inspiring them to be attentive, obedient and respectful in-

volves my attitudes, prayer life and acts of love (including punishment for wrongdoing/wrong attitudes). Being content and showing gratefulness is encouraging to him. Finding little expressions of love (such as favorite foods to serve him) keeps our intimate life in good repair.

We encourage each other, but I haven't ever really thought about how. I am always there for him and for whatever endeavor he is into, be it craft work, yard and garden, travel, children. He is retired and wants the companionship of an at-home wife, but he also allows me to pursue my interests and career both in the workplace and at home. In return, I try to accommodate him with a schedule that allows me to continue working but gives us maximum time together for our leisure-time pursuits.

I try to always ask about his day and if something has been amiss or troubling, and perhaps give suggestions how it might be improved or helped or encourage him to do. I always make a point to ask the night before what is on his agenda for the next day or even next week and encourage him to "hang in there" or "have a great day." Also, I always tell him I love him several times during the day—like before he leaves and when the day is over. I also try to let him know how much I appreciate it when he does things for me or generally keeps the house, yard and cars in tiptop shape.

My father was an alcoholic that we all "practiced" diligently to keep happy—at all costs. It was hard work, and

I now struggle against this aspect! It's a hard balance.

My husband is an artist. I encouraged him to quit his 9 to 5 steady job in order to use the gifts that God has given him. That was almost four years ago—financially it has been a struggle, but we have both grown by leaps and bounds in learning to trust the Lord.

I pray over him when he is asleep (probably six years ago he was not walking with the Lord). I used Colossians 1:9-14 (all the women in my prayer group have used this with miraculous results!). Here are the words:

> For this reason, since the day we heard about you, we have not stopped praying for you and asking God to fill you with the knowledge of His will through all spiritual wisdom and understanding. And we pray this in order that you may live a life worthy of the Lord and may please Him in every way: bearing fruit in every good work, growing in the knowledge of God, being strengthened with all power according to His glorious might so that you may have great endurance and patience, and joyfully giving thanks to the Father, who has qualified you to share in the inheritance of the saints in the kingdom of light. For He has rescued us from the dominion of darkness and brought us into the kingdom of the Son He loves, in whom we have redemption, the forgiveness of sins.

I encourage my husband by reflecting on spiritual issues and acknowledging that he approaches Christianity from a different angle than I do. I encourage him by verbalizing his strengths that I love as a parent, husband and artist.

As a woman, I was taught to support my husband in any way possible, and he would return the favor. I watched my mother for years soothe my father and continue to encourage him to follow his dreams. Sometimes that seems so hard to do.

Society likes us to believe that we need to look out for #1. As women, we should not allow any man to have dominion over us. This worldly view does not fit the teaching of our Lord. The decision to do what was right and not what was best is still a rather conscious thing.

What I did find when I made the decision to support my husband was a great joy. Now, when he tells me his dreams, I don't wonder what is going to happen to me. I try to be his sounding board—a springboard for him to bounce new things off of. If I remained rigid and worried, I could never help him obtain his dreams. The wonderful thing about it is that all I had to do is hang on and ride the ride.

I'm not saying that everything has turned out the way it was dreamed up. But it has been an adventure that I would never want to replace. My support has allowed both him and me to venture out, to follow the dreams that the Lord has given us.

Simple things like listening about his day, his dreams and his hopes. Praying with him and for him. Hearing out his ideas for our future without wondering what is in it for me. These are things that I try to do to support my husband.

I pray for and with him. I began working to help alleviate some of his responsibilities and time spent earning money. We have more time together now.

It is an encouragement to him when I go with him to the job site on the weekends to finish up a job.

I encourage my father frequently. I send him random letters (not a Christmas or birthday letter) and reminisce of times when I was a child and the things that he did that impacted my life, or I thank him for wisdom imparted to me and how it has helped me when it came time for me to raise my children. I call him often.

He was encouraged when I urged him to share his navy days with my son. It caused him to open up and share his grief of lost comrades with his family. He also brought up triumphant times.

When my husband and I first met, he talked about going on an out-of-state hunt with his father before his dad couldn't go anymore. Last year the opportunity came for him and his dad to go hunting (elk) in the Colorado Rockies. I encouraged my husband to go and tried to help him find ways of financing his trip.

When they got back my husband was just like a little boy in a candy store. He had been able to fulfill a longtime dream and bag a huge six-point bull elk, the head of which I'll be living with for years to come, as he wanted to get it mounted.

In turn, he brags about how great his wife is to all the guys he spends time with and encourages me in other things that I do. He also tells me constantly how grateful to God he is that we are married.

First off, a wife knows how her spouse really feels. Honest, pure love and acceptance shine through a quiet spirit and loving demeanor. I make it a point to see the best in my spouse and encourage, encourage, encourage. We enjoy a very close and loving marriage in part because of this. I am also very thankful for my spouse and I very regularly let him know it. In other words, he knows he's appreciated.

I encourage my husband by acknowledging him and praising him for the accomplishments he has made. I suggest new ideas or skills to pursue and commit to trying them with my spouse. When faced with a decision, I help him see the various options he can take and support his decisions. I help him see the positive sides to situations without accusing him of being negative and pessimistic.

My husband and I have been married for close to seven years. My role as an encourager is one that I am always working on. There were a few years when my husband was really struggling with what he wanted to do with his life. This was a question I had in my own life, but it was a greater barrier for him. I encouraged him then by being supportive of ideas he had as he thought through options. I gave him a gift of a gym membership, which he had not had for a year or two, because I know that in his life, the physical discipline sets the pace for other areas of his life.

Since this time, he has pursued a graduate program and is just a few months from completion. My support has been financial and emotional as he has taken on a difficult academic/internship schedule. His grades are excellent and he has been graciously guided to a field where his gifts are wonderfully evident. I remind him of this and of his journey so that he can be encouraged by his growth as a person on many levels. While at times I play the martyr, I have also grown. I try to see beyond the immediate sacrifices and am then able to celebrate his sense of direction and purpose and our growth as a couple, laying the foundation for our future.

Other ways I have tried to encourage my husband are less verbal and more practical. I am slowly learning to choose his "side" when we are faced with responsibilities through church, family, school and so on, and he makes a choice not to participate. In short, I don't try to make him go places and do things unless it is what he wants. We are very independent with independent interests and activities, so when there are shared areas, it is difficult to bite my tongue; but as I do, it has been an encouragement to him—knowing that I am supporting his choice for how he uses his time. He does the same for me, and it has been very positive.

To encourage my husband, I try to treat him as I would wish to be treated. Recently, my husband had an interview, and I knew that he was putting a lot of pressure

on himself to get the job. But to me, he is more important. I told him that I love him and that some job was
not going to make that big a difference in our lives. He
may not have gotten the job, but I feel that it was so
very important for him to hear those words that I am
not putting additional pressure on him. That I believe
in his talents, work ethic and sweet spirit. That I know
him well enough to say that truly if they did not hire
him, that was their loss.

I also try to encourage him by encouraging his interests and activities, like allowing him space for his
Men's Meeting once a week. Sometimes I have to say
that when I come home tired, this is really the last thing
I look forward to in my home, but I know that it is important to him; so I try to allow him the time and space
for his meetings.

I also pray for him. When we pray together, I pray
that the Lord will help him in the areas that he has
shared with me. I pray for things that he is concerned
about.

I encourage my husband by supporting him in all that he
does. I let him know that I am praying for him. I thank
him for the things he does for me when he goes out of
his way to do it. I lift him up in the presence of others
and let them know how wonderful and kind he is.

I have on occasion let him know how smart (intelligent) I think he is. I've even made the comment to
others that for a person who has never had any professional training, i.e., college, he is very knowledgeable
about the Bible. He's just very wise and smart.

He is a very kind, smart, gentle, loving husband and father, and he has a lot of patience. I tell him this periodically. When I tell him verbally or in actions how I feel about him, I can see his face light up and the tension release.

I have such a loving and sensitive husband. I try to always be aware of when he does things for me. I will compliment and thank him for fixing dinner, taking out the trash, changing the bottled water, keeping his desk straight and making the bed. But most of all, I let him know how much it means that we spend time in God's Word and pray together. I love him so. He's the best. I respect and admire him.

My husband and I have known each other since September 1985. We were friends and nothing else until three years ago. Oddly enough, today is our second wedding anniversary. We never dreamed in a million years that we'd marry each other. We're still in awe of that fact.

We know each other backward and forward. He was, and still is, my best friend through our adolescent years, my first marriage, my first child's death and my second child's birth; and now he is his "Daddy." He was there for all of it. And vice versa. I know his dreams and goals and support him in everything he does, unless I feel like it will be harmful to him physically, emotionally or spiritually, or to us.

I encourage him. He is very hard on himself. He sets his expectations very high, but it keeps him successful at work. He's in construction and uses his high standards to be a good leader. He is an excellent husband and father, but he doesn't see himself that way. We know and understand our faults as well. We see each other's strengths and weaknesses. We never argue; we just have discussions. I could go on and on.

My dad and I have a very similar relationship. I was brought up in an open-minded, open-hearted home. I never saw my parents fight. They would have discussions and weren't afraid to have them in front of my sister and me; and at times they even included us. My parents have been married 28 years this May. I pray our marriage is similar to theirs. I love my husband like my mom loves hers. She taught us how to be a good wife like she is. She's a beautiful woman, and I pray we can learn more from her as we already have.

I don't encourage my husband like I should. But my experience is that men like to be encouraged by making them feel important. They also like to feel appreciated; the more they are appreciated, the better they feel about themselves. Men usually don't feel appreciated. They work a job all day and come home, and it goes on day after day. Humdrum life. When you tell them how important they are in your life, they try harder to please you and hold up their head a little higher. Damaging words cause the opposite effect. When he comes home, he needs to be told he was missed and that I am glad he is home. I want him to know he's important.

My form of encouragement to my husband has been to let him know that he was created in Christ's image, and whether or not he believes it, God has forgiven him and does see him as a new creation; old things are passed away.

I also let him know that God has given him power and talents and that as he steps out in faith, God will give him the desires of his heart. Believing and receiving!

My father died a horrible death, and I guess the best encouragement I gave my dad is that when everyone else was afraid to hug and kiss him, I kissed him and hugged him and let him know no matter what, I would never stop loving him! Never.

I make my husband meals, tell him how much I appreciate him, buy him things he needs/wants and make him special gifts. I write him notes, call him during the day to tell him how much I appreciate him, and listen to him. I am his biggest fan!

One of the ways I encourage my husband is by speaking positively to him in public and especially in front of my two daughters. At a job that I had in the past, I was actually criticized by a group of coworkers because I never complained about my husband. They did not appreciate me not taking part in their miserable men stories. While my husband is not perfect, I have often told my girls to look for husbands just like their daddy. Sometimes he hears these compliments and sometimes he doesn't, but I know he is well aware of his girls' love and respect for him. They truly do feel that Daddy "hung the moon." I sincerely feel that he is one of the best fathers I have ever known and I work to make him aware of that. I try to let him know when he does special things—especially things my father did not do for me—and how meaningful those actions are to our girls.

The times that it is most difficult to encourage my husband is when he is feeling depressed and angry with himself. It is during these times that I try to keep the home environment quiet, ask little or nothing from him, and listen intently when he does share his feelings. Sometimes he doesn't talk, and I know he needs me to confirm that he is in control, that he is a great man and that I desire to pursue him in the physical relationship. Actually, I know that the latter is probably my best encouragement of all for him during these times.

I often forget that he is encouraged by my telling him how handsome he is, and sometimes I just let him know how glad I am that I married him. When I see other men at church and how they respond to their wives, I tell him how glad I am I didn't marry any of them.

My sister's mother-in-law made a very negative statement about my husband's weight once during a family gathering. While I've been raised to keep angry feelings inside, I let my displeasure out with this woman, and she became quite upset. She left the gathering in a huff, and I was mortified at what I had done. My husband's feelings were not hurt by her statement, but I think he was surprised and pleased when he heard about my quick defense.

I know I can never outdo my husband in this area. He is the master of encouragement and has helped me and my self-esteem tremendously. This writing has made me aware of my need to do more.

H. NORMAN WRIGHT

I mentioned the strength of my husband in his presence when I led a Family Enrichment Seminar for our congregation. I write down his strengths or my appreciation to him in as many ways as his age on his birthday cards, every year.

When I am proud of my children, I say to them where my husband can hear, "You look like your dad on that point! I am proud of you!"

My way of encouraging my husband is to wake up at 6:30 each morning to cook him a hearty breakfast. He feels very much cared for and loved (so he says). I also verbally express my affection for him. I also help him with his church responsibilities. Since I have a background in banking, he feels that I can be of great help to him, so I do try to help. I didn't have a very close relationship with my dad. He didn't show much emotion and was mostly quiet (except on moral issues). I don't recall doing much to encourage my dad.

I try to thank him for all the good, kind things he does. I try to not take his creativity for granted, nor his efforts to help me however he can. I respect him, his spiritual leadership, his integrity, his perseverance. I block off time for us to spend together, alone, to revitalize and recharge.

I encourage my husband by supporting/joining him in church activities. I listen to his ideas, concerns, and such. I help him brainstorm plans for his church work.

I hold him when he comes home from work and especially after a hard day. I prepare meals he enjoys. I plan dates with him, especially on the two mornings a week when I don't work and he can go into work later.

He is not particularly spontaneous and likes me to plan unexpected outings or dates. He loves Snickers candy bars, and I buy these for him sometimes. I rub his shoulders and sometimes his feet. When he comes home, I encourage the children to welcome him enthusiastically so he has a big welcome from us all. I also verbally tell him I love and need him, especially when we are intimate.

Sometimes I feel that I encourage him by not telling him about mundane, irritating things and just handle them myself and not overburden him with such things.

I spend lots of time with him and try to schedule activities he will enjoy. I ask for his advice and opinions. I pass on compliments he has received from others. I help him in his career efforts whenever I can. I keep a calm and peaceful home that is always in good order and clean. I promote happy relationships within our family (he was raised in a difficult and contentious environment) and lots of family celebrations together. I remember to remind him of things that he forgets (appointments, and the like). He is not highly organized by nature!

I try hard to be a sounding board for him about his job and feelings about his coworkers. I tell him what a great father he is and tell him that the time he spends with his children is important because they need a father's input and outlook on life.

I listen carefully, and I do less talking. I support him in his interests. It's easy because they are also mine. I tell him often that I love him and appreciate him. I show respect for him because I honestly feel it.

There are many ways in which I hope I encourage my husband. We've been married for 30 years, and during that time I've learned so much and I know I will learn a lot more.

First, I always try to compliment my husband daily. I find specific things to affirm him in. As a pastor's wife I encourage him by supporting his ministry. Not just verbally, but by being involved—using my gifts and abilities to enhance his ministry. Submissively supporting him whether I necessarily always agree with him or not. I say good things about my husband in front of others and then let him know I did.

I also try to keep him sexually satisfied, which I've found is a part of encouragement. I allow him to be the spiritual leader and in doing so am encouraging him in his role in our family. Do I do all of these things perfectly and consistently? No. But, with God's help I am trying to be an encourager.

I write out thoughts and feelings about him in creative ways and give them to him as gifts.

I pray for him and with him.

I focus my attention on our kids so that he can relax. I show consistency in my parenting so that he does not have to be the "heavy" when the kids misbehave.

I kidnap him for a getaway trip to amusement parks. We play and eat junk food all day.

I make sure I'm fully dressed (clothes, makeup, hair) with a fresh look when he comes home at night.

I leave messages on his work recorder to say how much I love him and miss him through the day.

I make appointments to discuss problem issues that usually he automatically clears time for.

I don't yell; it completely shuts him down.

I have always thought it most important for my husband to always know he's the love of my life. That I believe he is #1 in my life! I pray for him and try to support him, especially when the world tries to shatter him. I try to keep the home front running as smoothly as possible, so he doesn't have to be concerned about household stuff. I don't bother him during his naps. I let him rest in peace. (Ha!) I try to let him know that the family and I totally respect his opinions and input. I tell him I love him on a regular basis. Hugs, kisses, pecks!

I think the way I best encourage my husband is by making our home an oasis for him. When I try to define oasis, several ideas come to mind, but the most significant description is an acrostic of "oasis":

Open
And
Safe
In
Side

If our home can truly be the one place that is always open and safe for my husband, I believe he will be an encouraged man. He knows he is loved, accepted, wanted and admired just as he is, even on the less-than-best days.

My husband's job keeps him out late many evenings. He has expressed the leap of joy in his heart when he walks in and sees the bedroom light on. He knows he will have the opportunity to talk, share and connect before going to sleep. Where I used to think nothing about going to bed early without him, now I make it a habit to wait up for him and look forward to our time together.

I also try to give genuine compliments to my husband at home. I brag on his fathering, his handiness, the way he has completed jobs. At church I compliment his activities, his finesse in hard situations and his insights.

I encourage my husband by listening to him. I have talked to our four children about giving him space when he comes home so that he has some time to unwind. That gives us time to talk about his day. I desire to know all about it; the people he's talked to, the meetings he had, what he's created today. I defend him and lift him up to others. I listen to him when he's discouraged and help him find the answers he's searching for. I confront him when he is wrong.

My husband needs a lot of encouragement. He is a touch person. Hugs and kisses and pats on the back do wonders for him.

I need to tell him often of my love and affirm the things that he does and says. I try to encourage him to do things that I feel are his strengths. When he helps at home or with the kids I try to tell him how much I appreciate it. I don't give my husband enough encouragement but those are the ways that he seems to need and those are the ways I try to contribute.

I encourage my husband by being there for him. I attend his ball games and other things that are important to him. I take a day off from work each week so that I can spend it with him in order to refresh him and uplift him in his life.

It is important to him to spend time with me. He says that it recharges his soul's batteries and helps him to be able to effectively do the things that his work demands from him. So I carve out time each week to spend especially with him doing activities that please him. I also let him take his naps when he needs to.

My husband is very important to me, and I value him greatly. When I can, I write little notes, make him special things, attend functions with him and spend time with him just because I know that I am pleasing and encouraging him.

Knowing that God has called my husband to minister in a specific geographical location, God is always my source of strength to encourage my husband. The Lord has given us a vision for our community, and we know that the vision will be accomplished. Therefore, I encourage my husband by speaking words of "reminders" to him. "The Lord has equipped you for this purpose. You can do it through the strength of the Lord."

When others have deserted him, I remain by his side. We discuss what we can learn from this experience and try to grow from it.

On my husband's day off, we escape from our little town and spend time together. I listen to his discouragements, his dreams. And we dream together.

I constantly pray, "Lord, help me to be the wife my husband needs."

I encourage my husband with verbal praise. Words of affirmation, gratitude. Especially when he does things for others. Also when he does things around the house (dishes, laundry, garbage)—I make sure to comment on it.

I encourage my husband by praising him when he does something special that I have not asked him to do. I thank him when I have asked for his help and he goes out of his way to help. I encourage him to reach out to others who have hurt him in the family. I let his family know when he has done a good deed so he knows I appreciate him.

This is a humbling experience for me because I don't feel I am encouraging my husband enough. I probably encourage others more than him. In reality I try to support him by praying for him on a daily basis. I also try to support him in ministry by using hospitality with people he is ministering to. I try to listen to him share dreams or frustrations and be a sounding board for him. I try to make our home a cheerful, pleasant place to come home to as a security from the stresses of life out there.

My husband knows I am behind him all the way. When he lost his job (after 13 years at a big company), he knew I didn't mind when he started his own company. We took on the new challenge.

I offered to go to work if he wanted or needed me to. We cut all corners possible—I buy store brands, read books from the library, make gifts, clip coupons, plus not shop at the mall too often. I praise his work in front of the children.

I do everything possible to make him know he is important—notes on the computer, hugs and kisses, never cut him down in front of anyone else, enjoy being with him, go out on dates, send him cards, tell him that I appreciate specific aspects of his personality. I also re-assure him that procrastinating with the ironing is not a reflection of how much I think of him.

It is different that he is the one who likes to sit down and talk every night. (Isn't it usually the other way around?) But I try to remember, so he doesn't have to remind me because it is so important to him. I also pray for him, the most important thing.

I encourage my husband with verbal praise. I laugh-ingly tell him he is the best husband I have ever had. I tell him he looks good when he dresses up for a date with me, and I always remember to thank him when we do something special, like going out to dinner or a movie.

It seems strange to answer how I encourage my husband and father when, from my perception, they encourage me far more than I encourage them. Their encouragement comes through verbal statements about how much they believe in me and by very concrete help they give to me. They seem to anticipate my needs and constantly help me in all aspects of my life—from the minute details to the big issues.

Positive praise works best. I thank him over and over again for filling my car with gas or for getting the oil changed. When he's slaving in the yard I bring him lemonade without being asked—keep the glass full! When he helps me in the kitchen, I give him lots of hugs and pats and compliments. Works every time. Also, praise, genuine praise, in front of our friends works miracles.

There is one area that we left out in our response to your survey of encouragement of wives to husbands. That area covers the subject of hearing loss, which becomes a problem to all of us sooner or later. To my husband it was "sooner."

Because our daughter became profoundly deaf from meningitis in her early years, we are well aware of the problems of the hearing impaired. But then came the situation of half-hearing and half-deaf to an energetic hearing man—my husband—who is independent, a natural born leader who loves to sing.

Fortunately, vanity is not a problem, so wearing hearing aids is no big deal. But leading the Sunday School class and not being able to hear prayer requests became humiliating and embarrassing. Barbershop singing has been a fun-filled hobby but is becoming more frustrating because of not being able to hear enough to harmonize. We now have a special phone that can be adjusted to a high volume, but even then some callers have voices difficult to understand.

These are a few of the obstacles we are trying to get over as we grow old together. My job of encouraging my husband falls into two obvious categories—physical and mental.

The physical: Seating guests so that light shines on their faces as we visit. Expression reading is something we begin to do to understand speech. For instance, my husband takes his binoculars to stage shows—he says he "hears" better with them!

Entertaining small groups so that one person at a time is speaking. A hubbub of noise only causes confusion. Being available to listen or speak on the phone if he cannot understand the other party. Trying to be subtle about interpreting in a group if he has not been able to understand what is being discussed. Speaking louder.

Try to be in the same room for communication. We have devised a signal. For instance if I need help with the computer I just "hoo-hoo," and hearing this he comes to me!

The mental: Patience and understanding and a SENSE OF HUMOR. Try to solve the frustration of getting communication mixed up because of not hearing the "whole." Relax and let it go. For instance, if he is heading for the door to do grocery shopping, I may yell after him, "Oh yes, get some milk too." His mind is on putting keys into the auto ignition, he hears my voice and assumes I am saying, "Drive safely!" Then he is on his way to the store only to return with no milk. It is easy to grumble in this situation and say, "But I told you . . ." "But I didn't hear you!" would be the response.

Know that hearing aids are not cheap and new ones must be ordered periodically because hearing usually decreases. Be willing to put new aids on the top of the list of material needs.

The spiritual: Being equally yoked, according to the Scriptures, and doing things together has been our anchor. We both know that God is in charge of our lives and that He will get us through our problems. Open communication is easy at times, difficult at other times. Praying gets me through this. I am not as open as my husband and tend to harbor hurt feelings. When all is said and done, these feelings are usually not warranted.

By the way, a SMILE and a locking of eyes of understanding get us through many difficult situations.

A Willing Cheerleader

The biblical teaching "Do to others as you would have them do to you" (Luke 6:31) does work! It is apparent that these women have discovered what encourages their husbands and in some cases their fathers. Let's summarize the content of their comments.

These women's responses involve listening, being grateful, being frugal, being available, accommodating, showing appreciation, being informed, offering suggestions, believing in his abilities, praising him, praying over him, supporting his dreams, listening to his dreams and hopes without being threatened by them, going with him to work, sending notes and letters, praying together, encouraging him to share his past experiences with his children, looking for the best in him, acknowledging accomplishments, clarifying issues for him, helping rather than accusing, reminding him of his gifts and abilities, taking his side, believing in his ideas with him, telling him "I love you" regardless, giving him space, supporting him, and telling him specifics of what is appreciated about him.

These women do not take their men for granted. They tell him he's missed, how God sees him and are willing cheerleaders. They tell their children how special he is, cook his favorite breakfast, block off time together, hold him, plan dates, handle irritating things for him rather than dumping on him, ask his advice and opinion, act as a sounding board, keep him sexually satisfied, dress for him, provide an atmosphere of safety, teach their children to give Dad quiet time, touch him, and are there for him.

Peggy Campolo shares how she encourages her husband, Tony:

In my own marriage, I learned long ago that my husband appreciates the time and effort I put into helping him with the letters and articles he writes or ideas he wants to discuss, more than he does any time I spend decorating (or even cleaning!) our house. Yet I have a good friend whose husband is simply delighted to have a beautiful setting to come home to each evening. She pleases him by fixing fresh flowers, frequently rearranging the furniture, and making their home a lovely place. Each of us has learned a different way of showing love for her own special person.

It's easy to do what you think your spouse should appreciate. The challenge is to figure out what he or she really wants, and the fun is to learn how to provide whatever it is better than anyone else possibly could.[1]

The possibilities are endless! Encouragement is one of the finest expressions of love.

DISCOVER THE ENCOURAGER IN YOU

1. As you read through the women's comments in this chapter, what was your response?

2. What did you learn about encouragement—what one thing stands out to you?

3. Did you notice that several women not only told of how they encourage their husbands but they told of the positive effects their encouragement had on their husbands? What did their stories inspire in you?

4. What are you doing to encourage your man right now?

5. What will you do differently for him in the future?

Men Whose Wives Encourage Them **Speak Out**

WOMEN ARE ENCOURAGING MEN. They tend to be nurturers and relational anyway. But it was helpful to hear men report about how their wives encourage them. The responses varied. Some were very basic comments; others were complex. What is encouraging to one man may not be encouraging to another. Therefore, you need to discover what your man needs and adapt your responses to him.

Encouragement is often a two-way street in the sense that it is easier to encourage when it is appreciated and reciprocated. I'm sure that some of these men who were interviewed were responding in such a manner that it was easy for the women in their lives to encourage them.

An example of this came from a middle-aged man who said, "My wife frequently affirms her love for me. She takes an interest in my interests. She may not necessarily join in, but she gives a listening ear. She usually tries to make my favorite meals.

"We talk to each other frequently—we both enjoy talking. I always call her while I'm away on business trips. We always touch base once a day during my trips. I help her in the kitchen as soon as I get home from work. I help set the table, do the dishes, and so on. I ask her for her input when I need to make a decision. She appreciates the fact that I value her opinion."

What woman wouldn't love to encourage a man like that! But regardless of the response of the other person, we are called to be encouragers. Our call to encourage is not dependent upon the other person's response.

A young man wrote: "My wife truly cares about me and lets me know that she cares. She listens when I talk, she supports me in everything that I do, and she is positive and joyful about life. We have fun together.

"My goal is to make my wife feel special and loved. I try to take every opportunity to tell her how much she means to me. I love to do the unexpected for her. I want to make life enjoyable for her."

WHAT THE YEARS HAVE HARMONIZED

The following responses came from a couple in their seventies. It was interesting to hear how a man thought his wife was encouraging him and then to hear her share how she tried to encourage him. The husband said, "During the more than 50 years of our marriage, my wife has developed some delightful patterns of behavior that encourage me.

"On occasion when I've been dressed up to go somewhere, she will say, 'My, you are handsome!' Several times she has complimented me on teaching a Sunday School lesson. Sometimes she will refer to me as 'Boss.' I take this with a grain of salt, for in the next sentence she'll ask me to take the trash out.

"Although she hasn't put a statue of me anywhere, she often does little things to demonstrate her trust, her respect and her love for me. Just as the pilot of the airliner revs up the motor to start down the runway for a takeoff, she will slide her hand under mine. As I am about to ask the blessing at a meal, she will put her hand on the table to be covered by mine. At a special time during a movie or play, she may circle my arm with hers—all little loving contacts—all initiated by her, and that's what makes these actions so special. What would I like her to do in the future? Just more of the same. You see, real love is an action—love so demonstrated is a true encouragement."

His wife added, "The first thing that comes to mind is that I try not to be discouraging. In our lifetime, as with most people married more than 50 years, we have had dramatic personal experiences. We found that when one was down, the other offered a balance of supportive understanding. The latter did not necessarily come in a verbal response but in a hug, pat on the back or holding hands.

"When my husband brought work problems home, I tried to listen. Our daughter made an interesting observation one time. She said, 'Whatever Mom was doing when Dad got home she would stop, sit down and talk (or listen).' I was unaware that this was my habit.

"I found that I have a sensitive husband. He is crushed by criticism. Being aware of this, I try to hold my tongue. But being human and a talkative person, things DO slip out. With effort, I many times say nothing, like when we are ready to walk out the door and the tie is totally wrong for the suit. But the times I do openly criticize, there is hurt and anger. We try to solve this by my setting out the clothes before he gets dressed. I now know that he really doesn't give a hoot what he wears as long as it is comfortable and has lots of pockets!

"I find it helpful to offer encouragement by planting positive seeds and withholding negative comments. My husband was in a profession (medical physician) that he had heard enough tragedy and unhappy stories at the office and needed a happy atmosphere to come home to.

"It is not difficult to offer an honest comment of admiration when my husband really looks great. I guess that would be a form of encouragement.

"My husband and I purposefully did not discuss our thoughts before we each wrote our comments. It was fascinating to later read each other's paper and find similarities. Oh yes, one more thought. A sense of humor has played an important role during the tense times. My husband is better at it than I, however! There is nothing like a good laugh!"

MEN SPEAK OUT

As you read the following pages of responses from men, ask yourself three questions:

1. Is this the way my man would like to be encouraged?
2. In what way am I doing this at the present time?
3. How might it affect our relationship if I responded in this way?

The most encouragement I get from my wife comes from the fact that she has stayed with me for 18 years. It is indicative of a commitment to the marriage above what I deserve. She is loyal and faithful, unconditionally. These things translate to me as a commitment to me that is a tremendous encouragement. She stands by me, supports me and defends me not only when others would consider it appropriate, but when they probably would not.

In a consistent pattern she compromises to do the things I like to do. She is always willing and ready to assist with projects that bring me recognition. Often these find her doing the majority of the work with little of the credit.

I can't think of anything else she could reasonably be expected to do to encourage me more.

Here is a man who appreciates loyalty, support, recognition and adaptability. In what way do you express these qualities toward your husband? The next two responses have some similarity and also reflect a common threat that many men struggle with—the fear that they have to change.

I'd say the greatest encouragement I get from my wife is her unconditional love. My wife allows me to be who I am freely without judgment, criticism or nagging. It's nice to have a wife who knows how to be a best friend as well. Praise the Lord! She is patient and waits for the right time to talk about things. She never puts me down in front of others.

My wife accepts me just like I am; she doesn't pressure me to change. She greets me when I come home in the evening. She always smiles and seems glad to see me. She seems interested in what I am doing at work. She compliments me on how I dress; she is glad to go places with me and we enjoy being together. She always trusts me, gives me the benefit of the doubt and believes the best about me. She is an ideal Christian wife!

As men go through their struggles in life, often it's a woman who helps them navigate the troubled waters. Men may appear self-sufficient and strong, but the reality is they need support.

When my wife notices that I am discouraged or frustrated, she will put her arms around me and pray for me. She thanks me often when I do something around the house. Often, she will leave a Post-it note in a place where I'll find it—and on that note is an encouraging love note. I'm not sure what I'd do in my ministry without my wife. She is a great, great help in many ways in the church. She gives such encouragement just by helping out, contributing her considerable gifts and skill in the church.

She encourages me by being there when I need to express doubts or frustrations. Just to know that she is there and shares common values/interests is a major source of encouragement.

My wife makes me breakfast every Saturday and Sunday. During the week she puts little notes in my lunch that tell me what she thinks about me.

With some of the crises that I have been going through, she has been there for me and she knows how much she supports me. Not only in words but also in her actions. With a hug or a soft touch at just the right time.

My wife helps me prioritize my activities and schedule. She also helps me to "lighten up" when I am feeling pressure due to over-committing my schedule. She is also great at counseling me on approaches and strategies to making my activities as focused and directed as possible.

When I am down my wife encourages me with positive remarks like, "I know you can do it" or "I'll be praying for you." When she says that she will pray for me that encourages me the most. I know she will, and it gives me the strength and confidence to face another day.

These are the things my wife does to encourage me:

1. She offers to help in my work tasks (i.e., visiting, phone calls, word processing).
2. She remembers family dates (birthdays, anniversaries, and so on), obtains presents, cards, reminds me to make phone calls to family.
3. She is a great lover.
4. She is willing to talk over issues and come to an agreement.
5. She is very understanding and forgiving when I disappoint her.
6. She works part-time and brings a salary home that helps the family.
7. She desires me to lead spiritually.

The way in which a woman talks about her husband publically or in private is important to a man. If a man discovers that his wife has shared intimate details about their life and problems with others, he could be uncomfortable around them. I've been in social situations in which a wife made fun of her husband in front of others; that is extremely painful. Read another encouraging testimonial:

My wife is always telling me that I have vision and that I'm wise. She also loves to meet with me on my day off to listen to my dreams for the future. My wife also encourages me by the way she speaks about me to others. She is complimentary about me to our young daughters. She often tells me when she thinks something I have done is good. She affirms qualities that she sees in me that are positive. It is encouraging to me as she understands what I have to deal with in all the pressures.

The following responses came from men of various ages:

To encourage me my wife welcomes me when I come home (instead of launching into some huge agenda). She enjoys sexual relations with me (instead of putting it off or showing little interest). She does not depend on me for all her emotional needs. (It encourages me to know she is growing in the Lord and in her friendships with other women.) She is cheerful, or at least able to share humor, even if things are a mess.

My wife is very supportive, nurturing and tolerant. She maintains a strong positive attitude. When I talk about things I would like to pursue, she is open-minded. I would gain additional encouragement from her if she would read information on depression and converse with me several times about the status of my coping with depression. This I would greatly appreciate.

My wife lets me know the good that I did. I think it really helps when she encourages me with specific wording. For instance, I like to hear, "That speech was great; I really like the way that you put it together. That third point really hit home. Good job!" Instead of just, "That was good."

She frequently expresses her love for me. Also she takes pride in what I do and praises me when things go well. She cares about my ideas and will talk with me and be open in her opinions and evaluations. I can ask for nothing more.

She protects me from people, meaning that she doesn't over-commit me socially. She supports me to others. She does a better job of raising our kids than anybody I've ever seen.

She thanks me for things I do for her. She compliments me on things I accomplish. She compliments me on my appearance.

Currently, my wife does several things to encourage me. I value her listening to me the most. She has also affirmed my strengths and praises me when I do something well. Every once in a while she will do that by a note or a card. While she tries to listen to me, she doesn't critique me or try to make a point with me when I really need her to listen. That is so helpful.

My wife and I have only been married a few months. She readily expresses gratitude for things I do around our home, for praying for her and thinking of her when I am considering a decision that may have an effect on her. She frequently tells me the things she likes about me or what I do (approval). If I mention something and am considering something, and she likes it, she says so, such as "That sounds like a good idea."

One of the best things my wife has done for me is to accept her role as helpmate. She desires and strives to make me successful as a husband, father and business-person. She is a quiet and submissive wife but is willing to tell me the things that she feels might be wrong or bad for me to do.

As a mother of our 10 children she has selflessly given up ambitions to excel in the world as a nurse or in other career options. Because she has chosen and dedicated herself to be a stay-at-home mom, she has freed me to provide for my family as God has called and ordered me to do.

Because she is committed to God, she has accepted the challenge to home school all our children. She is a diligent and hardworking woman who has prioritized her life to please God and help me.

My wife shows affection for me with a tender, caring touch or a kiss. She verbally encourages me. She gives respect to our marriage by being faithful to me, and she comes to church with me even though she may not feel like it. She blesses me when she tells me that she wants a baby. This is encouraging me to strive to do better in life.

Many ways of encouraging have been suggested—timing, meeting needs, a cheerful attitude, giving feedback, values, ideas, careful about committing her husband's time, listening, gratitude, affection, and concern over his appearance. It was interesting to hear the number of men who were encouraged spiritually by their wives' spiritual responses and involvement.

She compliments me on my endeavors, she encourages me when I'm down and she lets me know she loves me no matter what.

She worships with me, prays and studies with me. She shares a commitment with me that our greatest love is God.

She plans and dreams with me.

My wife is truly the encourager of my life. I will try to explain what I mean in as few words as possible. When I was called to full-time ministry in 1992, I was very apprehensive and fearful. I was doing effective part-time ministry and could not understand why God wanted me in full-time ministry. I consulted my wife, and she encouraged me to do the will of God. Since that day she has been at my side working as my partner in ministry, supporting me financially and with prayers and words of encouragement.

In my case, it's what my wife is not doing that's been an encouragement. As a professional singer, she has been in demand at other venues that took her away from our home and church on lots of weekends. That brought extra money and fulfillment for her, but it put a stress on our marriage.

About 13 months ago she began directing and leading a music ministry at our church—actually two of them. Her traveling declined. Coincidentally, our church began to grow significantly.

In August, our church board voted to hire her as the director of music ministries. She has traveled very little, and the church has seen its greatest growth ever. This has served to encourage me and fulfill both of us. We are working as a team and God is blessing our efforts.

Knowing that my wife continually and consistently spends personal time alone before the Lord in prayer and in Bible study on my behalf gives me mental, physical and spiritual strength. Her complementary attributes and character qualities help me feel a sense of completeness. I know she is the very best mother our children could ever have. Physically, spiritually, socially, even sexually she meets my every need as a helpmate.

At the present time, my wife encourages me primarily through her faith. She is able to see through our daily struggles, such as finances and over-commitments outside the family, by relying on God's presence in our lives. I typically think to myself that her faith is just immature and shallow, but then I realize that would more accurately describe my own faith. She models a faith in her lifestyle that encourages me. Her patience with our 14-month-old and her gracious understanding of me as I come home stressed and burned out are her primary ways of encouraging me.

To conclude this chapter, here are several responses from men who were very appreciative and articulate.

We have been married 41 years. My wife has always encouraged me and still does by telling me, "You can do it" at whatever task I'm embarking on. She also tells me I'm handsome. Also she gives me greetings cards on holidays, birthdays and anniversaries. For example, on the card for my recent sixty-third birthday, she listed on the card 63 very complimentary attributes she sees in me. Along with this, when I get frustrated or down, she tries to help me see the positive, brighter side.

She is always willing to join me at golf or fishing, and we both really enjoy the time together. Plus she is always willing to sit and talk over coffee on the deck in the morning or in the winter in front of the fireplace. This helps me to express my thoughts and concerns and helps me move ahead positively.

I like flying and hunting, and she is always willing to let me go and encourages me to enjoy whichever I'm going to do.

As for what I would like her to do, I'll be very happy if she just keeps on doing what she is already doing.

Much of what my wife does to encourage me consists of her conversation. After 20 years of marriage, I have never known her to say anything even slightly degrading about me. This covers our private conversation as well as public. She may disagree with me, or even believe that I am out-and-out wrong, but she always expresses these feelings in appropriate circumstances and in such a way as to let me know that she supports me as her husband.

She has the ability to admire the strong qualities of others without ever causing me to feel threatened or inadequate by comparison. Her spoken compliments seem to always spring from some sincere reservoir deep inside, never shallow or trite. Spontaneous, not a matter of rote.

I am also encouraged by the confidence I have in her faithfulness. She is a beautiful woman and has surely caught the attention of other men. However, she is very cautious of the manner in which she accepts compliments and is vigilant regarding the possibility of being placed in any type of compromising circumstance. The fact that she is this way not only releases me from any anxiety in this area, but it also increases my sense of worth to know that she holds her relationship with me as very precious.

It is not so much the grandeur of an infrequent event where I am showered with exclusive gifts and splendid activity but through touches such as praying together, receiving cards in my luggage on a trip, a note of congratulations on the first day of school; keeping mints in the glove box of the car; receiving that special call in the middle of a tough day; an invitation to lunch, a personalized token, a kind word, breakfast or a favorite meal; ensuring that I take my vitamin, get adequate rest and exercise; a friendly reminder that her love is constant and enduring; her commitment to fine grooming, attractive apparel, her soothing fragrance and earnest prayer prior to our special times together; her diligence in developing that internal beauty that is inevitably manifested externally.

Being able to look into the face of one more committed to Jesus than myself and receiving the benefits from that love relationship; her engaging in an upbeat conversation despite the circumstances; her forgiving spirit even when I have blown it; her willingness to refuse to remain angry, but to reconcile and resolve; her commitment to H.O.T. (honest, open and transparent) communication; her disposition that reinforces and leaves no doubt regarding her marital fidelity; her commitment to develop mentally, physically and spiritually; her willingness to participate on a marital team; the way she loves our child daily; that sparkle of hope that twinkles in her eyes; that radiant smile that inevitably draws a smile in return. It is the accumulation of the small, prayerfully crafted and thoughtful deeds that take place daily that ministers to me.

With my wife, I have received far above what I ever imagined in marriage; hence, I have no expectations other than for Jesus to remain in the center of our marriage ensuring that we increase our love for Him, which will naturally result in an increase in our love for each other. (With this, despite the challenges of life, the best is yet to come.)

Isn't it helpful to hear from men who are encouraged by the women in their life? What would the man in your life say about the way you are encouraging him? It may be a helpful topic for discussion. So start talking!

DISCOVER THE ENCOURAGER IN YOU

1. What emotions did you feel as you read through these comments?

2. If someone were to ask your husband right now how you encourage him, what would he say?

3. Which of the men's comments stood out the most to you as something you would not hear from your husband?

4. What words would you most deeply desire to hear from your husband?

5. You may be the like the women described in this chapter. But if not, there are some attitudes and actions you need to ask God to remove; and there are some new attitudes and actions you need to ask God to cultivate in you. Spend a good amount of private time reflecting on all that you have read in this book, and then ask God what needs to change in you. When you have some answers, ask Him to change you. Then start writing down your thoughts on the following:

- New ways of thinking about my husband to change our home environment for the better
- Genuine praise I will begin speaking to my husband on a regular basis
- Sacrificial acts and ways of being that I will pursue to create a deeper friendship and intimacy with my husband

A wife of noble character who can find? She is worth far more than rubies. Her husband has full confidence in her and lacks nothing of value. She brings him good, not harm, all the days of her life.
PROVERBS 31:10-12

The Power of a **Praying Woman**

PEOPLE TODAY ARE INTO POWER. PERHAPS IT'S ALWAYS BEEN THAT WAY. Most of us, though, have never really availed ourselves of a means of power that can change lives—our own and others'. There is, indeed, tremendous power to change lives through prayer.

How are you praying for the men in your life—your husband, boyfriend, father or son? Would you call yourself a woman of prayer?

God's Word has so much to say to us about prayer. God wants us to talk with Him. He is just waiting to respond.

> "It shall come to pass that before they call, I will answer; and while they are still speaking, I will hear" (Isa. 65:24, *NKJV*).

> "Then you will call upon Me and go and pray to Me, and I will listen to you" (Jer. 29:12, *NKJV*).

> "Call to Me, and I will answer you, and show you great and mighty things, which you do not know" (Jer. 33:3, *NKJV*).

But we need to understand what prayer is. Stormie Omartian gives us a helpful description:

Prayer is much more that just giving a list of desires to God, as if He were the great Sugar Daddy/Santa Claus in the sky. Prayer is acknowledging and experiencing the presence of God and inviting His presence into our lives and circumstances. It's seeking the presence of God and releasing the power of God, which gives us the means to overcome any problem.

The Bible says, "Whatever you bind on earth will be bound in heaven, and whatever you loose on earth will be loosed in heaven" (Matthew 18:18). God gives us authority on earth. When we take that authority, God releases power to us from heaven. Because it's God's power and not ours, we become the vessel through which His power flows. When we pray, we bring that power to bear upon everything we are praying about, and we allow the power of God to work through our powerlessness. When we pray, we are humbling ourselves before God and saying, "I need Your presence and Your power, Lord. I can't do this without You." When we don't pray, it's like saying we have no need of anything outside of ourselves.

Praying in the name of Jesus is a major key to God's power. Jesus said, "Most assuredly, I say to you, whatever you ask the Father in My name He will give you" (John 16:23, *NKJV*). Praying in the name of Jesus gives us authority over the enemy and proves we have faith in God to do what His Word promises. God knows our thoughts and our needs, but He responds to our prayers. That's because He always gives us a choice about everything, including whether we will trust Him by praying in Jesus' name.

Praying not only affects us, it also reaches out and touches those for whom we pray. When we pray for others we are asking God to make his presence a part of their lives and work powerfully in their behalf. That doesn't mean there will always be an immediate response. Sometimes it can take days, weeks, months or even years. But our prayers are never lost or meaningless. If we are praying, something is happening whether we can see it or not. The Bible says, "The effective, fervent prayer of a righteous man avails much" (James 5:16, *NKJV*). All that needs to happen in our lives cannot happen without the presence and power of God. Prayer invites and ignites both.[1]

Praying for a man is not a means of gaining control over him. Prayer is a means of transforming the one who is praying and the one who is the object of the prayers. Prayer can encourage the one you are praying for, but it can also encourage and change you.

There may be times when it's difficult to pray for that man—it could be your husband. You may *not* want to pray for him. You could be angry or even bitter toward him, and the last thing you want to do is encourage or pray for him. But an amazing thing happens when you bring another person before the Lord. Your attitude begins to change. Bitterness decreases, anger diminishes, hardness toward the other softens. In time you can end up loving the person you are praying for. I have seen relationships restored between daughters and fathers, wives and husbands, mothers and sons. It may take time, but prayer is the means of restoration, growth and encouragement.

Stormie Omartian, in her most recent book, *The Power of a Praying Wife,* shares a struggle that she experienced with her husband's anger.

> I began to pray every day for Michael, like I had never prayed before. Each time, though, I had to confess my own hardness of heart. I saw how deeply hurt and un-forgiving of him I was. *I don't want to pray for him. I don't want to ask God to bless him. I only want God to strike his heart with lightning and convict him of how cruel he has been,* I thought. I had to say over and over, "God, I confess my unforgiveness toward my husband. Deliver me from all of it."
>
> Little by little, I began to see changes occur in both of us. When Michael became angry, instead of reacting negatively, I prayed for him. I asked God to give me insight into what was causing his rage. He did. He showed me. My husband's anger became less frequent and more quickly soothed. Every day, prayer built something positive. We're still not perfected, but we've come a long way. It hasn't been easy, yet I'm convinced that God's way is worth the effort it takes to walk in it.[2]

One of the ways that Joyce encouraged me over the years was through prayer. When I was traveling and speaking, I knew that when I called home each evening, I would hear her saying, "I'll be praying for you as you're teaching tomorrow." I'd also find notes stuck in my pockets (and elsewhere!) saying, "I'm praying for you" as well as a Scripture written out.

Over the years I've made it a practice to pray for my clients each day. I usually let them know that I will be doing this and ask if they have something specific they would like me to pray about during the week. I've had a number of occasions when a person has later shared that the only thing that kept them going was knowing that at least one person was praying for them.

If you're married, what are some ways you could pray for your husband?

Carole Mayhall, writing in *Today's Christian Woman*, suggested the following:

HOW TO PRAY "JUST FOR HIM":

Make it a point to commit five minutes a day to pray just for your husband. Pray a different Scripture for him each month, as well as other specific requests that God puts on your heart. And keep a prayer list specifically for him. The list might look something like this:

A. Colossians 1:9-11

- That he would be filled with the knowledge of God's will
- That he would have spiritual wisdom and understanding
- That he would live a life worthy of God
- That he would please God in every way
- That he would be strengthened with God's power for patience and endurance
- That he would have a thankful spirit

B. That he would develop a friendship with a committed Christian who would challenge him

C. That God would give him a hunger and thirst for Himself and His Word

Write down the answers when they come and date them.

After a friend of mine had been praying specifically for her husband for several months, she called me, excitement lilting in her voice. "Guess what!" she exclaimed. "Bill just told me a new coworker asked him if he'd be willing to attend a new early morning Bible study, and Bill said YES! And something else. I tried not to show my astonishment when Bill brought home a brochure on a Marriage Enrichment weekend and said he'd signed us up to go."

My friend and I rejoiced together in this new beginning.[3]

A woman shared her story of how God answered prayer for her husband. She said, "While visiting my friend Barbara in Germany last spring, I listened fascinated one evening as her husband, Russell, an Air Force officer, explained to a group packed into their dining room about the meaning of the Passover meal we were about to eat. As a Bible study teacher, he had spent hours preparing the lesson, the food and the table.

"After we'd eaten, I helped Barbara in the kitchen. 'Russ is really turned on to the Lord!' I exclaimed. 'I still remember the Sunday years ago when you asked me to pray for him. He was so wrapped up in his career he had no time for God, and he was so reserved—almost stiff in those days. But now, he is not only a mighty man of God, he's a terrific Bible teacher. What did you do besides pray a lot during the time he wasn't following the Lord?"

As Barbara shared, I jotted down her answers:

1. I had many intercessors join me in praying for him.

2. I was single-minded in my goal—determined that my words and my behavior would make him thirsty for

the Lord. I asked the Lord to keep His joy bubbling out of me.

3. Russ liked to show off our home and my cooking by having company over, so I often invited Christians to share meals with us. He enjoyed that—especially meeting Christian men, whom he found it fun to be around.

4. The children and I kept going to church.

5. Russ began to go with me to a Bible study—probably out of curiosity, but also because I had such joy. Then he started going to church with the family. Russ finally decided to make Jesus his personal Lord. He immediately had a hunger to know the Word of God and began spending hours each week studying the Bible. Now he's teaching a Bible study group which meets in their home.

I observed Russell's tender heart toward God during my visit with them, and thanked the Lord for doing such a "good job" in answering a wife's prayers for her husband.[4]

Recently I found a fascinating resource that personalizes passages of Scripture into prayer for a husband and wife. It's titled *Praying God's Will for My Marriage*, by Lee Roberts. It simply takes passages of Scripture and rewords them. By reading these aloud for a while, anyone can learn to do this for themselves. Here is a sampling:

I pray that my spouse and I will be swift to hear, slow to speak, slow to wrath; for the wrath of man does not produce the righteousness of God (Jas. 1:19-20).

I pray that my spouse and I will always love the Lord our God with all our heart, with all our soul, with all our mind, and with all our strength and that we love our neighbor as ourselves (Mark 12:30-31).

I pray that when my spouse and I face an obstacle we always remember that God has said, "Not by might nor by power, but by my Spirit" (Zech. 4:6).

I pray that if my spouse and I lack wisdom, we ask it of You, God, who gives to all liberally and without reproach and that it will be given to us (Jas. 1:5).

I pray that because freely my spouse and I received, freely we will give (Matt. 10:8).

I pray, O God, that You have comforted my spouse and me and will have mercy on our afflictions (Isa. 49:13).

I pray that my spouse and I will bless You, the Lord at all times; and that Your praise will continually be in our mouths (Ps. 34:1).

I pray to You, God, that my spouse and I will present our bodies a living sacrifice, holy and acceptable to God, which is our reasonable service. I pray also that we will not be conformed to this world, but transformed by the renewing of our minds, that we may prove what is that good and acceptable and perfect will of God (Rom. 12:1-2).[5]

Can you imagine the effect on your marriage relationship when you literally bathe yourselves with God's Word as a prayer? Try this for a one-month experiment. Then note the difference.

WOMEN IN PRAYER

Because this is a book for women, I thought it best to have women share their firsthand experiences of praying for the men in their lives. Consider the variety of ways that God answered prayer.

As I prayed for my husband it was a gradual process—I was a part of a group of women who interceded with me. I can't say there was one day everything changed; however, day by day, precept upon precept, there was a change! Now he is retired, and we pray together for our son and daughter. Retirement helped bring his focus from his work to our home.

After becoming a Christian at the age of 22, the desire of my heart was to have a Christian husband. My husband was always loving and kind, but year after year would go by without a commitment to Christ. I prayed and questioned and waited. He always attended Sunday School and morning worship services, but he was not a Christian. Often the Lord reminded me that His timing would come. Eight years later, during a revival service, my husband surrendered his heart to the Lord and has joyfully walked with and humbly served Him every day since. The Lord took a truly wonderful marriage and turned it into a glorious one. Praise God!

The greatest miracle we've received is an extraordinary answer to prayer. Four years ago my husband was diagnosed with a malignant brain tumor. After surgery, we were told he would have maybe five years to live. We requested prayer from all our family and friends. It was only prayer that strengthened us each day as God worked in our lives and taught us how to cope and not to fear. We were willing to accept His will whatever it may be. As I watched my once big and strong husband become so weak, I remember once in desperation (or was it selfishness) calling out to God, "Lord, I want my husband back." He had always been my protector and my provider; now I was forced to take on so many of his roles. I'm so glad God knows me so well; He understands my temperament and was not offended when I became demanding. God lovingly answered our prayers. To this day my husband is cancer free. I think that surgeon just may become a believer.

I began to pray for my husband because there were many times that I felt he was beginning to lose hope, enough to seriously consider ending his life. As difficult as it was for him, I tried to encourage him to know that God was taking us through this crisis for our betterment. The results from prayer have been miraculous to me.

He is working . . . the doctors said he wouldn't be able to work and would need to be on disability for life.

We are communicating . . . this is something we have struggled with in our marriage and have been forced to do to avoid additional stress. We are in counseling together and both of us realize that God is definitely at the controls.

God does listen. He knows every heartache and pain. He knows exactly what we will encounter. These are some of the things I was able to share with him and still do.

Every time my husband left to play golf, I grew more and more resentful. It took the better part of a day to play that silly game. A game that seemingly caused him more frustration than enjoyment. I had plans for us together at home. I wanted my husband to be able to relax, but at the same time I wanted him to be a better father to our teenage son. It seemed that my husband wanted only to improve his golf score. Why couldn't he just "relax" at home? I was jealous that golf seemed to have his full attention.

I remember one day I brought my resentments to the Lord in prayer, "God, please help my husband to want to spend more time with our son and me instead of spending so much time away on the golf course." A picture flashed through my mind of how I wanted God to answer that prayer. I pictured my husband at home with us giving us all the attention that I thought I had earned. I continued my prayer, "Lord, I believe it is Your will that my husband and I spend time together." I finished praying, listening for an answer. The answer that came was not what I expected. It was almost audible, "Take golf lessons."

The idea followed that instead of me changing my husband, I should instead join him so that I would understand him better. My jaw dropped at the very idea of having to bend my schedule any further to accommodate my husband's playtime. But when the thought of taking golf lessons came to me again and again, I began to yield my will to God's and prayed, "Lord, please provide a way for me to take golf lessons that will work for all of us." Several days later, I saw an ad in our newspaper for golf lessons. Two people could take the lessons for the price of one, so I enrolled both my son and me. We learned golf's fundamentals, just enough to begin playing. My son and I practiced at a local short course. Our games together turned out to be an unexpected blessing. Time alone on the golf course away from the telephone and television afforded us time to talk and walk through some of the deep issues that teens face. The three of us have played together just a few times, but those days are happy memories. . . . I thank God that His ways are higher than mine.

This final story is about a son, but it's worth sharing:

I have had several exciting times of praying for a man in my life that stand out in my mind. On each occasion it was concerning a major life event. The answers God sent gave me the peace that a mother and/or daughter needed. I will share one with you.

This prayer time concerned my 19-year-old son enrolled at the University of Santa Barbara, California. The time was the height of the Gulf War, and the United States was passing a law to reinstate the draft of young men. At that point in my son's life, where he was with the Lord and where the Lord was taking him in school, the worst thing in his life would have been to be drafted and taken out of school. Of course, my own heart as a mother cringed at the thought of his being drafted, so I began praying about it and, I might add, pleading with the Lord to protect my son. Several days later, my son called and left a message on my answering machine that he had lost his wallet. It was missing overnight, and he related that he looked everywhere for it, several times. Now, my son lived in Isla Vista, a college town. He said he went back to his car in the morning, and there was his wallet lying on top of the vehicle right where he had probably laid it when he got out of his vehicle. He said, "Mom, it was just as if God had put His thumb on it," and kept the wallet there until my son came back and saw it. It gave me peace that in the midst of events of the world, God would protect my son. If you know Isla Vista (or any other busy college town), and the number of kids that would be riding bikes by my son's vehicle, you know there would be no way that wallet would still be on top of the vehicle overnight if God had not protected it all day and night.

What is your story? Perhaps by praying for the man in your life, you could add your thanks and give a similar account. God does answer prayer. Lives are changed by prayer. Prayer for your spouse is a wonderful way for both of you to be encouraged all the days of your life.

DISCOVER THE ENCOURAGER IN YOU

Are you a praying wife? Do you daily depend on God to find your strength to love your husband and others?

Prayer is such an encouraging way to experience God's work in your life. There is great release and reward in allowing Him to be your partner in all that concerns you. What better way to apply all that you have learned about how to bring out the best in your husband than to ask God to guide your steps as you cultivate your home environment?

Before you close the covers of this book, ask God to help you find new ways to encourage your husband; or perhaps you need to ask God to begin a brand-new work in you so that you can start encouraging your husband for the first time. At whatever point you are right now, bow your head and commit yourself to your Father's loving instruction.

PRAYER OF COMMITMENT

Father, I want to be an encourager to my husband. In so many ways, I don't know how to do that. But I do know that Your Holy Spirit can instruct me and guide me in my efforts to build up my relationship with my husband. Help me get past any ingrained habits of reacting and any wrong attitudes. I specifically ask you to help me ...
[Make this prayer your own].

BOOK TWO

Includes Small-Group Study Questions

Bringing Out the Best in Your Wife

Regal

From Gospel Light
Ventura, California, U.S.A.

Believe in
Your Wife

FROM TIME TO TIME, I'VE ASKED HUSBANDS THE QUESTION, "If your wife were to change something about herself, what would you like to see changed?" You can just imagine all the different answers I've received over the years; they've ranged from the most absurd and ridiculous to those that are quite positive and encouraging. Now and then I've heard, "Nope. It can't be done. She'd never change." Once in a while I've heard, "I'd like my wife to value herself more. I'd like her to see herself as God sees her. She has so much potential under the surface. I'd like to see that develop." Now there's a great answer! This husband wants his wife to become the best she can be. Is it possible? Yes! Can she do it on her own? No! Can you, as a husband, change your wife? Yes *and* no! You can't do it *for* her or force it to happen. But you can encourage change to happen. You have more influence on and power over change than you can imagine.

The bottom line is this: What you believe about your wife will determine what she becomes. When Ephesians 5:25 states that a husband is to love his wife as Christ loved the church (to love her sacrificially), it also means he's her cheerleader.

Every husband is given a power that can bring about change, growth and the fulfillment of potential in his wife. There's so much truth to these words:

No matter how beautiful a woman is, she will struggle with not liking something about herself. No matter how confident a woman seems, insecurities still haunt her at times. No matter how fulfilled a woman is in her calling in life, there will always be a part of her that wonders if she measures up. Some women struggle more than others, but all women long to be affirmed, appreciated and admired. Other than God, there's no one who can do more to build a woman's self-esteem than her husband. Your wife is in the process of becoming what you think of her![1]

When a wife tells her husband, "Thank you for believing in me," her husband is fulfilling his calling.

Have you heard those words from your wife? Does she ever turn to you and say, "Thank you for bringing out the best in me"? Does she say, "It's your encouragement that makes my life different"? Read what these wives say about how their husbands bring out the best in them:

He appreciates me! He tells me often how much I mean to him, and he thanks me for things I do for him. He compliments me in front of other people, especially in front of our children; when he does that I feel valued and loved. He believes in me! He validates my dreams—and believes I can do whatever God has called me to do. He never trivializes my role as a woman—but treats me as a true equal.

He believes in me. Shows compassion. Uses humor to defuse a disagreement. Is not afraid to admit he is wrong. Compliments me often. Likes my cooking. Talks to me. Listens to me. Makes me feel important. He would even watch a chick flick with me. He keeps himself healthy and looking good. Takes dancing lessons with me and then takes me dancing. Brings me flowers. Leaves me notes in my snack bag.

My husband is a wonderful listener. He has learned over the years that the way I process problems is by "fleshing them out" out loud—or talking them through. It helps just to have his undivided attention, and then the solution will come to me. I don't necessarily need the problem solved; just an ear.

He truly knows me and wants me to be the best God made me to be. We are so opposite from each other in most things, but we accept each other and don't try to change one another. He studies me—my needs, my desires, my strengths, weaknesses, joys, sorrows; and he meets those needs whenever and however he is led to. He encourages by words and actions, exhorts where necessary and treats me like I am God's gift to him. I am free to flourish as the person God made me to be without fear of taking anything away from my husband. I am so grateful!

Not all the responses from wives are positive. Some wives lament the lack of encouragement in their lives. Read some responses from wives who describe what they wish their husbands wouldn't do:

[I wish he wouldn't] get angry so easily over things that don't go his way, or when we disagree about something.

He tends to overreact and blow up over the smallest things. It makes him an unsafe person, and I can't relax and just be myself. I wonder when "Mount Vesuvius" will erupt next. It shuts down communication and damages intimacy and closeness.

Sometimes he gets into his sarcastic "guy talk" mode where everything is a "dig" or a negative comment (because with his years in the military, that is how they communicate). I wish he wouldn't talk that way to me. It's hard for him when coming out of that environment to adjust to home.

I really hate it when he dictates to me, like I'm an employee. It makes me feel like I'm stupid. I'm a highly educated woman, yet he can make me feel so stupid. I really hate it when he treats our kids badly. This is an issue with us. He seems to favor one over the other, and it really creates tension for us.

He makes promises and does not follow through. He often gets sidetracked and forgets what he promised me. This hurts my heart. Also he is so prideful when he knows he has hurt my feelings; he would rather wait out my hurt and resentment than come to me and ask forgiveness or talk things out, for he knows I will "get over it." But what he really does not know is that until it's resolved, the hurt and resentment are still there.

I wish he wouldn't walk away to do his thing when I'm in the middle of a conversation with him—for example,

he checks emails, phone messages or DVR programs—
and then comes back to me and expects to continue
where I left off when he decided to leave the room.

Many husbands do try to encourage their wives, and even
think they are doing so. But it's difficult to be an encourager if
you don't understand what encouragement really means.

ENCOURAGEMENT DEFINED

To be an encourager you need to have an attitude of optimism.
The *American Heritage Dictionary* has one of the better definitions of the word "optimist." It's a "tendency or disposition to
expect the best possible outcome, or to dwell on the most hopeful aspect of a situation." When this is your attitude or perspective, you'll be able to encourage others. Encouragement is "to
inspire; to continue on a chosen course; to impart courage or
confidence." Think back over the past years. Can you remember
practical and specific examples of what you've done that would
illustrate this definition?

You may think of encouragement as praise and reinforcement, but it's also much more than that. Praise is limited; it's a
verbal reward. Praise emphasizes competition, has to be earned
and is often given for being the best. Encouragement, on the
other hand, is freely given. It can involve noticing something in
a person that others take for granted, and affirming something
that others notice but may never think of mentioning. Bruce
Larson shared this experience:

Early one morning, I had to catch a plane from Newark,
New Jersey, to Syracuse, New York, having returned late

the previous night from leading one conference and on my way to another.

I was tired. I had not budgeted my time wisely, and I was totally unprepared for the intense schedule before me. After rising early and hastily eating breakfast, I drove to the airport in a mood that was anything but positive. By the time the plane took off I felt so sorry for myself.

Sitting on the plane with an open notebook in my lap, I prayed, "O God, help me. Let me get something down here that will be useful to your people in Syracuse."

Nothing came. I jotted down phrases at random, feeling worse by the moment, and more and more guilty. Such a situation is a form of a temporary insanity. It denies all that we know about God Himself and His ability to redeem any situation.

About halfway through the brief flight, a stewardess came down the aisle, passing out coffee. All the passengers were men, as women have too much sense to fly at seven o'clock in the morning. As the stewardess approached my seat, I heard her exclaim, "Hey! Someone is wearing English Leather aftershave lotion. I can't resist a man who wears English Leather. Who is it?"

Eagerly, I waved my hand and announced, "It's me."

The stewardess immediately came over and sniffed my cheek while I sat basking in this sudden attention and appreciating the covetous glances from passengers nearby.

All through the remainder of the flight the stewardess and I maintained a cheerful banter each time she passed my seat. She would make some comment, and I would respond gaily. Twenty-five minutes later, when the plane prepared to land, I realized that my temporary insanity had vanished. Despite the fact that I had failed in every way—in budgeting my time, in preparation, in attitude—everything had changed. I was freshly aware that I loved God and that He loved me, in spite of my failure.

What is more, I loved myself and the people around me, and the people who were waiting for me in Syracuse. I was like the Gadarene demoniac after Jesus touched him: clothed, in my right mind and seated at the feet of Jesus. I looked down at the notebook in my lap and found a page full of ideas that could prove useful throughout the weekend.

God, I mused, *how did this happen?* It was then that I realized that someone had entered my life and turned a key. It was just a small key, turned by a very unlikely person. But that simple act of affirmation, that undeserved and unexpected attention, had got me back into the stream.[2]

Encouragement is recognizing your wife as having worth and dignity even though she's imperfect, just like we all are. It means paying attention to her when she's sharing with you. It's listening to her in a way that lets her know she's being listened to. When a wife is encouraged, she does her best and becomes her best.

THE ART OF LISTENING

The road to a person's heart is through the ear. Men and women today have few people who really listen to them. Most of us are often more concerned about what we are going to say when the other person stops talking. This is a violation of Scripture. James tells all of us to "be quick to listen" (Jas. 1:19). Proverbs 18:13 states, "He who answers a matter before he hears [the facts], it is folly and shame to him" (NASB).

Many of us have outgoing circuits, but our incoming circuits are clogged. When one woman was asked what her husband could do to bring out the best in her, she said, "Listen—listen without being judgmental or biased; listen and be accepting. Listen just to understand me. Listen instead of criticizing me."

How you listen to your wife also needs to be tailored to her. Men and women have different listening styles, and it helps to understand what these differences are. Women tend to give more responses and feedback while they are listening. Those responses usually mean, "I'm with you" or "I understand" or "I'm connecting with you." They don't always mean, "I agree with you." On the other hand, we men tend not only to say less, but our feedback usually does mean, "I agree with you." Have you run into this difference between the way men and women give feedback? Most of us have. When you're listening to your wife, she may need less feedback from you than you think is necessary. You can't communicate with her like she's a man. Listening quietly to her may lead to a response like, "Thanks for really listening to me. It helps me keep my mind on track when I'm not interrupted."

It's true—poor listening skills have an impact on wives more than many husbands realize. One of the greatest longings of any person is to be listened to. The gift of being a good listener is one of the most healing gifts you can give your wife. Unsolicited advice isn't a healing gift; neither is thinking about what you are going to say while she is talking . . . and then interrupting or finishing her sentences. Other non-gifts are squelching her verbal expression of her feelings with reassurances, or taking the conversation off on a tangent that's interesting to you but has no connection to what your wife has said. You'll read more about this later.

True encouragement validates that what your wife is doing or saying makes sense. It's letting her know, "You matter to me." When you encourage your wife, you respect her as well. You rephrase negatives to positives by discovering the constructive elements in situations, such as identifying her strengths and focusing on her efforts and contributions.

This means that you find something of value to recognize when everybody else has despaired! Does this take work? You bet it does. But don't look at it as a chore; it's actually a privilege. Encouragement builds up your wife. It focuses on any resource that can be turned into an asset or strength.

Encouragement also means that you expect the best out of her. Consider what happened to this young man because his high school principal expected something more from him.

I remember vividly the day we had a school assembly. Three buddies and I went out behind the school auditorium. We all lit up. We knew we were safe: everyone else was in the assembly. And then, who should come around the corner but the principal. We were caught red-handed. My friends took off in three directions and left me just standing there. The principal collared me and dragged me down the hall in front of the auditorium just as the assembly was letting out. I thought I was going to die. Hundreds of kids saw me in this humiliating situation.

He took me into his office and chewed me out royally. It felt as if it lasted forever. Maybe it was only ten or fifteen minutes. I couldn't wait to get out of there. From that time on, I hated this guy. I waited for him to nail my buddies, but he never did. He knew who they were, but he did nothing. One day I saw him in the hall, and I asked why he hadn't gone after them. It wasn't fair that I was singled out.

Instead of giving me an answer there, he grabbed me by the collar, and dragged me back into his office. He sat me down, but the chewing out didn't even last a minute this time. I'll never forget what he said. "I wish your friends the best. I don't know what's going to happen to them, but you could be somebody. I expect more of you than this. You're coasting through life. When are you going to do something with what you've got?" He turned around and walked out. I felt like I had been slapped across the face. He was right; I was coasting. And there is only one direction you can coast—down.

I was a junior at that time. I started working a little bit in my classes and made a new group of friends. My senior year I had an *A* average. I had been getting *C*'s and *D*'s before. I decided I wanted to go to college, but when I applied, I couldn't get in. My grades were too bad in a previous term. My principal wrote a letter of recommendation on my behalf, and in response the university agreed to admit me on a probationary status. I chose the field I did because of this man. He became like a mentor, like a second father to me.

Two years ago I gave the eulogy at his funeral. I'll never forget him. I will always be different because of him. He gave me something to live up to.[3]

We've become skilled as flaw finders in our culture. But encouragement is just the opposite of a deficit-oriented approach. To be an encourager you need to go counter to our culture and not be "conformed to this world." Would your wife say you're more equipped to point out her mistakes, weaknesses or liabilities rather than strengths? Your answer speaks volumes, as one man discovered:

> When I married my wife, we both were insecure, and she did everything she could to try to please me. I didn't realize how dominating and uncaring I was toward her. My actions in our early marriage caused her to withdraw even more. I wanted her to be self-assured, to hold her head high and her shoulders back. I wanted her to wear her hair long and be perfect at all times. I wanted her to be feminine and sensual.
>
> The more I wanted her to change, the more withdrawn and insecure she felt. I was causing her to be the opposite of what I wanted her to be. I began to realize the demands I was putting on her, not so much by words but by my body language.
>
> By God's grace, I learned that I must love the woman I married, not the woman of my fantasies. I made a commitment to love Susan for who she is—who God created her to be.
>
> The change came about in a very interesting way. During a trip to Atlanta, I read an article in *Reader's Digest*. I made a copy of it and have kept it in my heart and mind ever since.
>
> It was the story of Johnny Lingo, a man who lived in the South Pacific. The islanders all spoke highly of

this man, but when it came time for him to find a wife, the people shook their heads in disbelief. In order to obtain a wife, you paid for her by giving her father cows. Four to six cows was considered a high price. But the woman Johnny Lingo chose was plain, skinny and walked with her shoulders hunched and her head down. She was very hesitant and shy. What surprised everyone was Johnny's offer—he gave eight cows for her! Everyone chuckled about it, since they believed his father-in-law put one over on him.

Several months after the wedding, a visitor from the U.S. came to the Islands to trade and heard the story about Johnny Lingo and his eight-cow wife. Upon meeting Johnny and his wife the visitor was totally taken aback, since this wasn't a shy, plain and hesitant woman but one who was beautiful, poised and confident. The visitor asked about the transformation, and Johnny Lingo's response was very simple, "I wanted an eight-cow woman, and when I paid that for her and treated her in that fashion, she began to believe that she was an eight-cow woman. She discovered she was worth more than any other woman in the islands. And what matters most is what a woman thinks about herself."

This simple story impacted my life. I immediately sent Susan flowers (I had rarely if ever done that before). The message on the card simply said, "To My Eight-Cow Wife." The florist (who was a friend of mine) thought I had lost my mind and questioned if that was really what I wanted to say.

Susan received the flowers with total surprise and bewilderment at the card. When I returned from the trip I told her that I loved her for who she is and that I considered her to be my eight-cow wife, and then I gave her the article to read.

I now look for ways to show her that I am proud of her and how much I appreciate her. An example of this involved a ring. When we became engaged I gave Susan an antique engagement ring that I inherited from a great-great aunt. Susan seemed very pleased and I never thought any more about it. But I had come out cheap, and that's how she felt. After 20 years of marriage she shared with me how she felt about the hand-me-down wedding ring. We had our whole family get involved in learning about diamonds. Susan found one that she liked. It was not the largest stone, nor the most expensive. I would have gladly paid more. I bought it and gave it to her at Christmas. "To my Eight-Cow Wife, with all my love!" But what this did for our relationship is amazing.

First, it changed me! My desires began to change. My desire now is for Susan to be all that God has designed her to be. It is my responsibility as her husband to allow her that freedom.

It also changed her. Susan became free. She learned who she is in Christ. She has gained confidence and self-assurance. She is more aware of her appearance, her clothes, hair and makeup, because she is free to be who she is.

Susan rarely buys clothes for herself. Last year for Christmas I told her this year I would buy her an outfit or some type of clothing each month. This has boosted her confidence in her appearance. She looks great because she wants to!

Susan really is an Eight-Cow Wife of whom I am very proud. We have been married now since 1971.

ENCOURAGEMENT AND ACCEPTANCE GO HAND IN HAND

Time and time again we hear about the positive aspect of an encouraging parent upon a child. I remember hearing an interview one day with Scott Hamilton, who has become a household name in professional ice-skating. During the 1992 Winter Olympics, Scott served as a commentator for the ice-skating events. During his time on TV, he shared about his special relationship with his mother, who died prior to his winning an Olympic gold medal. He said, "The first time I skated in the U.S. Nationals, I fell five times. My mother gave me a big hug and said, 'It's only your first National. It's no big deal.' My mother always let me be me. Three years later I won my first National. She never said 'you can do better' or 'shape up.' She just encouraged me."

A wife shared with me, "My husband is a very supportive person. He believed in what I could do even when I didn't, especially in the early years of marriage. Oh, he gave his opinion and lots of advice, but without being judgmental. He cared about me as a person, not just what I did or could do. In time I felt I could do anything I set out to tackle. But the best thing he ever gave me was his belief in me. He still does."

Encouragement means that you show faith in your wife and her potential. It means that you believe in her without the evidence that she is believable. That's hard for those who think, "I'll believe it when I see it."

Perhaps you have a dream for your wife. You're able to see things that she can't see, such as untapped potential. Have you ever heard of the four-eyed fish? It's an odd-looking creature. I don't think you'd want one mounted on your wall. It's a fish native to the equatorial waters of the Western Atlantic region. Anableps is the technical name of this fish. (Just don't name one of your children Anableps!) It means "those that look upward" because of the unusual eye structure. This unique creature has two-tiered eyes. The upper and lower halves of each eyeball operate independently and have separate corneas and irises. So, if you were to confront one in its natural habitat, you would see him with his upper eyes protruding above the surface of the water. This helps him search for food as well as identify enemies in the air.

Now remember, this fish also has lower eyes. These eyes stay focused in the water in the typical manner of most fish. On one hand the fish navigates in the water like other fish. But they have the advantage of seeing what other fish can't see because of their upper eyes. They see in both worlds. If you were like this, having four eyes, two for seeing what actually is and two for seeing what might be, you would be an unusual encourager![4] How are you doing this with your wife at this time in your life?

John Maxwell, in his book *Be a People Person*, says we need to anticipate that others will do their best. "When working with people I always try to look at them not as they are but as what they can be. By anticipating that the vision will become real, it's easy for me to encourage them as they stretch. Raise your anticipation level, and you raise their achievement level."[5]

Perhaps the best way to describe encouragement is through the example of gardening. I've raised flowers and vegetables for years. Some years were good; others I'd rather forget! At times I've raised tomatoes. There's a right way to raise tomatoes and a wrong way. The right way is to make sure you have good soil with plenty of nutrients. You need water, cultivation and fertilizers in the right amounts. You also need to stake the plant or use round wire cages for them to grow on. They need this support, or their branches will break. Sometimes you need to put up a protective cover and, above all, watch out for insects, especially tomato worms.

After you've done all this you can take several weeks off to do nothing, right? No, you have to care for tomato plants consistently rather than sporadically, or they won't produce a crop.

Giving encouragement is like caring for tomato plants. It takes work—constant, consistent work—for it to be effective.[6] When you're an encourager, you're like a prospector or a deep-sea diver looking for hidden treasure. Every woman has pockets of underdeveloped resources within her. Your task as a husband is to search for these underdeveloped resources in your wife, discover them and then expand them. As you discover the strengths in your wife, you'll begin to focus on them. You'll look at them and care about what you discover. At first what you discover may be rough and imperfect. Talent scouts and scouts for professional sports teams do this all the time. They see undeveloped raw talent and ability, but they have the wisdom to see beyond that. They look into the future and see what can happen if all that potential were cultivated and developed. Do you look at your wife that way?

Encouraging your wife means that you honor and respect her because you believe in her.

I entered sports late in life. I took up racquetball in my early forties. One of the reasons I kept at it was a young pastor who worked with me the first few months. At first, I was a bit discouraged, especially when I noticed the proficiency of some of the younger men. But Tom was patient and excited whenever I did something right. He encouraged me; he believed in my ability; he saw me for what I could become, and that made so much difference. Almost 20 years later, I still played. I gained confidence, and some of those younger guys didn't beat me anymore!

WHAT ENCOURAGEMENT BRINGS ABOUT

You are like the refiner's fire. What you notice and encourage can be refined in a positive way. Any movement that you see headed in a healthy, positive direction needs your attention and reinforcement.[7] You're saying, "Go for it. You can do it!"

One of the character qualities that lend themselves to being an encourager is gentleness. This quality means that when you discover where another person is vulnerable or sensitive, you're not hard, harsh or forceful. When you discover a tender, sensitive place in your wife, you protect it rather then step on it. As you consider ways of encouraging your wife, ask yourself:

- Am I gentle, especially with those sensitive areas?
- Am I treating her the way I would want to be treated?
- Am I building hope in her life?
- Does she feel safe around me with those sensitive areas?

A husband shared with me how he encouraged his wife to take some steps to move forward in her life:

My wife and I were accustomed to living on two average incomes when our first child was born and I began seminary. Both of us went to part-time work in order to adjust to our new family and the demands of school. Our reduced income also necessitated a move to a much less attractive house. In addition, it became necessary for us to be much more thrifty than either one of us had ever experienced. My wife is not naturally given to bargain hunting, coupon shopping or other cost-saving measures. Being naturally a bit of a tightwad, I realized that I needed to encourage change.

To encourage my wife to change her shopping habits, I did several things: (1) I prayed for her to be open to change and that God would show me what to do and say so that she wanted to change; (2) I very tactfully passed on cost-cutting ideas I was aware of or learned about; (3) I held up the virtues of cost cutting and the practices of other thrifty women we both knew, praising her each time she came home with a bargain; (4) I set an example of thriftiness and cost consciousness; (5) I allowed her to change and exhort me in this area as well; (6) I trusted God to change her, because I couldn't do it alone.

The challenge of living on less, especially with school and then a second child, was sometimes intimidating. However, we were still able to tithe to our church and continue to save, even while my wife was out of work following the birth of girl number two. My wife is not proud of her management of the household finances, but I am proud of her, and we both have a deeper appreciation for the way that God blesses those who are good stewards of what He entrusts to them. We've been blessed by freedom from the love of money and things—and by generosity of others in times of special need. We worked together constructively, and a potential threat to our relationship has brought us closer together and given us confidence in facing other challenges.

Perhaps you're like some men I've talked to, or I should say, men who have talked to me! They say, "Why do I need to be the one doing all the encouraging? I need it as much as she does, and I'm starving for some."

"This sounds just like what I've been hearing for years. We guys have to give, give and give. And if I do more of this, she'll just expect more!"

"This sounds one-sided to me. Many of us men go through life starving for some need fulfillment. Why don't you work with wives to get them to be more caring?"

These are good, honest questions. I have two responses.

First, this is *not* a book directed to women. It's written to encourage men to bring out the best in the women in their lives. We, as husbands, have a need to grow and develop as encouragers. In a marriage relationship, we often function as a thermostat. What we do affects the temperature of that relationship. Most men were raised in a way that handicapped them emotionally and made them relationally deficient; and I'm saying that about myself as well. We have much to learn! And we can do better (some of us have already learned to do better as a marriage partner). But there are other books and helps for women to read, including the companion to this volume—*Bringing Out the Best in Your Husband*. The book you are reading, however, is for men.

Second, as Christians, we don't really have a choice about whether we encourage others or not. It's not our decision to make. Scripture states that others will know that we are Christians by the love we show for one another. One of the ways we reflect this love is by being an encourager. Look at what God's Word tells us to do.

In Acts 18:27, the word "encourage" means "to urge forward or persuade." In 1 Thessalonians 5:11, it means "to stimulate another person to the ordinary duties of life."

Consider the words found in 1 Thessalonians 5:14: "And we earnestly beseech you, brethren, admonish (warn and seriously advise) those who are out of line [the loafers, the disorderly, and the unruly]; encourage the timid and fainthearted, help and give your support to the weak souls, [and] be very patient with everybody [always keeping your temper]" (*AMP*).

Scripture uses a variety of words to describe both our involvement with others as well as the actual relationships. The word "urge" (*parakaleo*) means "to beseech or exhort." It is intended to create an environment of urgency to listen and respond to a directive. It is a mildly active verb. Paul used it in Romans 12:1 and in 1 Corinthians 1:4.

The word "encourage" (*paramutheomai*) means "to console, comfort and cheer up." This process includes elements of understanding, redirecting of thoughts and a general shifting of focus from the negative to the positive. In the context of the verse, it refers to the timid ("fainthearted" in the *KJV*) individual who is discouraged and ready to give up. It's a matter of loaning your faith and hope to the person until her own develops. In what way does your wife need you to loan your faith to her?

The word "help" (*anechomai*) primarily contains the idea of "taking interest in, being devoted to, rendering assistance or holding up spiritually and emotionally." It is not so much an active involvement as a passive approach. It suggests the idea of coming alongside a person and supporting him. In the context of 1 Thessalonians 5:14, it seems to refer to those who are incapable of helping themselves. In what way does your wife need this kind of help at this time?

First Thessalonians 5:11 states, "Therefore encourage one another and build each other up, just as in fact you are doing." Hebrews 3:13 states that we are to "encourage one another daily." In the setting of this verse, encouragement is associated with protecting the believer from callousness. Hebrews 10:25 says, "Let us not give up meeting together . . . but let us encourage one another." This time, the word means to keep someone on his feet who, if left to himself, would collapse. Your encouragement serves like the concrete pilings of a structural support. In what way does your wife need this kind of support at this time? One of my favorite verses is Proverbs 12:25: "Anxiety in a man's heart weighs it down, but a good word makes it glad" (*NASB*).

The Word of God is clear about what we're to do. To be a consistent encourager we need to reflect the character qualities of 1 Corinthians 13. Here they are, amplified in a unique way:

- *Patient* (you are tolerant of frailties, imperfections and shortcomings in your wife)
- *Kind* (you are tender and thoughtful toward your wife)
- *Not jealous* (of genuine friendships with others or of the special gifts and talents of your wife)
- *Not boastful* (about personal appearance or achievements in an attempt to compete with your wife)
- *Not arrogant* (you are not disdainful of your wife's looks or achievements; you do not belittle your wife)
- *Not rude* (you are not inconsiderate of your wife's needs or feelings)

- *Not insistent on your own way* (you are willing to compromise, to consider your wife's needs and interests)
- *Not irritable* (you do not snap at your wife; you are approachable)
- *Not resentful* (you do not hold grudges; you are forgiving)
- *Not rejoicing in wrong* (you do not delight in your wife's misfortunes; you do not keep score or tally perceived wrongs)
- *Rejoicing in right* (you are truthful; you do not try to conceal things from your wife)
- *Bearing all things* (you support your wife in times of struggle)
- *Believing all things* (you consider what your wife has said before responding)
- *Hoping in all things* (you do not wallow in pessimism about your relationship; you keep a positive attitude)
- *Enduring in all things* (you do not give in to pressures of life; you are willing to stand by your wife when she's having personal struggles)[8]

If you want a wife of character, who responds to you, follow the directives in this Scripture passage. The classic Proverbs 31:10-11 Scripture passage reveals a key element of why the Proverbs woman is the way she is. The *New International Version* says, "Her husband has full confidence in her." The *New American Standard* version says, "The heart of her husband trusts in her." Perhaps *THE MESSAGE* version sums it up best:

A good woman is hard to find, and worth far more than diamonds. Her husband treats her without reserve, and never has reason to regret it. Never spiteful, she treats him generously all her life long.

What is in your heart for your wife today?

DISCOVER THE ENCOURAGER IN YOU

1. What is more typical of you—to tell your wife what she does wrong or what she does right? What behaviors bring out the worst response in you?

2. Think about various times when you know your words have influenced your wife's self-esteem, either positively or negatively. Try to remember what you noticed about her then—the way she dressed, the way she wore her hair and makeup, the way she carried herself. What conclusions can you draw from this about you as a catalyst for positive or negative change?

3. The word "encourage" (*paramutheomai*) means "to console, comfort and cheer up." In the context of 1 Thessalonians 5:14, it refers to the timid ("fainthearted" in the *KJV*) individual who is discouraged and ready to give up. It's a matter of loaning your faith and hope to another person. In what way does your wife need you to loan your faith to her right now?

4. Review the bulleted list of 15 character qualities that define love (from 1 Corinthians 13:4-7). Choose the characteristic that is most problematic in your relationship with your wife. Ask God to create in you the character quality you would most like to develop. Consider what kind of speech or actions would reflect that quality to your wife. (This will be a spiritual exercise to do over again and again as God shows you new ways to love and encourage your wife and empowers you to do it.)

5. How does the Proverbs 31:10-11 passage describe the way you view your wife? If it does not describe what's in your heart for your wife right now, what types of behaviors in you, gleaned from this chapter, could encourage her to become more like a woman who is "worth far more than diamonds"?

Husbands **Speak Out**

ONE OF THE BENEFITS OF WRITING THIS BOOK IS THE DISCOVERY OF WHAT MEN ARE DOING TO BRING OUT THE BEST IN THEIR WIVES. It's encouraging to hear about the creativity, candor and commitment on the part of so many men who are making a difference in their marriages. As you read these accounts, some of which are bottom line while others are quite expansive, ask yourself two questions: (1) *Am I doing something like this in my marriage?* (2) *Would I be willing to do this?* You may discover some new ways to respond, or you may end up feeling like you're doing a pretty good job already.

> When I understand my wife's feelings and emotions and support her by doing what she likes, she responds to me with gladness. Usually it takes a long time to figure out exactly what she wants, but once I realize it and act on it, she is very pleased. I show her my respect and encouragement through my actions.

> As a husband, I try to encourage my wife from time to time even though she often makes mistakes.

> I encourage her by spending time with her, rather than with a group of people or other people.

No question—die to self by living to meet her needs. Communicate better—listening is good, but attending alertly is better.

I need to take care of my wife's family (her aging parents) and her safety issues (doors locked/cars tuned up). I also need to keep her love-language gas tank full (quality time and words of affirmation).

Complimenting her continuously and genuinely is critical. I try to know her and know all the things she expects me to take care of. If I neglect to do things she expects me to do, I bring out the worst in her. I need to communicate everything with her. When she knows everything, she is very supportive; but when she feels left out she gets frustrated.

I demonstrate good leadership.

I don't attempt to make her be a certain way that she is not made to be. For example, she can't cook, so I don't pressure her to be a better cook.

I usually give her something, such as letters or flowers, to let her know how I value and appreciate her and her sacrifice for our family.

First of all, my wife and I have always tried to encourage the other to pursue individual passions in addition to our shared goals and dreams (kids, house, family). So, in the midst of all the pressures of getting married, having kids, buying a house, embarking on our careers and keeping the finances in order, I try to encourage my wife to do things that feed her soul. For my wife, that means taking dance classes on her own, doing creative projects with friends, and taking time to play the guitar and sing. It unleashes such incredible talent in her when she is simply free to dream a bit, even when there is limited time for both of us to do that. When she doesn't get time to do these small things, she starts to get into the grind of the day-to-day, and she soon starts to forget about those passions. I think the key for me has been simply to encourage her in these pursuits, and then I have to make the time for her to pursue these things outside of her time at home (even if it's only a couple hours a week). I have found that this gives her great joy and passion after long days at home with the kids. It charges her up and, as a result, she has reciprocated and allowed me time to do the same!

Second, my wife loves it when our house is clean, as many wives do (especially when they have three young children messing it up all day long!). And, to be honest, most days I don't worry too much about a clean house. I never understood why this was so important for women until I began to actively try to help my wife in this way. Now, I'm no Martha Stewart, but after many discussions about helping out around the house, I now do the dishes more often, take out the trash, and generally do more things around the house (it becomes habitual after a while). Sometimes when she's out working, I'll have the kids help me clean up the house and we'll get everything smelling wonderful. My wife's reaction to these small acts is beyond what I ever imagined they could be. She'll come home and, instead of immediately starting to clean the house, she'll stop and relax after a long day. In a busy week, these moments are important.

Finally, the most important thing I can do for my wife is to make time to be with her myself. It is very difficult in some stages of marriage to simply be together and talk and make that emotional connection. So it is crucial for us to set aside time every week just to talk and hear from each other. To be honest, for me it can be the easiest thing to forget about doing this some weeks. So when I set up a date night and call up a baby-sitter so that she and I can go out and sit down together for a couple of hours, that time is invaluable to our marriage. It brings out our best attitudes over the week following.

I encourage and praise her for all she does to support and nourish the family. I reinforce how important her role is as a stay-at-home mom. I provide as much support as possible with her tasks and with down time. I pray and fast the first Wednesday every month for her.

I talk to her and give her my full and undivided attention. I affirm her and the beauty she brings into our home. I do what she wants me to do—shop, spend time with her family, prepare for meals, clean-up, do laundry, vacuum the floors, plant roses.

I try to really listen to my wife without trying to "fix" the problems. I give her a listening ear. She is the happiest when I listen carefully and let her know that she has my full attention. I bring out the best in my wife when I just spend time with her, either by taking her out for coffee or to dinner or by planning something out of the ordinary "rat-race" of our lives.

She is very happy when I pitch in by doing the dishes (without having to be asked), or when I clean up my side of the bedroom, or when I show that I care about her sense of order and detail. If it were up to me, our home would look like an army warehouse, so I tell her how much I appreciate her design and decoration in the house, and I try to do concrete things to preserve and support what she has done.

My wife appreciates it when I treat her as a valuable friend whose discernment and wisdom I really need. Instead of invalidating her observations, I take them seriously, because I've learned in 25 years of marriage that if I don't take seriously her discernment about people and situations, I get into more trouble, grief and pain than is necessary!

She loves receiving gifts, so I give her little notes, flowers at unexpected times, and phone calls just to say, "I love you; you're the best part of me." She is excellent one on one. I try to put her in individual situations so she can use her strengths, and I constantly pray for God to use her, build her, encourage her and show her who she is in Him.

I help with the laundry, make dinner, and talk to her about her day at work. I listen, but I don't make suggestions on how I would try to fix something.

I help her with her chores *without being asked*. I constantly remind her how beautiful she is and how much I love her. I spend time with her—a *lot* of time.

To encourage her on a day-to-day basis, I do my part around the house and help the kids with homework or do activities with the kids. For a special time—either a special occasion or surprise—I plan a weekend getaway for just the two of us.

I encourage her by being the most Christian man I can be and leading the household through Christ. I try to set a good example for my kids. As I lift myself up and grow in Christ, so does my wife.

My wife just told me that what really turns her on is when I'm a good father and grandfather. We spend quality time together, and I try to do anything I can to make her feel important.

I give her words of affirmation. I compliment her attributes and daily activities and try to pay close attention to her everyday needs. I try to be close with her, clear in my communication and transparent. I pray with her and encourage her.

I make her favorite dinner as a surprise. I leave her sticky notes with messages about what a wonderful wife and mother she is. I arrange a shopping date with her friends for her to enjoy. I give the kids a bath without her asking. I fold the laundry when she walks away from it to tend to another chore.

I show her affection by hugging her and telling her that I love her. She likes affirmation ("nice dress," "you look good," "thanks for your support").

I encourage her by being present and actively listening without giving advice—which is a great way to validate her emotions. When she's stressed, I jump in and do extra chores. A clean kitchen and laundry room are a delight to her.

I encourage her and support her. I actively listen to her, especially at the end of the day . . . it does wonders.

I praise her.

I make sure that when she asks me to do a project, I complete it *as she would*. I make sure to double-check all projects.

I try to do something for her before she asks for it to be done. I talk with her and review her day—what went well; what needs to change.

I talk with her about how her day went at work, asking details as she shares to show my interest in her work and her relationships at the office.

I compliment her about what she is good at. This is hard for me to do, and it takes a lot of work on my part.

I remember our wedding date on a monthly basis! We have lunch together. I give her neck rubs and back rubs.

I allow my wife to be who she wants to be. I encourage her by allowing her to be creative and reach her potential. I support her mentally and verbally to help make her feel important.

When my wife tells me that something is broken at home, or that something is wrong with the car, or that we need to get insurance for the family, I respond. She feels secure and safe, because I act and minister to her concerns.

I frequently and consistently offer her encouragement and praise. I do this in a variety of ways: verbally, through Post-It notes (often in surprise locations—vanity mirror, in a book she is reading, on her laptop screen), and by sending text messages and emails. I try to mix it up and be creative, spontaneous and surprising. Romance her.

I try to do housework without being asked. She's a clean freak, and I'm not. She feels loved when I help out in that area.

I bring out the good within her. In our marriage we struggle at times, but in that struggle I turn to God for prayer and answers. She tends to follow my lead when she sees me do that.

I give my wife one day (or weekend) each month as a "you name it—I'll do it!" day. This includes doing projects, going on special visits, and doing the shopping. Every Friday night is date night, so I take her out to dinner or cook dinner for her.

I like to bring laughter, joy and love to our family. I try to find something she enjoys and dwell on it. I do things for her without being asked and tell her that I love her and enjoy life with her.

First, I encourage her by doing things to show her I love her. I make sure the house is cleaned up and that messes the kids and I make are minimal. Second, I tell her I love her. Always being encouraging.

I take her on a date about once a week—just the two of us. I try to get home right after work to relieve her of her mom duties as soon as possible. Every evening, I take time to sit down one on one and talk through her day.

I bring out the best in her by saying "yes, dear" to whatever she asks.

I show her that she has my full commitment—my full support. I try to be a good listener, work as a team player and have a full commitment in family things—church, kids, and so on. I feel that the greatest commitment as a husband is to show love and respect for her. We spend time together, but I also give her time for privacy. We pray together.

I've learned the following: (1) do not aim any jokes her way, (2) do not try to wash your own clothes, (3) do not ever complain about her not taking care of a certain item, (4) do not ever mention weight, dress or hair in a constructive manner.

I communicate and listen (initiate conversation) and try
to ask more open-ended questions. I acknowledge her role
and accomplishments and help out with the kids. I try to
be quiet and rely on prompts to communicate.

My wife is naturally negative, so I compliment her whenever she has a positive attitude.

I ask her what her needs are and how I can fulfill them. I
act on this information and make fulfilling these needs a
priority.

I want her to feel the freedom to make her own choices in
life. She is an awesome and godly woman, and I don't
want to be the bump in the road that takes her off course.
If I have any insights on how she can overcome her weaknesses, I share these in love. I need to do more things in
the home to give her time for herself.

My love language is to help—do the laundry, wash the
dishes, clean the kitchen, take care of the cars. I know
that sometimes I do too much, but it gives my wife the
freedom to do her tasks, send emails, go shopping, take
outings with friends, or study for women's ministry. In
what I'm doing, I'm supporting her role as a person, ex-
panded beyond just mother, cook and chauffeur. Also, I
listen to all the details of her conversation. She's smart
and intuitive, especially with the kids. I know that words
of affirmation are important to her, so I try to be spontaneous, telling her that she's beautiful, that I've missed
her, that I want her. Her family is important to her as

well, so we always make time for them and are generous toward them.

I encourage her in the areas of life where she feels inadequate. In many ways she still feels like a little girl, although she never acts like one.

I listen—and *think twice* before I respond.

I try to listen to her and let issues go by that are not worth arguing over. I support her in times when others come against her.

I take her out for an evening of dining and entertainment. We talk about her interests, her associations and her endeavors.

I don't forget anniversaries, birthdays, Christmas—and I speak silently.

I spend time on my knees before the Lord, praying and studying the Word (see Psalm 119:11), which changes me.

I encourage my wife in her endeavors and help her when she asks. I also compliment her.

I listen to her, show interest in what she's saying, and spend time with her.

I always encourage her in her endeavors, especially when she has self-doubts about her activities. I share in all the household work.

We have committed to have one date night each week since we married, and I have followed through. It's just the two of us—and we have seven children.

I tell her how much I enjoy her company over all else—sports and other hobbies. I go and do the things she likes to do (like shopping).

I ask, "Do you have anything for me to do?" and "Have you been okay today?"

I think it's important to be flexible. Don't have your own agenda—give and take. Be respectful and complimentary, and help her with anything she needs.

I try to treat her like a queen. I tell her she is beautiful and give her tools so she can feel beautiful. I tell her the things she did well and the things I like about her. I appreciate her artistic, creative bent, even though it may not be interesting to me. I read the Bible with her and have Bible study time with her, and we pray together.

My goal is to love her in the same way Jesus loves His bride. There is nothing that I would withhold from her that I could give or that would lessen her radiance. I respect her for all of her God-given talents. I tell her often how much I appreciate her. I trust her in every aspect of our relationship. I try to be a good listener and am learning not to try to fix her problems—it's more about letting her vent and work through them than it is about me solving them. We laugh together—a lot. I hold her.

I open doors for her. I help her with her coat and with her seat and all those other "old-fashioned" things that previous generations (who usually stayed married longer) chose to do. It may be noteworthy to mention that my wife allows me to do those things for her and appreciates them—so the relationship of these actions is in sync with our love. I am trying to further develop my sense of good timing for communication. I am trying to be more aware of my facial expressions and body language that she reads *so* well. I am conscious that I may be sending the wrong message or a message that I did not intend to display as I think through things. I am alert to our differences on parenting (mom kinds of love vs. dad kinds of love). I say all these things not as bragging on myself, but as an acknowledgment that her "bringing out the best" is somewhat reliant on my "giving her the best."

I have found that praying for my wife makes a difference—whether in her presence or on my own. My wife asks me to pray for her in certain ways—when she has some challenges she is working through or when she has certain needs. Just a crazy example: My wife and a neighbor have both struggled with weight at times, and so they walk (and talk) together. But unknown to them, I started praying for them—for their health, friendship and that God would honor their efforts to care for their bodies. Both had struggled with losing weight (her weight has never been an issue for me—but it was for her), but they began to lose weight. So I casually told my wife that I had been praying for them. Now whenever they walk for that purpose, they ask me to pray for them! (By the way, there is no guarantee for this weight-loss plan!) I also try to compliment my wife, whether it is her dress, her food, the way she cares for our family, the mother that she is, her care of our home, the character of her life, or whatever. These are just a couple of quick ways that I have found in our love relationship to show her how much she really means to me. These things cause her to light up, they encourage her, and I believe they bring out the best in her.

Recently, I have been convicted by the Holy Spirit to put my wife ahead of my job, where she should have been all of our marriage. That has made a remarkable change in our relationship. This change has made me feel much more secure in my marriage, which in turn has made my wife more willing to "fill my love bank" as I fill hers. Being more secure has opened the lines of communication. I now understand that she only wants what is best for me, and I only want what is best for her. Knowing this one fact has helped defuse many arguments and made it much easier for us to honestly communicate our feelings to one another. We also try to have a weekend getaway about once a quarter. Nothing fancy, just time to focus on us.

Communication. I take time to be with her.

I try to live my life with Ephesians 5:25 and 1 Peter 3:7 in view: "Husbands, love your wives, just as Christ loved the church and gave himself up for her. . . . Husbands, in the same way be considerate as you live with your wives, and treat them with respect as the weaker partner and as heirs with you of the gracious gift of life, so that nothing will hinder your prayers." I know that Psalm 23:3, "he restores my soul," outlines that my life is not for me, but for Him is a start. Then, longing to finish and to hear "well done" by both God and my wife, I do my best to surrender my all to Christ. When that occurs, I'm blessed to have a wife that responds to godly behavior in me, and not only returns godly behavior but also outgives me.

Before we married, I read Judson Swihart's book *How Do You Say, "I Love You"?* and learned about love languages. I bring out the best in her by investing love in her life in languages that she understands. (In her case, "spending time together" and "saying it with words.") I also show her constant appreciation for her love and dedication to our family. I think I bring out the best in her and make it easier for her to do her job of respecting and submitting to me when I love her as Christ loved the Church, and I am willing to give myself to her.

I pray for my wife in the mornings before we go to work and at night before we go to sleep. We take care of our grandchildren three days a week, and I help prepare meals for them. Also, on days that I have off, I fix meals and help clean the house. I encourage her in her teaching of ladies' Bible studies at the church we attend. I try to remember to tell her every day that I love her and that I appreciate her and what she does to help me do the things that I need to do.

I simply work to be her greatest cheerleader. I encourage her in her new ventures and in opportunities to use her God-given talents and gifts. I let her know on a daily basis how important she is in my life and that I'm more in love with her than ever. I constantly tell her how beautiful she is—both physically and in her heart. I make sure that she knows that we are in this until "death do us part"—that we will survive any trials that life throws at us because we're in this together.

I affirm my love for her daily and tell her how beautiful she is. I demonstrate unconditional love to the best of my ability. I praise her for being such a godly woman and tell her how fortunate I am to be married to her. I stress that we are on the same team and that our teamwork is critical to having a fulfilled life. I could write a book about how intelligent my wife is and how talented she is. She is a Proverbs 31 wife and mother. I love her.

I encourage my wife in several ways. First, I try to support her interests as much as possible. She does so much for our family. I always make myself available so she can participate in activities outside the family that help revitalize her. Second, I help around the house as much as I can (doing dishes, laundry, cleaning, helping with the kids) so she doesn't have the entire burden. Third, we always support each other as parents, even when we disagree on something. Fourth, I try my best just to love and honor her as my wife 100 percent of the time.

I try to actively listen to her. I champion the activities she is passionate about. I thank God for her daily in her presence. I express appreciation for all she does. I scratch her back each night as we are falling asleep, which is her favorite form of touch. I make her laugh. We have fun together. I bring her coffee in bed when she wakes each morning. I read a portion of Scripture and pray with her each day. We share mutual interests.

I think of ways to encourage her and then verbalize them. I may come into the room and "breathe in" out loud—as when you see something that is *awesome*—and I let her know she is. I may write her an email just saying how special she is. I appreciate her laughter and the way she loves the Lord.

I cherish her. I make it a point to understand what is most important to her, and I let her know through my words, actions and prayers that I will do whatever I can do to support her in those things. This often requires sacrifice, patience and humility. However, I don't do this to bring out the best in her but to demonstrate my love and bring out the best in me.

I constantly praise her both in private and in public, giving specific praise for her character and her skills, gifts and accomplishments. Those who have known me for 20 or 30 years have never heard me speak a critical word about her. Long-term, this may be one of the most specific strengths of our marriage. Meanwhile, my wife blooms in the garden of praise; she feels safe, sheltered and valued.

I consciously try to encourage and build up my wife's confidence, emphasizing her abilities and relationship skills. I also try to remove impediments to her by helping with meal preparation and, on occasion, cooking, cleaning, picking up our home, vacuuming and running errands—plus my "honey-do" list. Fortunately, I work at home. My wife is part of the women's leadership team at our church, is a trainer for table leaders for each session of Radiance (a woman's Bible study), and does premarital mentoring with me. She continues to grow in the Lord despite being an above-the-knee amputee and dealing with other health issues.

TWENTY WAYS TO BRING OUT THE BEST IN YOUR WIFE

I received the following list from one husband on how he brings out the best in his wife:

1. I serve the Lord with all my soul, heart, mind and strength and let God bring out the best in me.
2. I obey Scripture regarding my wife.
3. I tell her I love her (not as a foreplay audible).
4. I listen to her (even when I have to push the record button during a play-off overtime).

5. I love her even when she does not "deserve it."
6. I compliment her on her beauty, clothes, cooking, spirituality and marital "performance."
7. I give her flowers regularly (and not the cheesy ones).
8. I am honest with her at all times (but I avoid suicidal opinions).
9. I tell her I think of no other woman (i.e., no alternate fantasies).
10. I pray with her.
11. I don't insist on sex when she's tired.
12. I maintain a godly, peaceful atmosphere in our home.
13. I keep her laughing (self-deprecating humor works best).
14. When she's wrong, I have the character to admit it.
15. I remind her that opposites attract, and that I'm the smart one.
16. Date night is Friday night, and I don't flake out.
17. Rubdowns are good (and so is whatever happens after).
18. I get her something hot (wintertime) or cold (summertime).
19. I avoid criticizing her (an effective antidepressant).
20. "Sex starts in the kitchen," a cold (floor) metaphor for me, but I try to maintain the romance (very important).
21. Extra: I got turned on just making this list!

Now that you've read what others have said, what's your reaction? Did you gather some new ideas? Was it overwhelming? Were you encouraged or discouraged? If you had to summarize what you read or list the top six ideas, what would you say? Perhaps you're wondering, "Is all this worth it?" "Will it really help?" or "Our marriage is in too bad a shape at this point; I've given up." Well, it's never too late.

Listen to the story of a couple of friends of mine. At one point it was too late, but redemption occurred.

Here is Jim's story:

I wondered why I was asked to give my testimony, and then I realized that the pastor knew that Marie and I were divorced and then remarried. I first thought the reason they asked me to share was that out of all the people in the congregation I had done the worst job the first time around in marriage. But when we had the *Forty Days of Purpose*, one of the things I remembered from the book was when it talked about life as a metaphor. What immediately flashed in my mind is that it's a battle and a struggle. And it's always been a battle and a struggle for me.

Marie and I were both living in Los Angeles in what most people would call the ghetto. We met when my mother worked with Marie's aunt. They wanted me to take her to her prom and I said no because I didn't have any fun at mine. Then I saw her picture and said yes. Eventually, in 1966, we were married.

I always believed in God, but I never let Him into my life, and I always tried to fight all the battles and struggles myself. I was a basketball coach and was focused on winning, winning and winning. That's all I thought about. I brought all those struggles home and dumped them on her. Even though I was a leader at work, I really wasn't a leader at home. I just didn't know how to lead my family.

We were married 23 years before we got divorced in 1989, basically because I was such a poor leader. I did not give my wife the things she needed. I really didn't know exactly what those things were. We went through with the divorce and Marie went to Mexico City to study. I was a Christian at the time, but I wasn't walking with the Lord. But I prayed and asked Him to take over because I loved my wife and my family and I did not want this situation. God was faithful to me and restored my marriage a year later. We were only divorced for one year.

I think the major things I have learned are that I can trust the Lord to fight my battles and that He will lead me if I give Him that opportunity. I think the major change in my life is that I am more of a spiritual leader in my home. I think I support my wife more now.

I know that women need to be loved, supported and cherished. As men, that's really the role God has given us—and He sets an example when He loves, supports and cherishes His church. I'm trying to do a better job on that. I don't always do it, but the more that I can be in the Bible and listen to God speaking to me—because that's where He's speaking to me—and the more I can rely on Him, the more I can focus on my wife's positive gifts rather than on her negative traits and on trying to change her.

You see, that's what coaches do—we work on changing negative behavior so that we can get players to do the positive things so that we can be successful. But I know I shouldn't carry that home—and that's what I did for years.

Marie is a very intelligent, compassionate, loving and beautiful woman. We are very different. Last night, for example, she was reading her welding book and I was watching the De La Hoya fight. But we are meant to be together. The Scripture that I have relied on is 1 Peter 3:7, which says, "Live with your wives in an understanding way . . . show them respect" (*NCV*).

Here is Marie's response:

I really like the cherish part; Jim was always a hardworking, responsible man. I never had to worry about any of the material things in our life, but I felt way down on his list of priorities. It seemed like basketball was number one, two and three. He was very critical of me— whether it be my dress, my hair or the smudge on the table. It didn't seem like I could do anything well, and the irony of it was that other people thought I did many things well. But none of that sank into my heart, because Jim was the one I wanted to please. My sell-out to the Lord has made such an incredible difference in our lives. Now Jim's self-esteem was very wrapped up in what he thought of me.

My family had died. I was a young woman trying to raise a family—and without a foundation in the Lord. In fact, in our early marriage I was an atheist because of a lot of things that had happened to me. I was needy, and Jim wasn't able to show me the love he actually had for me.

I started to build up sadness and deep depression over the years, and after 23 years, I thought, *I can't go on any longer like this*. But crying out to the Lord is an amazing thing. It wasn't an overnight change, but it turns

out a church I was attending needed a singer and gui-
tarist and I was pushed into the role. That's where I
found out God was real, that Jesus Christ had died for
my sins and that He was there for me.

Jim and I reaching out to the Lord has made such
an incredible difference in our lives. Now Jim reads the
Word faithfully, and I can see that he's devoted his life
to God's plan. This has been a benefit to me and our
family, because God's plan is that we be united. That
has enriched our relationship.

Jim is now my biggest supporter. He helped me overcome my fear of going to school, so at the age of 44, I
went to college, got a bachelor's, master's, two teaching
credentials and two administrative credentials—when I
thought I never could pass one college class.

And then last May Jim pushed me into doing a con-
cert that was a magical experience—at an auditorium
with more than 600 people in attendance. I have found
that I can rely upon my husband not just for material
things, but for spiritual strength and for emotional
support. Now he enumerates my strengths to me and
to other people. He also helps me with my weaknesses,
as a spouse should do, and in an uncritical way.

It's an amazing thing. In a short sentence: There is
always hope in the Lord.

DISCOVER THE ENCOURAGER IN YOU

1. As you read the men's comments in this chapter, what was your response?

2. What did you learn about encouragement? What one thing stood out to you?

3. Several of the men not only told how they encourage their wives, but they also told some of the positive effects their encouragement had on their wives. What did their stories inspire in you?

4. What are you doing to encourage your wife right now?

5. What will you do differently to encourage her in the future?

Wives
Speak Out

IN POPULAR CULTURE, HUSBANDS ARE OFTEN THE BRUNT OF JOKES, which often revolve around the belief that they don't always know how to respond to their wives or they don't understand them.

I once picked up a small book in a store with the title *What Men Understand About Women*. To my surprise, I discovered every page was blank. The message was all too apparent. But was it true? Unfortunately, in many cases, it is the truth. Having spent 40 years counseling couples and conducting marriage seminars throughout the country, I've found that women are much more concerned about learning about marriage and the man they married. They want to grow in their understanding. There is also evidence in the fact that 85 percent of Christian books are purchased and read by women. If men would study women, and their wives in particular, with the same intensity they put forth (at least some of them) in getting an education, developing their athletic ability or becoming proficient in their vocation, marriage counselors would start going out of business!

It helps a man when he is given some direction. That's what this chapter is about. I look to surveys for a lot of my information; but to discover how a man can really bring out the best in his wife, I needed feedback from wives, and lots of them. So I asked a few questions and also looked to others' surveys, which also asked questions of women. And we found answers.

Scores of wives shared what their husbands did to bring out the best in them. It helps a man to find out what other men are doing so that he can think about it for as long as he wants, decide what he wants to do and then follow through. But remember that each wife is unique, and every husband will need to discover what works best for his own wife.

ENCOURAGING YOUR SPOUSE

Here are the responses that can shed some light on what you might do to encourage your wife:

> He communicates his love and appreciation for me daily—with email, texts, words, body language and physical touch. He shows me love physically on a regular basis: hugs, kisses, loving touches. He only uses kind, gentle words, because he knows I'm sensitive and he knows that words are my love language.

> He supports me emotionally—even when he thinks I'm wrong. He always backs me up. He encourages me in all my endeavors and supports my decisions. He's there to catch me when I fall.

> He compliments me, especially in front of others. He does things that show he has listened and paid attention to what I have said. He helps me when I ask. He's loyal and trustworthy. He gives me backrubs. He stands up for me and spends time with me.

> My husband encourages me to be creative and to have hobbies and special friends to do them with. He never minds when I spend money on myself to buy nice clothes (maybe because I don't do it very often).

He will take the time to stop and really listen to me and support my thoughts and feelings. He acknowledges and appreciates what I do for him. He compliments me and is impulsively demonstrative when I least expect it.

He really listens and responds to what I am saying. He doesn't try to fix it; he just listens and says things like, "I understand how you would feel that way" or "You are so right." He tells me he still thinks I'm beautiful and will say to me, "Good meal, babe."

What helps is his being a listener *at all times*. He is a good listener because he gives verbal affirmation—he praises and acknowledges my strengths as well as my weaknesses in a positive tone. He spends time with me—trips, coffee time, walks, date night.

When he is thoughtful of me, I'm encouraged. I don't feel that I'm in this family alone when he does his part by working and helping around the house and with the children. When he does these things, my attitude changes and I'm different.

He encourages me to set and follow goals. He gives constructive criticism in a loving way for areas I need to improve, and he likewise allows me to give him my thoughts on areas he needs improvement as a husband/father/son. He understands that staying home with two children under four years old is hard work. He knows exactly when my patience is running on low and keeps the kids to give me a break.

He is patient with me. I'm very emotional, and if I go off on something or about someone, he listens patiently. He lets me get it out of my system. Then, later that day (or even a few days later) after I've come to my senses about that topic, I'm more able to listen to his wisdom and discuss the issue rationally. He doesn't meet me with condemnation when I'm emotional or passionate about something. He quietly leads me to a more forgiving heart.

He is funny. He can change my mood and lighten me up by helping me to see the humor in a situation. He leaves me notes around the house to tell me he loves me. He calls me during the day for no reason but to say he is thinking of me. He says nice things about me in front of our friends.

He stays calm even when I am at my worst. Sometimes even I think I'm being unreasonable, but I can't stop myself until I see how calm he stays. He provides stability.

I feel encouraged when he says he appreciates all the things I do for our family and our home.

When he does things to show me that he loves me—holds me, rubs my neck and shoulders, shares deep personal things—I feel safe.

My husband supports my desires to serve and use my spiritual gifts, even when it requires a sacrifice.

He recognizes my need for time alone and my need for time with my girlfriends.

He always tells me he loves me and kisses me frequently. He tells me how beautiful I am even when I don't feel that I am. I need that.

He listens *without trying to fix things* for me. He makes me feel loved by wanting to spend time with me—whether it is traveling, camping, or something else.

He encourages me in pursuits that make me a better person and closer to God. He never criticizes me. He primarily encourages me and thinks things through before saying anything to me.

His being positive and being a Christian man and husband, in spirit and in action, sets a tone for our family. Being nice to people.

He lets me know clearly and lovingly what he wants and needs from me. I don't have to second guess or read into what he is saying.

He speaks respectfully to me and doesn't nag when I need to change something.

He is a great support to me when we care for our three young grandchildren three evenings a week. He fixes more than his share of meals, does housecleaning and plays board games with them. He also encourages me in my leading a ladies' Bible study.

My gift is teaching and speaking, and he encourages me to take advantage of opportunities and assures me the Lord is using me in this way. He reviews my talks and is honest if they don't make sense. He takes up the slack at home if I need more time. He's my biggest fan.

My husband pampers me, supports me emotionally, serves me and believes in me. His motivation in all of this is to be the leader in our home—always pointing us to Christ.

He really listens and tries to implement something I've said into an actual scenario. I feel at times that it would be easy for him to brush me off and my suggestions, but he doesn't.

He encourages me to share my opinion, which I don't volunteer. He draws me out.

He listens to me and validates me.

He shows how proud he is of me by complimenting me on my appearance or an accomplishment.

He brings out the best in me when he praises me for my accomplishments as a good, loving stepmother and mother. He acknowledges he could not do what I do—being a stay-at-home mother of three young children.

He supports me 100 percent in my endeavors. Through-out my four-and-a-half years in seminary, my husband worked crummy jobs with terrible hours so he could stay with our son. He's listened to my frustrations about being a young woman in ministry, and he's always been my cheerleader. And he's done all of this while also attending school and being shipped overseas twice in the military.

He forgives me immediately when I'm not at my best or when I'm being unreasonable. He supports me in my dreams and surprises me daily by doing household chores (does dishes, makes coffee, feeds cats) or by fixing me breakfast when I'm under pressure. He tells me I am his one and only and that I am beautiful! He listens to me without trying to "fix" it. All this makes me feel special.

He affirms the things I do and am interested in. He makes me want to do better and be better without pressure. I end up wanting to do well.

He encourages me and supports my attending women's Bible study, which keeps me centered. That affects our relationship.

At present, our children are both out of the house (we have a 21-year-old in college and an 18-year-old in the Navy). My husband helps our children understand that I am not trying to control their lives; I only need to hear their voices and small talk. Their voices, he tells them, are helping me cope with the separation a mother must endure as her children grow into independent adults.

My husband is a wonderful listener. He has learned over the years that the way I process problems is by "fleshing them out" out loud—or talking them through. It helps just to have his undivided attention, and then the solution will come to me. I don't necessarily need the problem solved; I just need an ear.

He notices and confirms that what I do routinely is important for him and our family. I don't need to hear this every day, but it is nice for him to notice and affirm the small things that I do over and over again. After years and years of marriage, my husband is great at complimenting my looks and liking the way I look. My husband does not belittle, put me down or say hurtful things to others about me. He is good about saying nice things about me in front of other people.

My husband is an energizer bunny, always moving. When he actually stops to hear what I have to say—and really stops—he really listens. I'm encouraged when he thinks ahead of me and finds something to help me out, like emptying the dishwasher, folding clothes or taking any kind of pressure off my plate. This takes my reactions down and calms me.

He makes me feel that I matter—that I'm special—when he places time with me above job, friends or chores. He encourages me when he is aware of my need to have one-on-one time with him because I need to talk, cuddle or just play. When I feel validated, I, in return, want to please him and help him in all things. When I feel left out, I close off and he does not get my best.

It works best when he listens to me and lets me get out all that I want to say. I want to complete all the details and then get his input. That's ideal. However, realistically, that is very hard for him. He wants to jump in, fix and guess at the conclusion. He gets impatient, doesn't want to hear the details, and wants me to get to the point . . . which is irritating. To bring out the best in me requires his concerted effort to listen to all I want to say, no matter how long or detailed it is.

When my husband shows me he appreciates even the little things that I do, it makes me happy and makes me want to do even more things for him. I find that I carry out my daily chores with more love and care when I feel appreciated.

When I am down, discouraged and just having a straight-out bad day, he will encourage me with the truth found in God's Word. He'll remind me that "our struggle is not against flesh and blood" (Eph. 6:12) and to "be strong in the Lord and in his mighty power" (Eph. 6:10).

My husband says "Thank you" to me almost daily for specific things I do, and that makes me feel appreciated. That, in turn, keeps me aware of what he is doing and what others are doing. I can put others first.

My husband is so willing to help me with the housework! Amen to that! We both work full-time at this point, and I just don't have the energy after working a full day to also tackle the housework, pay bills, shop for groceries and cook meals. My husband never gripes or complains when I ask him for help; in fact, he often sings or hums while he works, which cracks me up every time. In those moments, I feel especially close to him. Ninety-nine percent of the time my husband has the most amazing attitude toward the requests I ask of him. This has truly transformed my heart, because I had always struggled with my attitude in work and service-related things. My husband's positive attitude and constant support in our home have revealed Christ to me in a tangible way. I eagerly look for opportunities to serve my husband and bless him, and it is so easy for me because my husband has set the example by loving me as Christ loved the Church! That is the best thing a wife could ask for, in my opinion!

It was encouraging to discover how many men are really reaching out to build up and bring out the best in their wives. There are numerous ideas shared here that may help you respond in a new way to your wife. But remember that each woman is unique in her personality, needs, desires and spiritual gifts. Your task as a husband is to discover her uniqueness and respond accordingly. Just think of it as a project, and the discovery is giving you a road map on how to reach your destination.

TWO ADDITIONAL QUESTIONS

From a different survey, I discovered two other questions that women answered that deserve our consideration. The first question was:

What can a man do to make you feel good about yourself?

The answer that echoed from woman after woman related to their need for approval: "Women need approval. It's probably born in them—they need it in everything. That's why we take so much care to dress and put all this makeup on. We do it because we need approval—a compliment or acknowledgment that we're here and cared for by someone. That caring is one of the things I look for."

"Compliment me" was another answer I heard over and over again. Here are examples:

Give small compliments in any area. The way I've fixed the house, my clothes, my makeup. Be alert to what I'm doing. Notice.

Compliment me on how competent I am—like, "Gee, that was a really successful party we had" or "That was a nice trip, and I had a good time with you" or "That was a great piece of work you did."[1]

The second question that stood out as one of the easiest for the women to answer was:

If you had to give up hugging and caressing
FOREVER, or sex FOREVER, which would you give up?
The key word is "forever."

Ninety-one percent of the women said they would give up sex with a man before they would give up his hugging and caressing. The women gave this question less thought than any other question. Their responses were instantaneous, almost to the point of being automatic. There seemed to be no doubt in their minds. If they had to choose, they would choose hugging and caressing over sex.[2] You may not like the answer, but perhaps it's a good subject to discuss with your wife.

AREAS THAT COULD STAND IMPROVEMENT

In our survey, we also asked wives what they wished their husbands would *not* do. You're probably thinking, *That was a dumb thing to do.* Yeah, perhaps. But once again the women came up with some helpful material for their men to consider.

One of the problems we have as men is being defensive. We don't like to hear suggestions or even constructive criticism. And we don't like to admit that we're wrong. Years ago, I read some information about men and their reaction to being wrong. It went like this: *Men hate to be wrong.* When I read that, I thought about it for a while and then said, "I don't agree with that."

The next points were:

1. Men hate to admit they might have been wrong.
2. Men hate it when their wives know they're wrong before they do.
3. Men think they're being made wrong by their wives when they're not!

That last point really convicted me, because I've thought that. And when a man thinks that, he tends to overreact.

Proverbs 28:13 has good advice for all of us: "A man who refuses to admit his mistakes can never be successful. But if he confesses and forsakes them, he gets another chance" (*TLB*). It's true. Admitting when you've made a mistake does wonders for your marriage. Here are some other biblical guidelines:

> If you refuse criticism you will end in poverty and disgrace; if you accept criticism you are on the road to fame (Prov. 13:18, *TLB*).

> Don't refuse to accept criticism; get all the help you can (Prov. 23:12, *TLB*).

> It is a badge of honor to accept valid criticism (Prov. 25:12, *TLB*).

How Do Your Answers Match Up with Reality?

The following responses are from wives who were asked the question, "What are some things you wish your husband wouldn't do?" As you read these responses, consider whether any of these comments describe you. The responses have been divided into six sections, with somewhat similar responses grouped together.

Group 1

Tell his friends when I get angry with him. Read the newspaper when I am trying to talk to him. Tease his sons when they are being sensitive. Complain that I'm too sensitive. Go through the day without a hug or kiss.

Sit in front of the computer and work and spend a lot of time on it.

Procrastinate. Dominate the conversation. Leave his plate at the table.

Point out things I do or don't do and then say that it is not really important. If it is not important, don't point out the flaw.

Leave his trash on the counter.

I wish my husband would not forget the things that we've talked about.

Silly things—sometimes I feel he doesn't always need to have the remote control; however, over the years he has learned to share the choice of viewing.

Make me worship like he does. I have my own style of worship that is not like my husband's.

Discount my attention to details.

Volunteer "us" to do things without asking me first in private.

Leave me to fend for myself when we are in a crowd or at an event.

Group 2

Get angry, so easily, over things that don't go his way or when we disagree about something. He tends to over-react and blow up over the smallest things. It makes him an unsafe person, and I can't relax and just be myself. I wonder when Mount Vesuvius will erupt next. It shuts down communication and damages intimacy and closeness.

Not be so judgmental of others. Clam up and not talk about something that is bothering him. I wish he would not avoid conflict and that he would learn to walk through the communication process of talking out problems right away rather than waiting until they build up and can't be ignored.

Go silent when something is wrong. That makes me fearful and nervous.

Not be critical. Try to fix when I don't want it fixed.

Sometimes he can "nag" about things and put pressure on me to be on "his schedule." Always thinks he's the one that's right.

Putting things off. Being moody or snappish toward me.

Gets angry so quickly, doesn't have any patience for questions or conversation regarding finances.

Watches TV or raises his voice.

Complains. If and when he complains about something it makes me feel like he's complaining about me, our life, the things we do. . . . He becomes distant and defensive and we end up arguing.

Interrupts me. I wish he wouldn't be so defensive. He is always looking for an easier way. Now, that can be good, but also not good. It's frustrating when I want something done as *I* want it done and then he ponders and goes for a different plan because to him it was simpler and easier. If I object, then I'm unappreciative and he's then angry.

Overly critical, impatient—overly reactive and loses his temper over little stuff. Trivializes what bothers me and what I'm upset about. I've been married 29 long years!

WHAT'S ALL THE SHOUTIN' ABOUT?

The three main responses and concerns in Group 2 are probably some of the most common of all. Read the section again. Do you see yourself in any of these comments?

Anger—that feeling of irritation that is often expressed more in tone of voice and nonverbal expressions can deaden the love of a wife for her husband. Because many men struggle with these feelings and lack a feelings vocabulary, anger is often used in response. Anger can be used to protect oneself from others and keep them from getting too close. Anger is actually a secondary emotion and is usually caused by fear, hurt or frustration. For help with the issue of anger, as well as conflict, you may want to read *Mad About Us—Moving from Anger to Intimacy with Your Spouse*, by Gary and Carrie Oliver.

It's true that we as men tend to avoid conflict if at all possible. Sometimes we feel overwhelmed by the process, especially if we've never learned a healthy pattern of resolving conflict. Avoiding conflict doesn't make it disappear; it only makes it grow larger. If you try to bury it, you only postpone a bigger problem. Conflict is a part of marriage, but it can be healthy and productive.

Group 3

I wish that he would not be sarcastic with me.

I wish he would not allow his irritations with me to come out in the form of snide remarks. Especially when it has to do with aspects of me that have caused us trouble and that I am working on.

Sometimes he gets into sarcastic "guy talk" mode where everything is a "dig" or a negative comment (because with his years in the military that is how they communicate). I wish he wouldn't talk that way to me. It's hard for him when coming out of that environment to home.

Reacting before knowing all the facts. Making comments under his breath.

Use of sarcasm; it is hurtful and exhausting to decipher what is a joke and what is really honest underneath the sarcasm. Speaking in absolutes—i.e., "You always . . ." "You never . . ."

Being critical or getting mad at me. Being sarcastic—even in fun. Being pessimistic.

Those are some serious concerns. Let's take a closer look at them.

IT'S NOT ALWAYS WHAT YOU SAY, IT'S HOW YOU SAY IT

Every couple will voice complaints from time to time. That's normal, and complaints can be voiced in a way that your wife will hear them and not become defensive. For example, instead of focusing on what annoys you, talk more about what you would appreciate her doing. Your wife is much more likely to hear you and consider your request. Talking about what you don't like only reinforces the possibility of its continuing with an even greater intensity.

The principle of pointing toward what you would like also conveys to her your belief that she is capable of doing what you have requested. Doing this consistently, along with giving praise and appreciation when your wife complies, will bring about a change.

Criticism is the initial negative response that opens the door for the other destructive responses to follow. Criticism is different from complaining in that it attacks the other person's personality and character, usually with blame. Most criticisms are overgeneralized ("You always . . .") and personally accusing (the word "you" is central). A great deal of criticism comes in the form of blame, with use of the word "should."

Criticism can be hidden under the camouflage of joking and humor. When confronted about it, the person who criticizes will avoid responsibility by saying, "Hey, I was just joking." It reminds me of the passage in Proverbs that says, "Like a madman who casts firebrands, arrows and death, so is the man who deceives his neighbor and then says, Was I not joking?" (Prov. 26:18-19, *AMP*).

Faultfinding is a common form of criticism. It's a favorite response of the perfectionistic spouse. Criticism is usually destructive, but it's interesting to hear critics say they're just trying to remold their partners into better persons by offering some "constructive" criticism. Too often criticism does not construct; it demolishes. It doesn't nourish a relationship; it poisons. And often the presentation is like this description: "There is one who speaks rashly like the thrusts of a sword" (Prov. 12:18, *NASB*).

Criticism that is destructive accuses and tries to make the other person feel guilty. It intimidates and is often an outgrowth of personal resentment.

BEWARE THE ZINGER

Criticism comes in many shapes and sizes. You've heard of "zingers," those lethal, verbal guided missiles. A zinger comes at you with a sharp point and a dull barb that catches the flesh as it goes in. The power of these sharp, caustic statements is seen when you realize that one zinger can undo 20 acts of kindness. That's right, 20.

A zinger has the power to render many positive acts meaningless. Once a zinger has landed, the effect is similar to a radioactive cloud that settles on an area of what used to be prime farmland. The land is so contaminated by the radioactivity that, even though seeds are scattered and plants are planted, they fail to take root. Subsequently, they die out or are washed away by the elements. It takes decades for the contamination to dissipate. The kind acts of loving words following the placement of a zinger find a similar hostile soil. It may take hours before there is a receptivity or positive response to your positive overtures.[3]

Another form of criticism is called *invalidation*. When invalidation is present in a marriage, it destroys the effect of *validation* as well as the friendship relationship of marriage. Encouragement is wiped out. Sometimes couples get along and maintain their relationship without sufficient validation, but they cannot handle continued invalidation. This is yet another example of one negative comment destroying 20 acts of kindness.[4]

Invalidation is like a slow, fatal disease that, once established in a relationship, spreads and destroys the positive feelings. As one wife said, "The so-called friend I married became my enemy with his unexpected attacks. I felt demeaned, put down, and my self-esteem slowly crumbled. I guess that's why our fights escalated so much. I had to fight to survive." To keep love and your marriage alive, keep the criticism out.

The next step down the path of destruction is contempt—the intent to insult or psychologically abuse your spouse. That sounds harsh, doesn't it? But that's what happens. It's like using a mortar in a battle to lob shells into the enemy lines. But in a marriage, you are lobbing insults into the person who you promised to love. It's thinking negative thoughts and speaking negative statements where nothing is sacred. Name-calling, nonverbal actions, sneering, put-downs and mocking are all part of the pattern.

It is all too easy to focus on the things we don't like about our mates, especially when we are irritated with them.

THE POWER OF POSITIVE REINFORCEMENT

The only effective solution is to balance any necessary criticism with at least five times as many compliments and expressions of gratitude. These don't have to be elaborate. In fact, it is better if they are a simple "Hey, thanks for taking care of that" or "I really appreciated such and such" or even "Your hair looks especially nice today." Similar comments let your mate know that you *are* paying attention. And because everybody loves approval, your spouse will tend to replicate the behavior you are rewarding her for with her gratitude. Professionally and personally, I have learned the power of catching someone being good.

Think of the wonderful fruit this intervention could bear in your relationship. In my own marriage, I know how well I respond when my wife acknowledges something I have done for her or compliments my appearance on a particular day. Besides making me feel good, I like pleasing her, and so I try to do those things more often. I don't think I am unique in this way. Everybody loves approval, but husbands and wives tend to be more stingy with it than they should. As a result, spouses end up feeling unappreciated by and isolated from each other.

Exceptional couples understand how their partner's strengths *and* weaknesses help them become better people. While no spouse wants his or her mate to have shortcomings, the fact is, we all do. Even if we are working to overcome them, from time to time our partner is going to stumble into our flaws, and vice versa. In such times, it is a very mature spouse who can see the opportunity for growth these situations present.

I will never forget one elderly gentleman—and he was a gentleman—who was taking exceptionally good care of his wife. Moreover, he seemed not to lose his patience like so many caregivers sometimes understandably do. I myself have a difficult time watching those I love suffer even from a head cold and, to my shame, I often allow such things to make me an insufferable crab—as if I had anything to complain about. But this man was so patient and loving in his ministrations to his wife that I finally asked him what his secret was.

"We've had a lot of good years together, and part of it is I figure I owe at least this much to her. But the other thing is that I've never been a very patient person. I used to complain a lot. It was mostly my way of blowing off steam. Anyway, seeing all that she's going through, and considering everything I've had to do, what with taking her to doctors and getting up at night to change her diapers and everything else, the little irritations in life don't seem to bother me so much anymore."

He started to tear up. "After all these years, she's still teaching me things."

I would invite you to look at yourself when your spouse's weaknesses and vulnerabilities are exposed and see what they can teach you about yourself.[5]

Group 4

I wish he wouldn't cuss and act differently when he is not around me—or be negative.

Group 5

I wish he wouldn't watch TV while I'm talking to him.

I wish he wouldn't try to fix a problem—just listen.

I really hate it when he dictates to me, like I'm an employee. I am a highly educated woman, yet he can make me feel so stupid. I really hate it when he treats our kids badly. This is an issue with us. He seems to favor one over the other, and it really creates tension for us.

Group 6

When I ask him to do something for me he waits or puts it off until later, and then I either get frustrated and do it myself, or it doesn't get done. Buying me gifts are things *he* likes/wants.

I would like him to move away from the exercise equipment aisle when it comes to buying me a gift and away from Costco as the only store to shop at.

He shuts down when I cry because he doesn't know what to do (a hug would make such a difference—if he would offer). He thinks it is best to get busy when sad—not cry. It bothers me when he does not make eye contact with me when communicating—makes it seem like he is disinterested and/or distracted.

Sometimes he thinks and plans too much—which I know is a good thing. Maybe he could do less of that and be more spontaneous. (Although he is a lot better as we get older.) Talk less about money—examples: worries a little. Can be dismissive of what I think is a problem and he doesn't.

He overeats. He goes overboard with things in his life.

He brings home stresses from work. Puts himself down. Belittles what a great dad and husband he is. His tone of voice sometimes when he talks.

Talks down to me. Tells me I'm emotional.

He defines my feelings and emotions for me. He says, "Don't build me the clock; just give me the time."

I wish he would give me clear communication and get to the point.

Sometimes he is too focused on what he has to get done—bills, whatever. I would love to see him let down, play golf, enjoy free time; of course, maybe if I would pay the bills, maybe he would have more free time. (I doubt it, I think he would find other things to get done.)

He works so many hours, makes too many commitments, and doesn't spend enough time at home.

I have a hard time even coming up with something. I guess if he could "reconstruct" the bathroom after using it in the morning, that would be great. Towels, toiletries and such scattered for me to put away each morning. Makes me feel disrespected or that he didn't care enough to put them away and expects me to do it. But I know that's not his intention—but it still feels that way. And clothes on the floor in various places in the house. Still roommate-y kind of stuff after all these years. But that's all!

I wish my husband would not be late for everything. When we go anywhere together, I am the one who gets the kids up, diapered, dressed, fed, packs the diaper bag, get myself dressed, fed, put shoes and coats on, gather necessities together—all while he reads the paper and takes a long shower . . . only to get in the car at the time we are supposed to be arriving at our destination. When I sit in the car with the kids waiting, that also means I have not had a chance to do my last-minute things, like use the restroom just before leaving. I often have car rides where I am stewing inside and say nothing about the three-ring circus I have just gone through . . . all to keep him happy.

He makes promises and does not follow through. He often gets sidetracked and forgets what he promised me. This hurts my heart. Also his being so prideful when he knows he has hurt my feelings; he would rather wait out my hurt and resentment than come to me and ask forgiveness or talk things out, for he knows I will "get over it." But what he really does not know is that until resolved, it is still there.

I wish my husband wouldn't lose his patience with me whenever I happen to be driving. I am already nervous when driving and become even more nervous when he is a backseat driver.

What Changes Would You Make?

I discovered these women's concerns about their husbands by asking a different question: "If you could wave a magic wand and make one change in your man, what would you change?" Here are their responses:

Group 7

More self-control . . . reduce his temper.

That I could be number one in his life instead of number two to his work.

I would wand away his stubbornness.

I'd change his attitude about life, to take more time to smell the roses. Take time to remember anniversaries. Take a vacation. I think if he had taken more time with his family instead of chasing the dollar, we would still be married.

That it's all right to trust enough to fall head over heels in love with a woman.

I'd cut his domineering attitude.

I'd give him the ability to communicate better.

I'd have him not try so desperately to please his mother.

I would have him accept my independent spirit.

I would increase his self-confidence, which would cure many other problems.

I'd like for him to be more spontaneous.

I'd wave my magic wand and say, "Be more sensitive."

I'd like for him not to always criticize me.

I'd like him to be more of a partner with more involvement in decisions that affect our family.

I would have him forget my past.

I wish I could wave a magic wand and make my man feel inner strength enough to show his affection for me in public. In the store he walks far enough in front of me to make it appear we aren't together. When we eat out, he doesn't talk to me, but rather keeps looking over my head to see whoever else is there. That hurts. I want him to recognize me in public.

I want more hugging before sex, during and after. Especially after.

If I had a magic wand to wave, I'd make his working environment more pleasant. He loves his job but hates the workplace he's in.

I'd change his way of supposedly telling me he loves me. I'd prefer he showed me he loves me with true companionship. Actions speak louder than words.[6]

This last response is different but insightful. Perhaps this woman's journey and discovery will give you something to think about:

There are plenty of petty things that my husband does that annoy me, but those things are more my issues than his, because I am letting them annoy me in the first place. As for bigger issues, I wish my husband wouldn't pull away from affection so quickly. By affection, I mean things as simple as hugs and kisses. My husband is the king when it comes to serving me around our home, but his weakness is serving me with personal touch.

It has been a tremendous challenge for me to learn to be satisfied with so little physical affirmation, as that is one of my love languages, but it is most certainly not one of my husband's. I remember shortly after I got married that I was devastated because my husband had little need for intimacy at all. I wondered what was wrong with me, and I felt unattractive all the time because my husband didn't seem to desire me (not always, but more or less). I remember sitting at a Taco Bell (great food, too!) with my mom one day and my heart was so shattered at that point. I was sharing with her that I didn't know how to feel loved in a marriage that didn't provide the touch that I so longed for. I felt lonely; I felt ugly. My mom said something that I know was straight from heaven, because it pierced me to the core. She said, "Casey, if your husband didn't have arms, would you still expect him to hug you?"

I was annoyed initially, but I sat there thinking about what she said to me and I replied, "No, of course not." Then she told me, "Well, if God has not yet given your husband the emotional arms to hug you, is it healthy or fair of you to expect something that he cannot offer you at this time?" Those words sounded like jewels of wisdom pouring out of heaven for me. I was radically transformed after that conversation with my mom. I stopped expecting my husband to be something that he couldn't be, or at least wasn't at that point. I stopped hoping for things that would only disappoint me and bring bitterness between my husband and me.

Ultimately, I had to sacrifice my needs and lay them at the feet of Jesus—sweet surrender. Jesus sacrificed so much for me; His blood has washed away all of the horrible things that I have done in my life. The least that I can do with my life to honor that great sacrifice is to learn to do the same—less of me and more of Christ! I began to communicate to my husband when I needed a hug or a kiss, and though it isn't quite the same as getting affection spontaneously, it helped to satisfy my need for touch and it taught my husband new habits. My husband has always been willing to work on this area and that is what blesses me and keeps me pressing on in love. Communication was really the key to resolving that issue . . . and every other!

DISCOVER THE ENCOURAGER IN YOU

1. Read the statements about what women hate on page 71. What are the five things your wife wishes you wouldn't do?

2. Read the statements from the wives in answer to the question, "What are some things you wish your husband wouldn't do?" (Group 1) on pages 72-73. What are the three major concerns the wives expressed?

3. If someone were to ask your wife right now how you encourage her, what would she say?

4. What type of comments, and perhaps a specific comment, stood out to you as something you would *not* hear from your wife? What words would you most deeply desire to hear from your wife?

5. You may be like the husbands whose wives described how they encourage and bless them. But if not, there are some attitudes and actions you need to ask God to remove; and there are some new attitudes and actions you need to ask God to cultivate in you. Spend a good amount of private time reflecting on all that you have read in this chapter, and then ask God what needs to change in you. When you have some answers, ask Him to change you. Then start thinking of ways you can do the following:

- New ways of thinking about my wife and her needs to change our home environment for the better
- Genuine praise of my wife—or of things she does—that I will begin speaking to her on a regular basis
- Sacrificial acts and ways of being that I will pursue to create a deeper friendship and intimacy with my wife

Understand
Your Wife

THE HUSBAND WHO TAKES THE TIME TO UNDERSTAND HIS WIFE is a wise man and is more likely to bring out the best in her. Not only that, but he will fulfill the teaching of Scripture: "You husbands . . . live with your wife in an understanding way" (1 Pet. 3:7, *NASB*). I can't get more bottom line than that. You are different from your wife and your wife is different from you. You need some basic understanding of those differences in order to live together in the way God intended. It's all pretty obvious; nevertheless, those differences can lead to misunderstandings. Here are some examples:

> Take bathrooms, for instance. A man has six items in his bathroom: a toothbrush, toothpaste, shaving cream, razor, a bar of Dial soap, and a towel from the Holiday Inn. The average number of items in the typical woman's bathroom: 437. A man would not be able to identify most of these items.

> What about the closet? A man has about four pairs of shoes: sneakers, sandals, casual and dress. If a woman

actually counts, she'll find she has 34 pairs of shoes, but she only wears about four of them.

And how about public restrooms? Men use restrooms for purely biological reasons. Women use rest rooms as social lounges. Men in a restroom would never speak a word to each other. Women who've never met will leave a restroom giggling together like old friends. And never in the history of the world has a man excused himself from a restaurant by saying, "Hey, Tom, I was just about to head to the restroom. Do you want to join me?"

When a woman says she'll be ready to go out in five more minutes, she's using the same measure of time a man uses when he says the football game's just got five more minutes left. Neither of them is counting time-outs, commercials or replays.[1]

Fact: Women don't think or express themselves in the same ways in which you do. Not only does her body work differently than yours, so does her mind. You're thinking, *I know that, so . . .*

You've probably already discovered that you don't think the same way she does. There's a big difference. You can have several choices of how you respond to this fact but only one of them will bring out the best in her. You could become irritated or exasperated with the differences or see that her differences complement yours and fill up some of your empty places.

Dr. Phil, the talk show host who has become a household name, struggled with these differences:

I am embarrassed to confess to you how many years I spent being frustrated with my wife, judging and resisting her for doing exactly what God designed her to do. God didn't design us to be the same; he designed us to be different. He made us different because we have different jobs in this world, and yet we criticize each other for being who we are.[2]

APPRECIATE THE DIFFERENCES

Your job is to identify the differences and learn to celebrate them. Differences can be an exchange of strengths. Each of you needs one another's differences. See them as an opportunity to be stretched rather than confined. It's true that some of the differences can prove to be irritants and sometimes inconvenient, but that's looking at just one side of them.

Here's a big step to consider. No husband can know what his wife is thinking even if he thinks he does. What's the point of saying this? Well, it simply means it may not be wise to take everything your wife says as reflecting what she's really thinking or feeling. In other words, don't take it for granted that you know what she is thinking or feeling just because that's what she says she's thinking or feeling. Does that make sense? If you've been married for a while, you've probably discovered this phenomenon even if it doesn't make sense. So, what's the action step?

Drop any assumptions you have about her and pray for an abundance of flexibility, because you're going to need it. Accept unpredictability in your wife. Think about this—what do you really know about your wife? To understand her, you need to know her thoughts and beliefs, even if they change.

How does she feel about:

- Being a mother?
- What she wants to be doing 10 years from now?
- Her childhood?
- Each of her siblings?
- What her losses in life have been?
- Her dad?
- Her mom?
- Your family?
- Your involvement with your family?
- What concerns her about raising the children?
- What concerns her about how you respond to the children?
- What concerns her about your work?
- Her career?
- Material items?[3]

For every one of these areas you don't know the answer to, it's essential that you find out. How do you learn? Watch your wife. Watch and observe and listen with the same intensity you give to a football game or video game. You'll see and hear things that have been evident for years.

One author suggests this approach, which could be applied to many other areas of your marriage:

You might start your observations the next time you visit a supermarket with your wife. During this mundane chore, you can learn something about the way her mind works if you step back and let her take the lead.

Let her decide which items to buy, which aisles to peruse, and how long to stay. You'll soon notice something about the way she thinks and makes decisions. Her methods of shopping are more than just consumer habits—they're clear signs of her personality. If she takes time to check prices, choose the bargain of the day, and use coupons, you'll learn that she's careful about how she spends money; this is a clue as to why she gets so angry when you pick up the tab when you go out to eat with your friends. (Money is at the top of the list of things couples argue about.)

What else can you notice? Does she plan out her trip so that she ends up in the frozen food aisle last so those foods are less likely to melt, or does she haphazardly choose her items? If she goes for the ice cream first, you'll have some insight into behavior that may drive you crazy at home when she doesn't plan ahead or think of the consequences of actions in the same way you do.

You can learn a lot if you just watch. Does she know exactly what she wants, or does she browse? Does she use a list or buy on impulse? Does she use her sense of sight or touch to buy produce? If you don't know the answers to these questions, there's a lot you don't know about your wife.[4]

It's difficult for your wife to feel special if you're not around her that much. One of the tasks we all have is discovering the balance between being at work and being with our wife. Sometimes our priorities are out of balance, when we place our wife toward the bottom of the list rather than near the top. I've seen too many men end up with a destroyed marriage because of an affair, and I'm not talking about another woman. They have an affair with their job, their hobby, the Internet, their friends or the like. An affair can occur whenever you take the time and energy that rightfully belongs to your wife and invest it elsewhere.

BE FULLY PRESENT

One of the other ways to make your wife feel special is to make sure you're home whenever you're home. That's right—be sure you're home when you're there. Most men catch on to this concept right away when I mention it. They may not say anything, but their nonverbals tell me they know exactly what I'm talking about. We all do it. It's called preoccupation. Our thoughts are elsewhere. It's possible for some husbands to be at home yet never really be at home. What do you do when you're at home, and what do you talk about? Think about that.

Here's one way to be sure you're fully present at home. Set aside a period of transition between work—or any potentially stressful activity—and other parts of the day. This transition time is designed to provide a "decompression period" so that any pressures, frustrations, fatigue, anger or anxiety that may have been generated will be less likely to affect marital communication. Some husbands pray as they drive home, committing the day's activities to the Lord. Others visualize how they are going to respond to each family member. One man said:

> "I live 20 miles from my bank. I've clocked off the halfway mark between my home and my bank by a telephone pole. I take the first ten miles up to that

point to think about my job. But when I arrive at that pole, I switch my thinking to my family. I prepare for our time together. I mentally get ready to greet them and spend time with them. When I leave for work the next morning, I spend my first ten miles reflecting on my family. When I pass my marker, I begin to prepare mentally for the day." Not surprisingly, that man was winning at home and the bank.[5]

Some couples take 20 minutes when they arrive home to sit in a dimly lighted room and listen to a recording of their favorite music, with very little talking.

When you, or your wife, are overly tired, emotionally upset, sick, injured or in pain, never discuss serious subjects or important matters that involve potential disagreement.

Set aside a special agreed-upon time every day to take up issues that involve making decisions, family business, disagreements and problems. This "Decision Time" should allow for the relaxed and uninterrupted discussion of all decision-making and problem-solving activities. No other activities should be involved, such as eating, driving or watching television. Take the phone off the hook. It may also help to set a time to talk.

Some couples have found it helpful to save all complaints about their marriage, disagreements and joint decisions for the scheduled Decision Time when these matters are taken up. Jot down items as they arise. When you pose a problem or lodge a complaint, be specific as to what you want from the other person. Do you want anger, defensiveness, resistance and continuation of the problem? Or do you want openness, cooperation and a change on the part of the other person? The way you approach the problem will determine your spouse's response.

THE MOST IMPORTANT THING YOU CAN DO

What does your wife need, or what does any wife need? She needs you to listen—to really listen. We men think we listen, but many of us don't understand how to do it.

One of the greatest gifts you can give to your spouse is the gift of listening. It can be an act of connection and caring. But far too many only hear themselves talking. Few listen. Often when two people are talking, they are, for the most part, dialogues of the deaf. They're talking *at* one another. If you listen to your wife, she feels, *I must be worth hearing*. If you ignore your wife, her thought could be, *What I said wasn't important* or *He doesn't care about me!*

Let me give you a threefold definition of listening when it pertains to your wife talking to you:

1. *Listening means that you're not thinking about what you're going to say when she stops talking.* You are not busy formulating your response. You're concentrating on what is being said and you're putting into practice Proverbs 18:13: "He who answers a matter before he hears the facts—it is folly and shame to him" (*AMP*); and James 1:19: "Understand [this], my beloved brethren. Let every man be quick to hear, [a ready listener], slow to speak, slow to take offense and to get angry" (*AMP*).

2. *Listening means that you're completely accepting of what is being said, without judging what she is saying or how she*

is saying it. If you don't like her tone of voice or the words used, and you react on the spot, you may miss the meaning. Perhaps she hasn't said it in the best way, but why not listen and then come back later—when both of you are calm—to discuss the proper wording and tone of voice? Acceptance doesn't mean that you agree with the content of what she says. It means that you acknowledge and understand that what she is saying is something that she's feeling.

3. *Listening means being able to repeat what she's said and express what you think she was feeling while speaking to you.* Real listening implies having an interest in her feelings and opinions and attempting to understand those feelings from her perspective.

If your wife shares a frustrating and difficult situation with you, you may stop listening because you view it as complaining. Or you may listen more closely because you view it as an act of trust in you.

GENDER DIFFERENCES AND LISTENING STYLES

Lack of understanding of gender differences in listening and conversation creates problems. Women use more verbal responses to *encourage* the talker. They're more likely than men to use listening signals like "mm-hmmm" and "yeah" just to indicate they're listening.

A husband will use this response only when he's *agreeing* with what his wife is saying. You can see what the outcome could be. A husband interprets his wife's listening responses as signs that she agrees with him. He's thinking, *All right! Good deal! We can get that new sports car!* Later on, he discovers she wasn't agreeing with him at all. He didn't realize she was simply indicating her interest in what he was saying and in keeping the interchange going. His wife, on the other hand, may feel ignored and disappointed, because he doesn't make the same listening responses she does. She interprets his quietness as not caring.

A man is more likely than a woman to make comments throughout the conversation. But a woman may feel bothered after she's been interrupted or hasn't been given any listening feedback. This is why many wives complain, "My husband always interrupts me" or "He never listens to me."

When it comes to your communication style, here's a recap of some things to keep in mind:

- Men are more likely to interrupt another person, whether the person is male or female.
- Men are less likely to respond to the comments of another person and, many times, make no response at all, or give a delayed response after the other finishes speaking. One shows a minimum degree of enthusiasm.
- Men are more likely to challenge or dispute statements made by their wives, which explains why men may seem to be argumentative.
- Men tend to make more statements of fact or opinion than women do.

What can a man do to be a better listener? Remember this, although it may be hard to accept: If your wife doesn't *feel* as though you're listening to her, it's the same as if you're not listening to her. If you're like me, your first response to this statement is to argue with it. "Hey, of course I'm listening. It's just her perception. Forget it."

Go back and read what I said again and again and again until it sinks in.

Here's what will cause your wife to say you're a good listener. When your wife is talking to you, stand still when she's talking. Just stop and stand still. It's hard to talk to a moving target, to a man in motion. You may think you can listen and move, and that may be true, but she won't believe it.

Next, stop—stop what you're doing. Put down the remote after you've turned off the TV. Don't answer that phone or respond to the text message. Give her 110 percent attention.

The next step is to look . . . at her. Turn your body so you are facing her, unless you're driving. And now listen—take it in—don't interrupt or try to fix. When you're talking, don't let your eyes wander. If you don't have eye contact, you miss out. Remember this fact: *Most women tend to repeat what they've said when they don't have eye contact with you because they're not sure if you have heard them.* Sound familiar? Husbands complain, "My wife always repeats; I heard her the first time!" Wives complain, "His eyes were all over the place. He can't do two things at one time. How do I know he heard me?"

The Eyes Have It

Listen with your eyes as well. Because of my retarded son, Matthew, who didn't have a vocabulary, I learned to listen to him with my eyes. I had no other option. He would grab our hands and place them on his head or rub his head against us to show us something was wrong. We learned to read his body movements and his eyes to detect any seizure activity. I could read his nonverbal signals that carried a message. Because of Matthew, I learned to listen to what my counselees could not put into words. I learned to listen to the message behind the message—the hurt, the ache, the frustration, the loss of hope, the fear of rejection, the joy, the delight, the promise of change. I reflect upon what I see on a counselee's face—his posture, walk, pace—and tell him what I see. This gives him an opportunity to explain further what he is thinking and feeling. He *knows* I'm tuned in to him.

Listen to others' tone of voice. Listen to your own. Listen to how with some speakers it's tone of voice that makes the difference. It's not loudness that makes a difference; it's tone.

How do you end your phone conversations? You don't come out and say you need to terminate the conversation, or that you're finished, do you? You use the change in tonal quality to accomplish this. One of my Shelties taught this to me years ago. Prince had this unique ability to figure out when I was concluding a phone conversation. He'd show up during the last 10 seconds of the conversation with a tennis ball in his mouth. It was as though he was saying, "I know you're about through. It's time to play ball." I thought, *What's this? A psychic dog?* No. He'd figure out the change in my voice and put two and two together. (I just hate it when the dog is smarter than me!)

I hate to admit it, but when it comes to tone of voice or variation of tone, men have more monotonous tones than women. Men don't open their jaws as wide as women, so they tend to sound more nasal than women. And men use only three vocal tones whereas women use more than five. So men tend to use more choppy staccato tones that can come across as abrupt and perhaps less approachable, at least to a woman. Women tend to have more flowing tones. And a woman will tend to use vocal inflections to emphasize a point whereas a man uses loudness.[6] Sound familiar?

If your wife is one who gives the entire novel length story at some other time than during the story, let her know you do better and you can engage her better in conversation when it's presented in smaller chunks.[7]

When Silence Isn't Golden

And above all, don't go silent on her. One of the most vicious and destructive communication techniques is silence. It can be devastating. Each person in a marriage needs to be recognized and acknowledged. But when we retreat into silence, our wife feels her very presence, existence and significance is ignored by the most significant person in her life—you! In fact, many consider silence an insult!

Silence can communicate a multitude of things: happiness, satisfaction, a sense of contentment, and wellbeing. But more often than not it communicates dissatisfaction, contempt, anger, pouting, sulking, "who cares," "who gives a darn," "I'll show you," and so on; when silence prevails there is little opportunity to resolve issues and move forward in a relationship. "Talk to me," she begs and we may get angry or continue to withdraw through silence. Too many of us use silence as a weapon.

If you're feeling overwhelmed or at a loss for words (which is not uncommon for us as men), share this with your wife. Let her know that you're thinking or taking time to process your response, but you *will* respond in a few minutes or before a certain time. And we need to follow through and not hope that she will forget it. That won't happen! We all know that.

John Gray, who is most recognized for his books on *Mars and Venus* (relationships between men and women), gives some helpful suggestions:

> To support your wife in feeling more loving and accepting, here is some bottom-line advice for men:
>
> 1. When you suspect she is upset, don't wait for her to initiate the conversation (when you initiate, it takes away 50 percent of her emotional charge).
>
> 2. As you let her talk, keep reminding yourself that it doesn't help to get upset with her for being upset.
>
> 3. Whenever you feel an urgent need to interrupt or correct, don't.
>
> 4. When you don't know what to say, say nothing. If you can't say something positive or respectful, keep quiet.
>
> 5. If she won't talk, ask more questions until she does.
>
> 6. Whatever you do, don't correct or judge her feelings.
>
> 7. Remain as calm and centered as possible, and keep a lock on your strong reactions. (If you lose control and "spill your guts" even for a moment, you lose and have to start all over at a disadvantage.)[8]

One of the best ways of responding and showing that you're listening is by reflecting back what you hear. Take a look at the following statements:

- "Kind of made (makes) you feel . . ."
- "The thing you feel most right now is sort of like . . ."
- "What I hear you saying is . . ."
- "So, as you see it . . ."
- "As I get it, you're saying . . ."
- "What I guess I'm hearing is . . ."
- "I'm not sure I'm with you, but . . ."
- "I somehow sense that maybe you feel . . ."
- "You feel . . ."
- "I really hear you saying that . . ."
- "I wonder if you're expressing a concern that . . ."
- "It sounds as if you're indicating you . . ."
- "I wonder if you're saying . . ."
- "You place a high value on . . ."
- "It seems to you . . ."
- "You appear to be feeling . . ."
- "It appears to you . . ."
- "As I hear it, you . . ."
- "So, from where you sit . . ."
- "Your feeling is now that . . ."
- "I read you as . . ."
- "Sometimes you . . ."
- "You must have felt . . ."
- "I sense that you're feeling . . ."
- "Your message seems to be, I . . ."
- "You appear . . ."
- "Listening to you, it seems as if . . ."
- "I gather that . . ."

None of these phrases are definite. None state what you believe or feel. None of them tells the other what to do or think or feel. They merely reflect what you think your wife is saying and give her the opportunity to say, "Yes, that's it," or "No, that's not what I was saying."

Remember that a major need your wife has of you is very basic: "Talk to me!" It can't be put in a simpler way. If you really want to bring out the best in your wife, create an atmosphere in which she has the freedom to be totally open and transparent with you and can reveal her deepest feelings. As she talks with you, she's presenting you with a road map on how to respond to her. Here are some guidelines that work in carrying on a conversation with your wife.

A CONVERSATIONAL ROAD MAP

A caring husband converses with his wife in a way that enables her to reveal her deepest feelings. Through conversation he learns how to meet many of her needs. But the conversation *itself* meets one of her most important marital needs: She simply wants him to talk to her.

Here is a list that summarizes the way you can impress your spouse with conversation. We've dealt with all of them; now it's time to put them into action.

1. Remember how it was when you were dating? You both still need to exhibit that same intense interest in each other and in what you have to say—especially about feelings.

2. A woman has a profound need to engage in conversation about her concerns and interests with someone who—in her perception—cares deeply about her and for her.

3. Men, if your job keeps you away from home overnight or for days on end, think about changing jobs. If you cannot, find ways to restore the intimacy of your marriage each time you return from an absence, so that your wife can begin to feel comfortable with you again. (If your wife does most of the traveling, the same principle applies.)

4. Get into the habit of spending 15 hours each week alone with your spouse, giving each other undivided attention. Spend much of that time in natural but essential conversation.

5. Remember, most women *fall* in love with men who have set aside time to exchange conversation and affection with them. They *stay* in love with men who continue to meet those needs.

6. Financial considerations should not interfere with time for conversation. If you don't have the time to be alone to talk, your priorities are not arranged correctly.

7. Never use conversation as a form of punishment (ridicule, name calling, swearing or sarcasm). Conversation should be constructive, not destructive.

8. Never use conversation to force your spouse to agree with your way of thinking. Respect your spouse's feelings and opinions, especially when yours are different.

9. Never use conversation to remind each other of past mistakes. Avoid dwelling on present mistakes as well.

10. Develop interest in each other's favorite topics of conversation.

11. Learn to balance your conversation. Avoid interrupting each other and try to give each other the same amount of time to talk.

12. Use your conversation to *inform, investigate* and *understand* each other.[9]

DISCOVER THE ENCOURAGER IN YOU

1. Which of the following statements best describe you and your wife when it comes to talking and sharing?

   a. We say a lot but reveal little of our real selves.
   b. We reveal our real selves but we don't say very much.
   c. We say a lot and reveal a lot of our real selves.
   d. We say little and reveal little of our real selves.

2. Which of the following statements best describe you when it comes to sharing with your wife about what you are really thinking, feeling, wanting or not wanting?

   a. I keep my inner self well hidden.
   b. I reveal as much as I feel safe to share.
   c. I let it all hang out.

3. Which of the following statements best describe you when it comes to your wife sharing with you what she is really thinking, feeling, wanting or not wanting?

   a. She seems to keep her inner self well hidden.
   b. She seems to reveal as much as she feels safe to share.
   c. She seems to let it all hang out.

4. Which of the following statements best describe some of the ways you avoid deep sharing when you and your wife are getting too close?

   a. I laugh or crack a joke.
   b. I shrug it off and act as if it doesn't matter.
   c. I act confused—like I don't know what is going on.
   d. I look angry so that she can't see into me too deeply.
   e. I get angry or huffy, especially when I am feeling vulnerable.
   f. I get overly talkative.
   g. I get analytical—hiding behind a wall of intellectualizing.
   h. I change the subject so I won't have to deal with it.
   i. I act strong, together, above it all—especially when feeling vulnerable.

5. Why do you think you avoid sharing in this way? What is the effect of avoiding sharing in this way with your wife? What would you be willing to do to build sharing into your relationship?[10]

Romancing
Your Wife

LET'S TALK ABOUT ROMANCE—YES! Finally we get to the important stuff. But wait a minute; I said romance, not S-E-X. That's a part of romance, but sometimes we, as men, bypass the romantic part and move right on to sex. If so, we've left out what's really important to our wives. Women want to be romanced! Let's get to a bottom-line question: Would your wife describe you as romantic? Think about it for a minute. Would *you* describe yourself as romantic? If you answered yes to either question, why? Why would you be seen as romantic?

Perhaps we ought to take a closer look at romance so that you know what I'm talking about. So, what is it?

The word "romantic" has so many meanings, including:

- Has no basis in fact
- Imaginary
- Marked by the imagination or emotional appeal of the heroic, adventurous, remote, mysterious or idealized [each of these could be a paragraph in and of itself]
- An emphasis on subjective emotional qualities
- Passionate love[1]

Romance is made up of fantasy, emotion and non-rational delights. It's really something different from the ordinary. It's a special time or event for two individuals.

I consulted a national survey for the answer to what women in general say is the most important to them in a relationship. They said, "We need to feel appreciated, wanted and loved."[2] The bottom line is they want affirmation! Your wife needs to know that she's special to you. When this occurs, you're helping her to be her best.

Wives want to feel loved, appreciated and respected *for who they are*. Those are their own words. What can you do to make your wife feel that way? You can learn as much as you can about her. You may think that you already know everything about your wife, but most of us don't. For example, what would you say are five actions a husband could do that a wife would say are the most important to romance? (Remember, you're answering this from a woman's perspective.)

Based on a national survey, here is what several hundred women said. The survey listed a number of actions that men could take, and women were asked to rate actions from 1 to 5 according to their romantic value, with 5 being the most important to romance. Here are those that received the highest rating:

- He touches me with tenderness (4.7)
- He snuggles after making love (4.6)
- He treats me as the most special person in his life (4.6)
- He is available when I need help (4.6)
- He gives emotionally (4.5)
- He shares his thoughts and dreams with me (4.5)
- He arranges for us to have time alone (4.4, higher for women with children)
- He knows what makes me happy (4.4)
- He keeps in touch when we are apart (4.4)
- He is gentle in his lovemaking (4.4)

- He listens to me intently (4.4, higher for married women)
- He treats me special when I am sick or down (4.4)
- He gives me love notes, cards, poems for no special reason (4.3)
- He is playful when we are alone (4.3)
- He undresses me with loving care (4.3)
- He remembers our anniversary or special day (4.2)
- He tells me he loves me (4.2)
- He surprises me with small tokens of love (4.2, higher for women with children)
- He compliments me (4.2, higher for married women)
- He includes me in his plans (4.2)
- He arranges a romantic dinner in or out (4.1)
- He gives me flowers for no special occasion (4.1)
- He initiates spontaneous sex (4.0)[3]

Now that you've read the list, go back and use it to enrich your marriage and begin to bring out the best in your wife.

1. Look through the list and consider which actions you do at the present time.
2. Look through the list and consider how frequently you do these things.
3. Now think about which 10 of these would be the most important to your wife.
4. Finally, ask her—yes, ask her—which of these she would like you to do more often. You may think you already know, but let her decide. Sometimes what we do as husbands isn't enough, or it's so subtle that it doesn't connect. Believe me, clarifying this area can put a smile on both of your faces.[4]

NONSEXUAL TOUCH

Here's another major insight that wives reveal. This one may shock you. Wives constantly say they don't receive enough touch—gentle, nonsexual touch. I was married for 48 years to a wonderful woman, and then she died of brain cancer. When your partner dies, you tend to think of what you wish you'd done more of, and this is one of my regrets. I wish I had done it a hundred-fold, as it would have meant so much to Joyce.

What would your wife like to hear about when you talk? Wives have suggested that they want to hear about:

- How wonderful she looks
- How you miss her
- How good it is to be with her
- Plans for your future together
- What you like about your relationship (to meet her personal dreams, goals, and so on)
- Her interests (encourage her in them)
- How you met (reminisce about the wonderful beginnings)
- Why she's special to you
- Positive things about the restaurant (or in whatever place you and she are together)
- Her accomplishments
- Her day
- Her ideas
- The appreciation you have for all she does[5]

If you respond with these items, she knows she's a priority. She knows she's in your thoughts. This works.

Romance was a major part of my relationship with Joyce—before and during marriage. We tried to be creative and not predictable. For example, we created a romantic atmosphere in our family room at home. For our twenty-fifth wedding anniversary, instead of spending money on a trip, we had our backyard landscaped to resemble a miniature mountain scene. We had a little (four-foot) hill, a waterfall and a trickling stream that feeds a couple of pools. There was a small footbridge and pine, birch and liquid amber trees, which provided us with ample fall colors. Our mountain scene could be viewed from our family room through sliding glass doors.

Some evenings, Joyce and I would play one of our favorite John Denver albums (that dates us) on the stereo, turn out the lights and sit together on the couch holding hands, listening to the music of the record and the waterfall. The outdoor lights accented the waterfall and the trees. We may have sat there for 30 or 40 minutes, not saying much, but listening and enjoying and feeling very content and comfortable. It was a romantic time for us. There were other times of romance, too, but I'm not going into detail on those!

WHAT MAKES ROMANCE?

A romantic relationship can have a number of important ingredients. First, romance often includes the element of the unexpected. The routines and tasks of our daily lives consume most of our time and energy. An unexpected romantic surprise can help break up the routine and monotony of the day. Surprises also carry the message, "I'm thinking about you. You're on my mind. I want your day to be different."

Romance Is Surprising

Presenting flowers for no special occasion or no special reason adds to the sense of romance. I enjoyed creating surprises for

Joyce. They ranged from the humorous to the serious. Because we enjoyed eating out together, I would often search out a new restaurant that I thought she would enjoy and take her there without telling her where we were going. I even took her on brief trips that were a total surprise to her. Sometimes she opened a cupboard to find a banner I'd placed there that said, "I love you."

You may have your own routine established for creating special romantic surprises. That's important. But beware: Anything that is repeated month after month, year after year or decade after decade may become humdrum. Surprising your spouse with dinner out at the same restaurant every payday may not be as romantic after 20 years! Why not look for new restaurants, activities and ways to say "I love you" that keep the excitement of the unexpected in your romancing?

Romance Is a Time for Two

A second element in a romantic relationship is called dating—something you used to do and hopefully still do. Dating means selecting a specific time to be together and making plans for the event. Sometimes a couple mutually plan the activity, or one person may be appointed to plan the date.

Most of the time, romantic dating is just for the two of you and not a crowd!

We asked wives what they *don't* want to talk about on a date. Now, you may wonder if these suggestions are necessary. Based on what women have said, they are, and they will not only save you some grief but also will build up your wife and your relationship.

Just imagine that you're at a quiet, quality restaurant, and that you have two hours to eat and connect. What will you talk about? Let's consider what your wife *doesn't* want to hear. On a date, wives don't want to hear about:

- Children or in-laws
- Your work
- Your involvement in something that doesn't involve her
- Anything negative—what you don't like
- Ongoing disagreements
- Tasks at home
- Money issues
- What's wrong at this restaurant
- What you've accomplished

Talk about yourselves. Make it a fun time. Laugh and enjoy each other and be a little crazy. When you go to a restaurant, let the host or hostess know that you and your spouse are there on a date.

Dates ought to center on an activity where you can interact together. If you attend a movie or play, plan time before or after the show to eat and talk together.

I've been impressed with some ministers who have made an announcement like the following from the pulpit: "If any of you ask my wife and me to attend a gathering on the first or third Friday of the month, we will thank you for the invitation, but we will have to decline. Those nights are our date nights together and we do not let anything interfere with those special evenings. And if any of you would like to know what we do on a date, you're free to ask!" An announcement like that may send some shock waves through the congregation. Couples in leadership, however, who make romance a priority, provide healthy role models for all the couples in the congregation.

Romance Isn't Always Practical

Third, because romance is often emotional and non-rational, a romantic relationship sometimes includes the impractical. You may splurge on an outing or a gift, which you know you can't really afford, but the romantic value makes it worth scrimping in other areas to pay for it. Or consider an out-of-the-ordinary event like inviting your spouse to a "famous" French restaurant in the countryside. Pack an inexpensive picnic dinner and take a tape recorder with some French songs and a picture book on France from the library to look through together.

Impractical romantic happenings are moments to remember. And that's what romance is so often built upon—good memories. Store your hearts with romantic memories and they'll carry you through the difficult times.

Romance Gets Out of the Rut

A fourth element in a romantic relationship is creativity. The French picnic dinner is an example of creative romance. Discover what delights your wife and make those delights happen in many different, creative ways. Even the way you express your love to your wife each day can be varied and innovative. If your wife can predict what you will say, how you will respond, what kind of gift you will give on special occasions, then you're in a romantic rut.

I like what Joseph Dillow tells husbands about being creative lovers. He has developed the following lighthearted test to help husbands evaluate their creativity in romance. Give yourself 10 points for each item on the following list if you have done it once in the past six months. If you have done any item on the list two or more times, give yourself 20 points.

Lover's Quotient Test

- Have you phoned her during the week and asked her out for one evening that weekend without telling her where you are taking her? Mystery date.

- Have you given her an evening completely off? You clean up the kitchen; you put the kids to bed.

- Have you gone parking with her at some safe and secluded spot and kissed and talked for an evening?

- Have you drawn a bath for her after dinner? Put a scented candle in the bathroom, add bath oil to the water, send her there right after dinner and then you clean up and put the kids to bed while she relaxes. (My wife says in order to get any points for this you must also clean up the tub!)

- Have you phoned her from work to tell her you were thinking nice thoughts about her? (You get *no* points for this one if you asked what was in the mail.)

- Have you written her a love letter and sent it special delivery? (First class mail will do—emails and texting don't have the same impact.)

- Have you made a tape recording of all the reasons you love her? Give it to her wrapped in a sheer negligee!

- Have you given her the day off? You clean the house, fix the meals and take care of the kids. (My wife says you ought to get 30 points for this!)

- Have you put a special effects stereo recording of ocean waves on tape and played it while you had a nude luau on the living room floor? (If this seems a little far out for your tastes, you could substitute by either removing the stereo effects or having a popcorn party in the privacy of the bedroom instead.)

- Have you spent a whole evening (more than two hours) sharing mutual goals and planning family objectives with her and the children?

- Have you ever planned a surprise weekend? You make the reservations and arrange for someone to keep the children for two days. Tell her to pack her suitcase, but don't tell her where you are going. (Just be sure it's *not* the Super Bowl!) Make it someplace romantic.

- Have you ever picked up your clothes just one time in the past six months and put them on hangers?

- Have you given her an all-over body massage with scented lotion and a vibrator?

- Have you spent a session of making love to her that included at least two hours of romantic conversation, shared dreams, many positions of intercourse and much variety of approach and caresses?

- Have you repaired something around the house that she has *not* requested?

- Have you kissed her passionately for at least 30 seconds one morning just before you left for work, or one evening after you walked in the door?

- Have you brought her an unexpected little gift like perfume, a ring or an item of clothing?

- Have you replaced her old negligee?

I have given this ridiculous test to men all over the country. Let's see how your score compares with theirs:

200–360: Lover. You undoubtedly have one of the most satisfied wives in all the country.

150–200: Good. Very few make this category.

100–150: Average. This husband is somewhat typical and usually not very exciting as a lover.

50–100: Klutz. Too many men score in this category. I hope you'll begin to move up soon.

0–50: Husband. There is a difference between a "husband" and a "lover." The only reason your wife is still married to you is that she's a Christian, she has unusual capacity for unconditional acceptance and there are some verses in the Bible against divorce.[6]

While the test shouldn't be taken too seriously, it does outline a plan of attack to increase your creativity level. I realize that many things on the list may not fit your temperament and your marriage relationship. *Make up your own list.* The idea is simply to encourage creativity in a fun way.

Romance Begins in the Mind

Fifth, romance involves daily acts of care, concern, love, speaking your partner's love language, listening and giving each other your personal attention. Such acts convey a message of acceptance and thoughtfulness to your spouse. You see, romance begins in your mind and not in your sex gland. Too many people, especially men, tend to let their physical drive take the lead in romance all the time. Rather, a thoughtful, caring attitude will create romance even when your glands are stuck in neutral.

Romance Is Defined by Commitment

Sixth, romance involves commitment. Every day of your life as a couple is marked by highs and lows, joys and disappointments.

Let's go back to affection. Affection and romance go hand in hand.

Affection—when you read this word, what comes to mind? For many men, it's sex. Let's eliminate this word "sex" from our vocabulary for a while. Now describe what affection means to you. Does it have the same meaning to your wife? Are you sure? The reason I'm pushing on this question is this: For a wife, affection is actually the "cement of your relationship." To most women, affection symbolizes security, protection, comfort and approval. When you show your wife affection, you're sending her several messages:

> "I'll take care of you and protect you. You are important to me, and I don't want anything to happen to you."

"I'm concerned about the problems you face, and I am with you."[7]

Hugging, touch, cards, flowers, invitations can all be expressions of affection, but they frequently and consistently need to be a part of the equation, rather than once in a while. This is both reasonable and attainable. By answering the following questions, you'll have a better understanding of this part of your relationship.

1. On a scale of 1 to 10, with 10 being "very affectionate," how affectionate am I toward my wife? How would she rate me?
2. Is affection the environment for our entire marriage?
3. In the past, have I tended to equate affection with getting sexually aroused? Why hasn't this worked?
4. In what specific ways do I show my wife affection?
5. Would I be willing to have her coach me in how to show her more affection in the ways she really likes it?[8]

Being consistently affectionate—and not just at those times when one is interested in sex—is a highly valued positive response. Sometimes nothing is shared verbally. It can be as simple as sitting side by side and touching gently or moving close enough that you barely touch while you watch the sun dipping over a mountain with reddish clouds capturing your attention. It could be reaching out and holding hands in public. It can be something thoughtful, unrequested and noticed only by your partner.

When your wife has had a rough day, you may choose just to stroke her head or rub her shoulders instead of talking about what happened. Being so understood by you and meeting her needs gives her the assurance that she has indeed married the right person.

Nonsexual touching as well as sexual is important. Hugging is an important element of touching. And hugging is a vital expression of love. I know. I went for 15 years without receiving a hug from our son Matthew. It wasn't that he held back or didn't care. He wasn't capable. Matthew was a profoundly mentally retarded boy who died at the age of 22 and had the mental ability of about an 18-month-old. He lived in our home until he was 11 and then moved to Salem Christian Home in Ontario, California.

For years, Joyce and I affectionately reached out to Matthew with hugs and kisses, but he did not respond. Through this process we learned to give love without receiving love in return. And we accepted Matthew's limitation even though we eagerly looked forward to the time when we might receive a hug from him.

Then one day we wrapped our arms around Matthew and, for the first time, felt his arms reaching around us and squeezing. It is hard to describe how precious Matthew's hug was to us after living without it for so many years. After that first hug there were several other times when Matthew would respond with his simple embrace. And sometimes we held out our arms and said, "Matthew, hug," and he reached to give us a hug. Please—never take the expression of a hug for granted.

How would you respond to a doctor who prescribed that you receive four hugs a day? Physical hugging is very therapeutic. Hugging can lift depression and breathe new life into a tired body. When you are physically touched, the amount of hemoglobin in your body increases significantly. The surge of hemoglobin tones up the whole body, helps prevent disease and speeds recovery from illness.[9]

Do you hug your spouse? Do you receive hugs? One of my favorite quotes is, "Every marriage needs to be picked up and hugged and given personal attention."[10] Hugging is a significant way to bring out the best in your wife.

Affection is demonstrated in many ways and displays. Years ago, I heard the story of a couple who had been invited to a potluck dinner. The wife was not known for her cooking ability, but she decided to make a custard pie. As they drove to the dinner, they knew they were in trouble, for they smelled the scorched crust. Then, when they turned a corner, the contents of the pie shifted dramatically from one side of the pie shell to the other. The husband could see his wife's anxiety rising by the moment.

When they arrived, they placed the pie on the dessert table. The guests were serving themselves salad and then went back for the main course. Just before they could move on to the desserts, the husband marched up to the table, looked over the number of homemade desserts and snatched up his wife's pie. As others looked at him, he announced, "There are so many desserts here, but my wife so rarely makes my favorite dessert that I'm claiming this for myself. I ate lightly on all the other courses, so now I can be a glutton."

And a glutton he was. Later his wife said, "He sat by the door eating what he could, mushing up the rest so no one else would bug him for a piece, and slipping chunks to the hosts' Rottweiler when no one was looking. He saw me looking at him and gave me a big wink. What he did made my evening. My husband, who doesn't always say much, communicated more love with what he did than with any words he could ever say."

ACTS OF CARING

Of course, there are many other ways to take positive action to show that you care. I raise flowers all year long, and I knew Joyce enjoyed seeing them inside the house. Often, after I made the morning coffee, I would cut her a rose and put it in a vase by her cup. It almost became automatic, but the motivation was the same. And often when I traveled, Joyce slipped a love note into my pants pocket.

Perhaps you're in the store and you see a favorite food your spouse enjoys, and you buy it for him or her even if you hate it; or you decide to stop at the store for an item, and you call your spouse at home or at work to see if there's anything he or she wants or needs. You are "other" thinking rather than "self" thinking. You follow through with the scriptural teaching in Ephesians 4:32: "Be kind and compassionate to one another."

An act of caring can be a phone call to ask if your wife has a prayer request. Acts of caring can mean remembering special dates and anniversaries without being reminded. I am amazed at the number of wives who have been deeply hurt by their husband over the years because he did not remember anniversaries or even birthdays.

And the men's excuses are so lame. I've heard, "I just didn't remember" and "I need to be reminded" and "We just didn't do that in our family." That's all such responses are—excuses! If the husband is sitting in my counseling office, I simply ask him if he forgets to go to work or to get involved in his hobby. Reluctantly, he says no, and I go on to let him know that I believe he is capable of learning something new that will benefit both his life and his wife's. We then talk about how he will do it. We don't accept excuses when it is obvious that change can occur.

SHOWING APPRECIATION AND EMPATHY

Another positive is being appreciative. This means going out of your way to notice all the little positive things your wife does and letting her know you appreciate her. It also means focusing on the positive experiences and dwelling upon those rather than the negative (more will be said about this later). Working toward agreement and appreciating the other's perspective is important. Compliments convey appreciation, but they need to be balanced between what a person does and who she is. Affirmations based on personal qualities are rare but highly appreciated.

Showing genuine concern for your wife when you notice she is upset builds unity and intimacy in your relationship. You may not be able to do anything, but sharing your desire to do so may be all that is necessary. When your wife shares a problem with you, don't relate a similar problem you once had, tell her what to do, crack jokes to cheer her up, or ask how she got into that problem in the first place. Instead, listen, put your arm around her, show that you understand, and let her know it's all right for her to feel and act the way she does.

I'm sure you've heard the word "empathy" time and time again. This is the feeling of being with another person both emotionally and intellectually. It's viewing life through your wife's eyes, feeling as she feels and hearing her story through her perceptions.

In marriage you have a choice to respond with empathy, sympathy or apathy. Sympathy is being overly involved in the emotions of your wife. It can actually undermine your emotional strength. Apathy means you couldn't care less. There are no in-betweens.

Empathy, however, includes rapport—knowing how your wife would feel in most situations without her having to explain. You'll experience something together at the same time through the eyes of your wife.

THE LIGHTER SIDE

Having a sense of humor and being able to laugh, joke and have fun gives balance to the serious side of marriage. Some of what you laugh at will be private, and some will be shared with others. Sometimes the memories are some of those hilarious incidents that happen even though your partner didn't think it was so funny at the time.

Several years ago, while speaking at a family camp at Forest Home, California, such an event happened to Joyce and me. We were staying in a nice cabin, and since I'm an early riser, I went down to the dining hall for an early breakfast, knowing that I would bring her back some fruit and a muffin. I entered the cabin and was just about ready to go into the bedroom with her food when the door of the bathroom was flung open. Joyce, fresh out of the shower, said, "Don't go in there! It's still there! Don't take my food in there!"

I was shocked and said, "What? What's in there?"

"In there!" she said again, almost in tears by now. "It's still in the bedroom. It was terrible. And don't you dare laugh. It wasn't funny!" I still didn't know what she was talking about, but saying to a husband, "Don't you dare laugh!" is like a subtle invitation that may get played out later.

Finally, she calmed down and told me what happened. She had been in bed, drinking her coffee, when she decided to reach down and pick up her slippers. She found one, lifted it up and then thrust her hand under the bed to find the other one. Now, Forest Home was using new mousetraps that consisted of a six-by-six-inch piece of cardboard with an extremely sticky substance on it. When a mouse stuck in it, it was stuck permanently and would eventually die. Well, you can guess what happened. Not only did Joyce put her hand directly on the goo substance, but it also contained a bloated dead mouse! It was gross! (I have a picture of it.) As she said, she went ballistic with screams, trying to dislodge this disgusting creature from her hand.

As Joyce was telling me all this, she was shaking her hand and demonstrating how she had tried to dislodge the mouse from her hand. The more she did this the funnier it got. I was biting the inside of my mouth to keep from smiling while remembering those fateful words, "Don't you dare laugh. It's not funny." I think she saw my struggle, because with an exaggerated put-out look, she said again, slowly, "*It's not funny.*"

That's all it took. I was a dead man, and I knew it. I laughed until the tears rolled down my face. I did take the mouse out and get rid of it. I also told Joyce that I would have gone into hysterics as well if that had happened to me, and that she had every right to be upset. After several hugs, she said, "I guess it was pretty funny at that." This became one of our favorite stories.

We also have many funny memories in which I was the source of the amusement. Joyce had a whole list of them.

Positive marriage shares the sense of shared joy. You share your wife's excitement and delight and you want her to be aware of what you're experiencing as well. Joy is a sense of gladness, not necessarily happiness. It's also a command from Scripture: We are to "rejoice with those who rejoice" (Rom. 12:15).

ACCEPT ONE ANOTHER

Accepting each other for who you are and what you say is the goal. Acceptance means letting your wife know that even though you don't agree with what she is saying, you are willing to hear her out. It means freeing your wife from being molded into the fantasy you want her to be. It's more than tolerance. It's saying, "You and I are different in many ways. It's all right for you to be you and for me to be me. We are stronger together than we are separately, as we learn to complement one another." This doesn't mean spouses won't help to change each other—that's inevitable. But the purpose for which it's done, and the method, makes a world of difference.

DISCOVER THE ENCOURAGER IN YOU

1. Romance—are you good at it or not? The bottom line is that some men are and some men aren't. Let's discuss what you know with a couple of questions (you can ask your wife to discover if you answered correctly or not):

    • Romance to a woman means:

    _____

    _____

    • Romance to my wife means:

    _____

    _____

2. What is romantic about you and your wife's daily life to-gether? What actions on your part create romance for you? What actions on your spouse's part create romance for you?

3. Describe a romantic getaway you would like to experience with your spouse. Where would it be? What would you do? How would it be different from your daily life? What would you wear? Where would you eat? What would be the décor, music, fragrances, conversation topics, and so on?

4. What would it take for this to actually happen? How could you create at home what you just described?

5. When you and your wife were dating, how did you create and sustain romance?

6. Which of the following statements best describe your cur-rent estimation on the degree of romance in your marriage?

   a. Our life together is one sustained romantic "high."
   b. We are romantic, but at times I feel we are getting less and less so.
   c. We have a romantic side of us that we can turn on when we want to.
   d. Maybe someday we will be able to be romantic.
   e. We're too old for romance.
   f. Romance? Who needs it? We are sensible and stable.
   g. We have more important things to do than get in-volved with romance.
   h. What's romance?

6. Which of the following statements best describe your relationship when it comes to romance?

   a. I am the romantic; my wife is practical and realistic.
   b. My wife is the romantic; I am practical and realistic.
   c. Both of us are romantic, but in our own way.
   d. Neither of us has a romantic bone in our body.

7. How do you feel when you get romantic and your wife doesn't respond? How do you feel when she gets romantic and you don't respond?

8. Which of the following statements best describe some of the reasons you are unable to get romantic with your wife?

   a. I am too critical of her.
   b. I feel she is critical of me.
   c. I hold too many resentments from the past.
   d. My mind is elsewhere, like on daily practical concerns.
   e. I'm concerned that she might reject me or not respond when I become romantic.
   f. I like to get romantic first because I am more of an initiator than a responder.

9. What is one way you would like you and your wife to be romantic at this point in your marriage?[11]

God's Plan
for Husbands

THIS IS A CHAPTER MOST MEN WILL LIKE. IT'S BRIEF, BLUNT AND TO THE POINT.

Whether you like the content or not . . . well, that remains to be seen. It's not meant to lay a burden on you, elicit guilt or point a finger at you. It's meant to help in your understanding of marriage and clarify your calling as a husband. It's meant to help you in your journey of being a positive support to your wife.

Let's begin with a question. You may need to stretch your memory a bit.

Why did you marry your wife? Your answer might include one or more of the following statements spoken by other men:

- "I wanted to share my life with someone."
- "I wanted someone to help make me happy."
- "I wanted to spend my life with someone I love and with someone who loves me."
- "I wanted to be happy and I wanted her to be happy."
- "I didn't want to spend my life alone."
- "I wanted to make up for all that was lacking in my own home."

- "I wanted to be faithful to God and love someone He wanted me to love."
- "I didn't want to end up alone, especially when I get older. Marriage is a security."

Did any of those answers resonate with you? Although personal happiness is part of the marriage equation, if that's all you think of as the reason you married, you need to go down a bit deeper. Let's take a look at what marriage is and discover its purpose.

Marriage is . . . a gift.

Marriage is . . . an opportunity for love to be learned.

Marriage is . . . a journey in which we as the travelers are faced with many choices and are responsible for these choices.

Marriage is . . . affected more by our inner communication than our outer communication.

Marriage is . . . often influenced by unresolved issues from our past than we realize.

Marriage is . . . a call to servanthood.

Marriage is . . . a call to friendship.

Marriage is . . . a call to suffering.

Marriage is . . . a refining process. It is an opportunity to be refined by God into the person He wants us to be.

Marriage is . . . an opportunity to reflect God's image.

When we marry for personal happiness and satisfaction, and then, for whatever reason, these start to diminish or have never met our standards, we tend to begin entertaining all sorts of unconstructive thoughts. I've heard people complain, "Why didn't He make men and women different than He did? It would make marriage so much easier." But why should God make it easier? Did He create marriage to make us happy or to make us holy?[1]

I talked with a couple in their late twenties who had been married for five years. In the third year, they had considered divorce. This is what they told me:

> We entered into marriage with high hopes and great expectations. Finally, we'd found someone that would make us happy. I had this dream but it ended up being more like a vapor. She didn't measure up, and neither did I. We always wanted more. We wanted the other to be better. We began to criticize and demand: "You're not meeting my needs. You're not the person I thought I was marrying." And then one of us mentioned the *D* word. We looked at one another and said, "No, never. There's got to be a better way."
>
> So we began to ask, *What does God want for our marriage?* After a hard two years, we've discovered a new way of living. Each morning, we ask, "What *will* please God in our marriage today?" The more we do this, the more satisfied we are with one another. The other way didn't work. This does. I'm just sorry we didn't start out that way.

God's Purpose for Marriage

The purpose of marriage is to please God. We need to remind ourselves of this each day, then take note of our words and actions and ask, *Does this please Him?* This is a safeguard. It provides a hedge of protection around a marriage.

We all need to discover God's design, not our own, for marriage. Marriage matters to God. He had a purpose in mind when He created marriage. God had two relational goals in mind. First, He created a person in His image so that He and the image-bearer could be in fellowship together. Then, seeing the aloneness of this first image-bearer, God made another like the first *and* like God, so they could *both* be in fellowship with each other *and* with Him.

God's Image-Bearer

God has a plan—and it happens in marriage—for transforming each of us into *image-bearers*. The bottom line is that that's what you are. What would happen if you looked in the mirror each morning and said, "I am an image-bearer"? We are called to reflect the glory of God in the marriage relationship. Unfortunately, this is not what most couples have in mind as their purpose when they enter into marriage. They have another purpose.

But God's main purpose is *not our* happiness.

Your marriage is not only going to change you, but it will also transform you. Have you heard the term "whistle-blower"? Depending on who's doing the talking, the phrase may be expressed with appreciation or scorn. It's a term used to describe someone who has revealed or exposed the truth about a person or a situation. A whistle-blower brings to light what was previously hidden. That's what marriage is, a whistle-blower. Marriage exposes and reveals who you really are when you enter into that covenant relationship. All the hidden places—and yes, defects too—will be made obvious. You'll be "found out." But that's all right! It's a great place for the process of transformation to occur!

A Transformed Heart

Transformation. It's an interesting word. Transformation is the heart of marriage. Yet many Christian couples have never integrated a pattern of Christian growth into their marriage. This is unfortunate because the two are so closely intertwined. They really can't run alongside one another on parallel tracks.

Scripture says that we are to be conformed to the image of Christ (see Rom. 8:29) and that Christ is to be formed in us (see Gal. 4:19). The results of this process should be evident in the marriage relationship. They're part of the script.

Both of you—you and your spouse—are quite different but equal in the eyes of God. In the New Testament, Paul reiterates this when he says that in Christ there is neither male nor female (see Gal. 3:28). This impacts the way you are to treat one another. We're called to *glorify* one another, not degrade.

If we were to see our spouse as someone to be used or abused, we're not responding to our spouse to the glory of God. We can insult the image of God in other ways as well. A friend of mine described it in very practical terms: "When you take someone for granted, you demean him or her. You send the unspoken message, *You are not worth much to me.* You also rob this person of the gift of human appreciation. And to be loved and appreciated gives all of us a reason to live each day."

When the gift is withdrawn or denied over the years, a person's spirit begins to wither and die. A couple may endure this hardship and stay married for decades, but they are only serving a sentence. In long-term marriages where one spouse or both are continually taken for granted and not built up, a wall of indifference arises between that husband and wife.

So the first question to ask yourself is, *What is it like being married to me?* Take some time to reflect on this question. Take a day, or better yet, take a week and carry a 3x5-inch index card around with you. When a thought comes to mind, write it down. When you ask yourself a question, it's like looking into the mirror. You'll see areas where you can say, "I'm doing all right there." But you'll discover other areas where you'll say, "I need some work."[2]

Now the hard question. Ask your *wife* to answer this question for you: "What is it like being married to me?" Have her take several days to process the question before answering. If you really want some help, you could ask, "In what area or areas would you like to see some improvement?" If you ask this, assure her that no matter what she suggests, all you will say is, "Thank you for letting me know this."

Every movie and every play has a script to follow as well as a writer, producer and director. Well, we have a script for our lives and our marriage. Where there are many different writers, producers and directors in the movie world, there is only one Writer, Producer and Director in your life and in your marriage—and that Person is God.

How to Lead in Your Marriage

According to His script, a husband has several callings, one of which is to be a leader, or "the head of the wife." Let's concentrate on this one. What does that mean? It doesn't mean control, passive noninvolvement, asserted superiority or taking advantage. On the contrary, a husband must never use his role as leader for selfish benefit. To do so would deviate from God's plan.

A husband must never put his wife into a straitjacket of compliance, or she will wither and so will her love for him. Even recent secular research has shown that what kills the love of a spouse for the other is in direct violation of Scripture—i.e., attempting to control rather than serve your partner. In the book *The Power of a Praying Husband*, there's great insight.

The power of a praying husband is not a means of gaining control over your wife. We all know that never really happens anyway. That's because God doesn't want us controlling other people. He wants us to let *Him* control *us*. When we humble ourselves before God and let *Him* control *us*, then He can work through us. God wants to work through you as an instrument of *His* power as you intercede in prayer for your wife. The power in your prayer is God's.[3]

A husband is to lead sacrificially in his marriage by example, not by ordering or constantly instructing his wife. He is never, and I mean *never*, to tell his wife what the Scriptures say *she* is to do. Rather, his only focus is to be on loving his wife as Christ loved the church—that is, sacrificially.

In practical terms, this could mean, among other things, volunteering to bathe the kids or massage his wife's feet, turning off the football game and talking with her, or going shopping with her—even after he's put in a 12-hour day at work.

Sacrificial love involves participating in something that is important or a favorite of hers, even if it's relatively unimportant to you or definitely not one of your favorites. It may mean doing any of the following (although it's not limited to any or all of them):

- Initiating prayer with her without concern that your prayers may be briefer and more bottom-line than hers
- Learning to say these three phrases: "You were right," "I was wrong" and "I am sorry"
- Calling her when there is any delay in plans
- Practicing Proverbs 31:28-29 (praising her) consistently
- Accepting her communication style and opinions as different from yours, and not necessarily wrong

- Accepting her femaleness and celebrating the differences that come from it
- Asking for her opinion
- Discovering the uniqueness of her personality in order to understand her and communicate better
- Asking what TV show or movie she would like to watch

THE LEADERSHIP THAT GOD SUPPORTS

The issue of the man's leadership in the home has been a concern for years. Book after book has been written on this subject, including *Passive Men, Wild Women* and *Husbands Who Won't Lead and Wives Who Won't Follow*. We're talking about biblical headship—specifically the authority of the man to lead.

A man's motives for leading a marriage spiritually can sometimes be diluted by personal reasons, but when he allows God to lead him, and when his heart is open to God and His purposes, then his headship receives God's support.

So what does that kind of leadership look like in practical terms?

Serve

The authority God gives men to lead is built on service. This is a difficult balancing and juggling act for many. The problem is not with the teaching of male leadership, but with the man who misuses the teaching that he is to lead so that he can serve his own needs and desires. Some men behave like drill sergeants, snapping out orders at their wives and children, which doesn't reflect Scripture, but their own selfishness and insecurity.

The truth is, a husband is called to think of others—particularly his wife—first, ahead of himself. That's not easy for many men. For one thing, the idea of being a servant-leader runs counter to the thinking of our present-day "me" culture. But with some hard work and sacrifice, it can be done.

I've seen both kinds of leadership. I've seen the self-appointed "dictators" who distort scriptural teaching for their own benefit. The result of this kind of leadership is that marriages and families suffer and fragment. But I've also observed men who are servant-leaders whose families flourished as a result.

Love

God's script also calls the husband to be not just a servant-leader but also a lover, meaning that his headship of his family is not to exhibit dominating control but the sacrificial love of Jesus.

And how did Christ love when He was on earth? He was single-minded in His mission of love as He spent time with the disciples where they were weak. He defended the disciples, praised them before others and revealed Himself to them. And why did Jesus do these things? He was concerned about the church's well-being and future glory.

That is how a husband is to love his wife. A husband represents Jesus in the home, and his role is to bring out God's glory in his wife and lift her up—for *her* wellbeing. That is leadership that leaves a wife feeling special, valued and loved.

So how specifically can a husband do that? There are many ways; one of the most important is a husband's putting his wife first over children, parents, siblings, work, TV and hobbies. Doing this will strengthen a marriage. Conversely, not doing it will weaken a marriage.

Another thing a loving husband can do is learn his wife's "love language"—in other words, the ways she tends to hear, express and receive love from others—and package his love in a way that speaks to her and meets her needs.

We are also to love our wives unconditionally, the same way God loves all of us. We're not to love her "because she . . ." but "regardless." When you love your wife sacrificially and unconditionally, she will more fully realize God's love and regard for her, and this in turn brings glory to Him.[4]

God expects us to care for one another. A husband who neglects or demeans his wife robs her of what God wants for her and robs himself of growth and development as well.

Regarding couples caring for one another, Bryan Chapell wrote:

> Because two people who marry are to be one, if either part damages, demoralizes or degrades the other, then neither will be completely whole. Just as a basketball deflated on only one side still cannot fulfill its purposes, so a marriage with one side diminished will deprive both persons of fully being and doing what God desires. God has designed the similarities and differences of a man and woman in marriage to complement and support the spiritual growth of both. Neither part to the marriage can develop fully if either one is denied his or her personal potential.[5]

What an opportunity you and I have! It's very much like Jesus' redemptive work on behalf of the church in that a husband is not to live for himself, but should live to be used as a channel of God's goodness in his wife's life. We're to respond, react, speak and think toward her in ways that enable her to develop who she is and to develop her gifts as a way to bring glory to God.[6]

An encouraging man does this. He's a man who sincerely tells his wife, "I believe in you," "Go for it" and "How can I help you?" We are to do everything in what the Bible calls the "fullness of Jesus Christ," and that includes being married. Colossians 3:15-17 instructs us how we can equip ourselves with that fullness:

> Let the peace of Christ rule in your hearts, since as members of one body you were called to peace. And be thankful. Let the word of Christ dwell in you richly as you teach and admonish one another with all wisdom, and as you sing psalms, hymns and spiritual songs with gratitude in your hearts to God. And whatever you do, whether in word or deed, do it all in the name of the Lord Jesus, giving thanks to God the Father through Him.

LETTING CHRIST LEAD THROUGH YOU

Let's take a more detailed look at what living in the fullness of Christ means.

Let the peace of Christ rule. This could be paraphrased, "Let the peace of Christ be umpire in your heart amidst the conflicts of life. Let Christ's peace within be your counselor and decide for you what is right." The peace described here is not just the peace you feel when you have conflict. It is a sense of wholeness and wellbeing, a sense that God is in control and guiding you.

Who or what rules in your life? The indwelling peace of Christ is indispensable when it comes to blessing your spouse and bringing out God's glory.

Let the Word of Christ dwell in you. How do we allow God's Word to take up residence in us? By reading it, studying it and memorizing it.

I've seen angry people, frustrated people, anxious people and obnoxious people changed because of the power of God's Word dwelling in them. God's Word has the power to change any of us, and it has the power to bring out the best in a marriage.

When you read the Bible, ask the Holy Spirit to make it part of your life. A chapel speaker I once heard at Westmont College said, "If you take one chapter from the Word of God and read it out loud every day for a month, it will be yours for life." He was right. It works.

Do all in the name of the Lord Jesus. Everything we as Christians do—good or bad—is a reflection of Jesus Christ. Our obedient, loving behavior in our marriage reflects His presence for all the world to see. But when we react and respond in a way that is contrary to what is in the Scriptures, and contrary to our relationship with Jesus, it reflects that He does not fully occupy our life.

Paul's command to do all in the name of the Lord Jesus follows a series of commands in Colossians 3:5-14. He warns us about behaviors we are to put off because they do not reflect a person who knows Jesus Christ. He tells us to get rid of sexual immorality, impurity, lust, evil desires, greed, anger, rage, malice, slander, filthy language, and lying (see vv. 5-9), because none of these behaviors reflects the presence of Christ in our life. When we engage in any of these things, we've rewritten the script. Ridding ourselves of them will prepare us to do all in the name of Christ.

We are called to replace these negative behaviors with words and deeds that clearly exemplify that we know Christ: We are to reflect compassion, kindness, humility, gentleness, patience and forgiveness (see vv. 10-14).

The Bible says, "Husbands, likewise, dwell with them *with understanding*, giving *honor* to the wife, as to the weaker vessel, and as being *heirs together* of the grace of life, that your *prayers may not be hindered*" (1 Pet. 3:7, *NKJV,* emphasis added).

Part of dwelling with your wife *with understanding* means recognizing that your wife is in need of your covering—your protection and love. And because you are *heirs together* of God's grace, you need to *honor* her in your thoughts, words and actions. When you don't, your *prayers are hindered.* This means *all* of your prayers, not just those for your wife. Many men have not seen answers to their prayers because they have not learned this key step. One of the best ways to honor your wife is to pray for her from a heart that is clean before God.[7]

In the Bible, God commands, "All of you be of *one mind*, having *compassion* for one another; *love* as brothers, be *tenderhearted,* be *courteous*" (1 Pet. 3:8, *NKJV,* emphasis added). Paying heed to these five directives can change your life and your marriage and make you the man and husband God wants you to be.

FIVE DIRECTIVES FROM GOD

1. Be of One Mind

It's horrible to have strife in a marriage. It makes us miserable. It affects every area of our life. And it's probably the closest thing to hell we'll ever know on earth. If it goes on long enough, it can destroy everything.

2. Be Compassionate

Have you ever seen your wife suffering, but you don't know what to do about it? Some men become impatient. Others feel so at a loss or overwhelmed by it that it causes them to withdraw. If you recognize that happening to you, ask God to give you a heart of compassion. To be compassionate toward your wife is to have a deep sympathy for any area in which she suffers and to have a strong desire to alleviate that suffering.

3. Be Loving

Jesus loves us with fidelity, purity, constancy and passion, no matter how imperfect we are. If a man doesn't love his wife in the same way, he will abuse his authority and his headship, and as a result will abuse *her*. Because you are one with your wife, you must treat her the way you would your own body. You have no idea how much your love means to your wife. Don't withhold it from her, or one way or another you will lose her.

4. Be Tenderhearted

Is there anything about your wife that bothers you? Is there something that she does or says, or *doesn't* do or say, that irritates you? Do you find yourself wanting to change something about her? What happens when you try to *make* those changes occur? Rather than be impatient with your wife's weaknesses, ask God to give you a tender heart so you can pray about them. Ask Him to show you how her weaknesses are a complement to your strengths.

5. Be Courteous

Do you ever talk to your wife in a way that would be considered rude if you were speaking to a friend or business associate?

Are you kind to everyone all day at work, but then you take out your frustration, exhaustion and anger on your wife when you get home? Do you ever allow criticism of your wife to come out of your mouth in front of other people?

Marriage is hard enough without one of the parties being rude, cruel or inconsiderate. Nothing makes a marriage feel more like hell on earth. Nothing is more upsetting, defeating, tormenting, suffocating or provokes the emotions; nothing does more to bring out the worst in us than a marriage where one of the partners is lacking in common courtesy.

Praying about these five simple biblical directives will transform your life and your marriage. No matter how great your marriage is, God wants it to be better. Because God tells us to "be transformed," there is always room for improvement (Rom. 12:2).[8]

Now, having said all that, how do you see these positive qualities of unity, compassion, love, tenderheartedness and courtesy reflected in *your* marriage relationship?[9]

DISCOVER THE ENCOURAGER IN YOU

1. What have you learned from the chapter about your calling as a husband?

2. What does it mean to be an image-bearer of God in your marriage?

3. What, if anything, surprised you about how God defines leadership in marriage?

4. What is your action plan to be a better leader of your family? Describe.

5. How will you pray for your wife?

Questions
Men Ask

OVER A PERIOD OF MANY YEARS, I'VE HAD NUMEROUS DISCUS-
SIONS WITH MEN ABOUT MARRIAGE. I wish I'd made a list of all
the questions and concerns they've asked me. There are a few
concerns I've heard again and again that we'll address here.
That's what this chapter is about. Three issues stand out that
have an effect on your relationship with your wife as well as
helping to bring out the best in her.

QUESTION #1
Why don't we men ask for suggestions from our wives?

Part of the reason is that men look at the facts and usually ignore the element that women focus on—the human dimension.
Women like to figure out how their decisions will affect not
only themselves but also those around them. They enjoy eval-
uating numerous possibilities as well as reflecting upon their
feelings. They enjoy asking questions, gathering information
and searching for solutions. Because of their concern for others,
after they make a decision, they may agonize, "Was it the right
decision or not?" "What if it hurts others, or someone doesn't
approve?" Usually when a man makes a decision, it's been cast
in cement. Does any of this sound familiar yet?

Women seek the opinions of others more than men do.
They enjoy including others in the decision-making process,
whereas a man deals with a situation within the privacy of his
mind and then consults others. If he receives favorable feed-

back, he moves ahead. If not, he'll reconsider. He rarely asks for help—in any arena—because he wants to feel self-sufficient.

A classic example of this is the man who drives somewhere and gets lost. You know what I'm talking about. A wife will suggest stopping at the nearest gas station or making a phone call to get directions or checking the car's GPS if it's available. To the man, this means admitting he's out of control and can't solve his own problem. To him this feels like failure. If he does stop for help, who usually goes in and asks for assistance? You guessed it, his wife.

Feeling out of control is one of the main causes of stress in a man's life. Consider some of the other sources of stress, based on our feeling out of control:

- We are stressed when we're forced to ride in the passenger seat rather than have control of the automobile. I felt that especially when Joyce drove.
- We're stressed when we have to wait for a table at a restaurant or in line for a movie. So what do we do to reduce this stress? We frequently choose to forego the meal or movie to regain our sense of choice.
- We get infuriated by road construction and exasperated at "stupid" drivers who distract or detain us, especially those using cell phones or putting on makeup (or both at the same time!).
- We dread funerals and therapy, and sometimes equate the two as depressing reminders of life's uncertainties and our own frailty.
- We postpone dental and doctor appointments or other procedures that require us to put ourselves in others' hands.

- We're terrified of illness or injury that may interfere with our ability to be in charge of our daily life.
- We prefer requests to demands, and free choice to requests—and we'll demonstrate this by saying no to demands for things we might have actually enjoyed. (I hate this one. It's too convicting—I've done it!)
- We prefer dogs as pets over cats because dogs are more responsive and can be controlled. Cats are independent and get into power struggles with us.[1]

There's another reason we men tend not to ask for suggestions. Most men dislike being wrong, being told they are wrong, even considering they might be wrong, or the worst scenario of all, discovering their wife knew they were wrong before they did! For most men, it's the ultimate in feeling helpless and humiliated. (I've seen exceptions to this based on the security a man finds through a personal relationship with Jesus Christ, allowing Christ to refine the man's attitudes and beliefs.)

To sum it up, we men are afraid of being wrong. Fear makes us expect the worst, misinterpret what others say and act overly defensive. When a wife offers unsolicited advice or suggestions, often it's not perceived as helpful. If a wife says, "Oh, not that way, honey, try it this way instead," many men hear it as, "That's the wrong way. Can't you figure it out?" When she suggests stopping and asking for directions, he hears, "Dummy! How could you get lost? You can't even figure this out."

Because of our defensive filters, husbands and wives often hear something different from what was actually said. It's not so much a matter of being right or wrong as it is a lack of understanding. Marriage provides the opportunity for education, clarification and refinement.

One husband told me, "During the first five years of marriage, I was defensive when Mary made suggestions or gave me any feedback. One evening, when we were out to dinner, she asked me, 'What do you hear me say when I give you a suggestion or some advice?' I thought a minute and I said, 'I guess I resist it a bit. I'm defensive ... and I think you're saying I'm wrong and I'm not doing it right.' Mary said, 'Do I use the words, "You're wrong" or "inept" or "incompetent" when I offer my suggestions?' and I said, 'No, but I guess I hear that; I guess I'm afraid of being wrong.'

"Mary went on to say, 'Could I say it in a different way to make it easier to accept?' At first I was going to say that might be the answer; but then I realized the problem was not with Mary, but with me, and I told her so. I suggested that I try not to assume she was saying or implying I was wrong. She smiled at me and said, 'That'd be great. I don't like to feel I'm wrong either ... so I have an idea of how you might feel. Perhaps we could both see the other's suggestions as an opportunity to grow and become even more proficient than we are now.' That was a great and enlightening evening for us!"

How can this information about decision-making and asking for help be useful to learn? How about talking over your decision-making styles? Encourage your wife to use her style and you affirm the positive features of it. Be willing to try your wife's style in order to understand her perspective, as well as to expand your choices. Don't interpret her questions as a challenge or as stalling. Be open to something new.

It also helps when your wife understands and accepts that you may not ask for help immediately. You like to mull it over for a while, but tell her what you're doing so she doesn't feel you're ignoring her! And if you need her help, ask her. It's a sign of strength and wisdom rather than a weakness to seek help and guidance. The book of Proverbs states:

> My son, if you will receive my words and treasure up my commandments within you, making your ear attentive to skillful and godly Wisdom, and inclining and directing your heart and mind to understanding [applying all your powers to the quest for it] (Prov. 2:1-2, *AMP*).

> Lean on, trust and be confident in the Lord with all your heart and mind and do not rely on your own insight or understanding. In all your ways know, recognize, and acknowledge Him, and He will direct and make straight and plain your paths. Be not wise in your own eyes; reverently fear and worship the Lord and turn [entirely] away from evil (Prov. 3:5-7, *AMP*).

> The way of a fool is right in his own eyes, but he who listens to counsel is wise (Prov. 12:15, *AMP*).

> He who refuses and ignores instruction and correction despises himself, but he who heeds reproof gets understanding (Prov. 15:32, *AMP*).

QUESTION 2
What if I want my wife to change in some areas?

I can think of a dozen comebacks to this question, but I thought better of them. So I'll just share a wise quote:

> We try to change people to conform to our ideas of how they should be. So does God. But there the similarity

ends. The way in which we try to get other people to con-
form is far different than the way in which God works
with us. Our ideas of what the other person should do or
how we should act may be an improvement or an impris-
onment. We may be setting the other person free of behavior patterns that are restricting his development, or we
may be simply chaining him up in another behavioral
bondage. The changes God works in us are always freeing,
freeing to become that which He has created us to be.[2]

Stop and read that again. If your request fits this, then go for
it. If not, then you know what to do.

Whatever change you want your wife to make needs to be ad-
vantageous for both you and her, as well as for the relationship.
It's not your responsibility as her husband to take on the job of
reformer. The Holy Spirit can do that much better. Your task is to
request change with your wife and provide an atmosphere of acceptance and patience that allows God freedom to work. Then
learn to trust God to do the work.

Scripture does *not* say that in order to bring about change in
another person we criticize, tear down, put down, undermine self-
esteem or find fault. Consider these Scripture passages. In fact,
read them out loud:

Do not judge and criticize and condemn others, so that
you may not be judged and criticized and condemned
yourselves. For just as you judge and criticize and condemn others, you will be judged and criticized and
condemned, and in accordance with the measure you
[use to] deal out to others, it will be dealt out again to
you (Matt. 7:1-2, *AMP*).

Then let us no more criticize and blame and pass judgment on one another, but rather decide and endeavor never to put a stumbling block or an obstacle or a hindrance in the way of a brother (Rom. 14:13, *AMP*).

Fathers, do not provoke or irritate or fret your children [do not be hard on them or harass them], lest they become discouraged and sullen and morose and feel inferior and frustrated. [Do not break their spirit.] (Col. 3:21, *AMP*).

If you're a faultfinder, you'll drive your wife away from you. Too often, legitimate requests get swallowed up by finding fault. Here are some reasons why faultfinding is so destructive to your marriage:

Faultfinding will wound your wife. Constant verbal and nonverbal criticism says, "I don't accept you for who you are. You don't measure up, and I can't accept you until you do." In more than 40 years of counseling I've heard so many people in my office cry out in pain, "My husband's criticism rips me apart. He makes me feel like dirt. I don't feel accepted. And right now I'm still looking for someone who will tell me I'm all right." A wounded spouse becomes afraid or angry and retaliates through overt or covert withdrawal, resentment or aggression.

Faultfinding really doesn't change your wife. Why do something that doesn't work? Though she may appear to change her behavior in response to your criticism, her heart rarely changes. Some wives simply learn to cover their inner attitudes with compliance. Then resentment grows and love dies.

Guess what? Faultfinding is contagious. A fault-finding husband teaches intolerance to his wife. So both of you learn to be critical and unaccepting not only of each other, but of yourself.

Faultfinding actually reinforces negative traits and behaviors. When you pay undue attention to your wife's mistakes or even irresponsible behaviors, you tend to reinforce instead of eliminate them.

Healthy marriages have a common ingredient—mutual education. Mutual education means that both of you must become skilled teachers as well as receptive learners. The reason for this is to develop a greater degree of compatibility. If you neglect this education process, your relationship could be in jeopardy.

Mutual education is a gentle process. It involves positive modeling of the desired attitudes or behavior, gentle prodding, being sensitive—not blaming or rebuking. It focuses on the positive, and you want to manage that change so the end result is positive.[3]

I'm sure these things are what you want, too.

I've included some firsthand statements telling how change actually happened in a relationship. This is what one wife said:

I'll admit I'm not the most open person to change. But I guess I've changed quite a bit. I'd like to think it was all my decision and my choice to change, but in reality, Bill was the instigator. And part of it was that he believed I could change and he created a safe atmosphere to do some things differently. It was okay if I failed.

I had some frustrations in both business and social gatherings. I tended to be too accommodating with others and often I would end up regretting my decisions. When I talked them over in advance with Bill, he asked me a question I've now learned to ask myself, "Is this what I want at this time, what I *really* want, or what I think I should want to make others happy?" Since he worked with me on that, I've changed my responses to others.

When we went out socially, I always felt pressure to talk with everyone and make sure they were having a good time. It was really draining, and I'd come back from parties or dinners at church second-guessing myself and wishing I hadn't gone. Bill started asking me the question, "Are you having a good time? If not, why not?" during such an event and it really got me to thinking. He also asked me, "Are these people really expecting you to do all you do, or are these your own expectations?"

Sometimes those questions irritated me, but in his gentle way, Bill forced me to challenge my beliefs and then evaluate them. I've learned that I was making a lot of unfounded assumptions as well. Yes, I've changed, but I have to give Bill a lot of credit.

Take in the words of this husband:

Adjusting to marriage was a difficult process for my wife and me. The first three years were miserable, and we felt more like adversaries than allies. We were both on a crusade to change one another. It wasn't working. Then we decided to try an idea that we read about. We each made a list of all the things that bothered us about each other.

They weren't easy to read. In fact, reading them was more difficult than hearing them. We each read some things we had never heard before.

The next step was different but great. We put our lists in the fireplace and burned them. As we watched them burn and crumble into dead ashes, we just sat there in silence, holding hands and thinking. It had been a long time since we'd had a positive time together like that.

We then made individual lists of all the good things we could think of about each other. It wasn't easy since our focus had been on the negatives. But by the next day our lists were finished. We shared our new lists with one another and then we made a commitment to read this list and affirm one another daily for at least one of these positive traits. But it didn't end there. We posted the lists in the bedroom and continue to add to them as we discover new positive traits. Now when either of us suggests a change for the other, we're more open to considering it since it's expressed in the context of a positive relationship.

If you choose to do this, how do you think this step would impact your marriage? It's worth considering.

CREATING A CLIMATE FOR CHANGE

Let's face it. There will be times when you would like your wife to change. But what guidelines create a climate for change? Your request needs to be reasonable and attainable. In other words, is it something that's possible for your wife to change? If you want to see a basic personality change, forget it. An extrovert will always be an extrovert, and an introvert will remain an introvert. But responses can be modified.

If you want your wife's attitude to change, don't count on it. Can she change your attitude? Doubtful. If you want your wife to "feel what you feel" and feel with the same intensity, you're reaching for the impossible dream. However, you can ask for a change in behavior that can *affect* personality expression, attitudes and feelings. But your request should give you an affirmative response to the question, "Will this request enhance our relationship and create a greater depth of intimacy?" This is the fundamental purpose for change.

The authors of *Two Friends in Love* give us some guidelines:

> When change is needed in our traits and personalities, it is beyond the realm of the man-inspired, man-prompted characteristics. Those that are God-given do not need touching up. They are the way they are. They only need to be acknowledged and appreciated. However, in the man-related realm, when there are characteristics that should be reworked because of the harmful effects they're having on the marriage, exercise great care in the way you handle change.[4]

To create a climate for change, you will need to be persistent and patient. You'll need to keep trying in a creative, sensitive and loving manner, even when it doesn't seem to work. And you will need to be realistic and not expect too much. That's patience.

Will your request for change help your wife as well as you? Will you both become a stronger person? Will it increase Christian growth and maturity? Or is the request not that important after all? If you ask yourself these questions, you can become a skilled teacher, and both of you can assist each other in the growth process.

When I conduct premarital counseling, I ask a number of confrontational questions. In the initial session I ask, "What passage of Scripture would you like your fiancé to implement that will make him or her an even stronger and more mature person?"

You can imagine some of the responses. About half of the individuals need a week to think about the answer. After they select a passage, I share my reason for the question. I tell them it's helpful to run a request for change through the grid of Scripture to see if the Word of God has anything to say about it. (Even if Scripture is silent on the subject, the request may still be legitimate.) Consulting Scripture can help a person refine his requests for change.

For example, if we want our spouses to change something in their character, Galatians 5:22-23 is the ultimate model of the qualities we can encourage our wives toward. We should desire the same qualities for ourselves!

But the fruit of the [Holy] Spirit [the work which His presence within accomplishes] is love, joy (gladness), peace, patience (an even temper, forbearance), kindness, goodness (benevolence), faithfulness, gentleness (meekness, humility), self-control (self-restraint, continence). Against such things there is no law [that can bring a charge] (*AMP*).

Following this passage will certainly bring out the best in each of you.

Question #3
Sometimes I wonder if my wife and I are from different planets. I'll say something totally different from what she hears, even a compliment. And sometimes I don't get what she's trying to get across to me either. It didn't seem this hard when we were dating. Were we just blind and deaf then or have we changed that much, or what? Help!

Let me answer that with an experience my wife and I had several years ago. It really showed the uniqueness of men's and women's communication styles. We were visiting historical Williamsburg in Virginia, a fascinating and charming setting that preserves our colonial history. When we took the tour of the governor's mansion, the tour guide was a man. As we entered the large entry door, he began to give a factual description of the purpose of the room as well as the way it was furnished. He described in detail the various ancient guns on the wall and pointed to the unique display of flintlock rifles arranged in a circle on the rounded ceiling. When he said there were 64 of them, some originals and others replicas, I immediately began counting them (which is a typical male response—we're into numbers). The guide was knowledgeable and he gave an excellent detailed description as we went from room to room. He seemed to be quite structured and focused. I thought it was great.

We had to leave before the tour was completed to meet friends for lunch. Because we both enjoyed the presentation so much, we decided to return the next day and take the tour again. What a difference! This time our guide was a woman. We entered the same room and she said, "Now, you'll notice a few guns on the wall and ceiling, but notice the covering on these chairs and the tapestry on the walls. They are . . ." And with that she launched into a detailed description of items that had either been ignored or just given a passing mention the day before. And on it went throughout the tour.[5]

It didn't take much to figure out what was going on. It was a classic example of gender differences. The first tour guide was speaking more to men and the second guide was speaking more to women. Actually, we ended up with the best tour imaginable because we heard both perspectives. What a benefit it would be to the tourists if the guides incorporated both perspectives into their presentations!

You're not alone in your struggle with communication. For years I've asked men and women in seminar settings to identify what frustrates them about the communication style of the opposite sex. Here's a listing of some of the women's responses:

They don't share their feelings or emotions enough. It's like they grew up emotionally handicapped.

They seem to go into a trance when they're watching sports or when I bring up certain subjects. They're not able to handle more than one task or subject at a time.

Men seem to think they can do things better, even when they can't, and they won't take any advice, even if it helps them.

They don't listen well. They're always trying to fix our problems.

Men need more intuition—get off the factual bandwagon.

Men need to learn to enjoy shopping like we do. They just don't know what they're missing.

Men need more sensitivity, concern, compassion and empathy.

I wish men weren't so threatened by women's ideas and perspectives.

They're so over-involved in their work and career. They want a family but they don't get involved.

Sex—that's the key word. Don't they think about anything else? They're like a microwave oven. Push the buttons and they're cookin'. Their on button is never off.

Here are some other responses that were recorded in a group setting:

Men think too much. There's more to life than thinking.

I wish he didn't think he always had to define everything. I feel as if I've been talking to a dictionary. Every week for the past year my husband has said, "What do you mean? I can't talk to you if I don't understand your words. Give me some facts, not those darn feelings!" Well, sometimes I can't give him facts and definitions. Man shall not live by definitions alone!

I don't think men understand the difference between sharing their feelings and what they think about their feelings. They tend to intellectualize so much of the time. Why do men have to think about how they feel? Just come out with it unedited. He doesn't have to respond like a textbook or edit everything he shares. I wonder if the emotional side of a man threatens him? Of course you can't always control your emotional responses. So what?

My husband is an engineer, and you ought to be around when his engineer friends come over. The house is like a cerebral, cognitive conference! All logical facts. They walk in with their slide rulers and calculators, and it's as though the house were swept clean of any emotional response. They talk, but they don't disclose. They share, but on the surface. They're safe and secure. Sometimes I have this urge to come into the room and start sharing emotions with all sorts of emotional words and then start crying to see how long it would take for some of them to bolt out the door, jump out the window or hide their faces behind a magazine. Why, I could even threaten 10 men inside of a minute. I never realized what power I had. I think I'll do that next time they're over.

What about men? What frustrates them about women? It's generally the opposite of what women say frustrates them about men. Here's what the men said about women in this survey.

They're too emotional. They need to be more logical.

How can they spend so much time talking? When it's said, it's said. So many of them are expanders. I wish they would get to the bottom line quicker and at least identify the subject!

They're too sensitive. They're always getting their feelings hurt.

Why do they cry so easily? It doesn't make sense to me.

I think most women are shopaholics. Their eyes glaze over when they see a shopping mall.

They're so changeable. I wish they'd make up their minds and then keep them made up.

Maybe they think we can read minds, but we can't. I don't think they can either.

What's wrong with the sex drive? Sex is great, only they don't have that much interest. It takes forever to get them interested.

They think they have the spiritual gift of changing men. They ought to quit. We can't be fixed and we don't need to be.

They're so involved with other people and their problems.

Women are moody and negative. You can't satisfy them.

I wish they would leave some things alone. They're always trying to fix something that isn't broken.

Here are some additional responses men have shared in seminars:

I understand her need to talk about us and our relationship. I happen to think there is a right way and a wrong way to talk about things. If you're not careful, the whole thing can get out of hand. It's best to be as rational as possible. If you let it get too emotional, you never can make any good decisions, and if it gets too personal, someone could get hurt. A little bit of distance goes a long way where a lot of these things are concerned.

It's important, first, to set out clearly what the issues are. I don't think women do this very well. They latch on to the first thing that comes to mind, and get totally emotionally involved in it. The next thing you know, you're arguing about everything under the sun, and no one is happy. I believe in a clear definition of the problem at the outset. If she can tell me exactly what is bothering her, we can deal with it logically. If she can't do that, then there's no sense even talking about it.

As we consider some of the unique characteristics of men and women, let's keep two things in mind. First, there are some generalizations that pertain to men and women. But there will always be exceptions in varying degrees. Second, the characteristics unique to men and to women are not negative. It is *not* a fault to be either way. Some of the characteristics will be more pronounced in some people because of personality type as well as upbringing. The problem arises when people feel they are always right or that the way they do things is the only right way. They don't care about understanding and accepting the opposite sex the way they are. The more flexibility a person develops, the more his or her marriage will benefit.[6] And your wife will feel understood and encouraged.

Getting Fluent in a New Language

Let's go further in this communication process. When you communicate with your wife, realize that you're talking with a foreigner, and both of you need to learn one another's language. It's as though you each have a secret code that the other needs to decipher.

I was at a board meeting for a university, and one of the guest lecturers for a marriage conference was Dr. Emerson Eggericks, author of *Love and Respect*. In the few minutes he had to speak to us, he talked about those gender differences. A husband and wife can make the same identical statement but mean two totally different things. For example, if you're going to an event, and you hear your wife say, "I don't have a thing to wear," do you believe that? Do you take it literally? Is that what she really means? What about you? If you said, "I don't have a thing to wear," what does that mean?

A woman's statement, "I don't have a thing to wear," usually means, "I don't have anything *new* to wear or that I want to wear"; whereas your statement usually means, "I don't have anything *clean* to wear." I'm sure you could come up with a list of words and phrases that you both use with different meanings. Clarifying what you mean and asking clarifying questions of your wife will do wonders for the communication process.

Men and women have very different approaches to communication. When a man starts a conversation, it is generally because he perceives there is a problem. If there is no perceived problem, he feels no particular need to talk. His wife, on the other hand, has a constant desire to talk with her husband. She wants to connect him to everything in her life and assumes he wants to connect her to everything in his life.

"Connect" with Me

When your wife begins a conversation with you, assume that she needs to connect the issues of her life together. She doesn't need you to work your male logic into her thinking process. She simply needs you to help her make the connections. That's all. Assist her, not fix her. You will do well if you view the conversation as a journey she is going to lead you on. Pack your bags, go on the journey and encourage her to take the conversation wherever she wants. Many men refuse to do this because they are afraid that if they give their wives permission to talk until they are done, the end will never come. This just isn't true. Most men don't know this, however, because they have never helped their wives finish a conversation.

Your wife is driven to connect. Because she is aware of all the issues of her life, and because it is impossible to fix every issue in her life all at once, she approaches things differently than you. Before she looks for solutions, she interacts with each part of her life and experiences the appropriate emotion of each issue. Things she should be upset with, she gets upset about. Things that are sentimental bring soft words and flowing tears. Things that are exciting bring giggles and enthusiasm. Things that are intense bring focused concentration. Each issue gets its own emotional reaction. That is why she can experience such a range of emotions in one conversation. Just because you, as a man, cannot keep up with her does not mean that your way is better. If you are willing to serve this need of hers, you'll be married to a much happier woman. You'll know when she is done connecting things together because she'll let out a deep sigh and may say something like, "You understand me like no one else in the world" or "You are my best friend. Thanks." You may not really understand what she is going through, but it will definitely make her life better.

A common complaint from men is that their wives ramble on . . . and on . . . and on . . . and on seemingly with no point. Because the man cannot figure out where the conversation is going, he feels powerless to do anything about it. A sense of failure sets in, and he concludes that his wife is unreasonable and unable to think through issues.

A new perspective is needed. Men, to help you understand your wife's need to finish conversations, imagine if everything in your life ended early. What if you were never able to finish a meal because it was taken away from you when you were halfway through? What if every sporting event you watched on TV was turned off five minutes before the end of the game? What if every sexual encounter ended before its climax? What if every project you started had to be abandoned before you were able to finish it? How are you feeling? Can you sense the frustration and irritation this would bring? If life were actually like this, your anger would always be close to the surface, and your motivation to keep pursuing these activities would be shattered.

This is the way your wife feels when she's not able to finish conversations with you. She experiences the same frustration and irritation. Her motivation to keep talking is threatened but her need to talk with you won't go away. She builds up hope that this time you will be interested, only to have it shattered by your insistence on getting to the point. The game has ended early, and the project must be left unfinished and unattended. You can avoid this irritating chain of events by simply taking some time to listen to your wife on a regular basis. She will keep things more connected, and your life will be easier.[7]

One of the greatest gifts you will ever give to your wife is communication—the kind both of you can understand. Think about this: Communication is to love what blood is to the body. Without it, there's no relationship. It may be helpful to review some principles of communication.

The Word of God is the most effective resource for learning to communicate. In it you will find a workable pattern for healthy relationships. Here are just a few of the guidelines it offers:

- "Some people like to make cutting remarks, but the words of the wise soothe and heal" (Prov. 12:18, *TLB*).
- "Pride leads to arguments; be humble, take advice and become wise" (Prov. 13:10, *TLB*).
- "A wise man controls his temper. He knows that anger causes mistakes" (Prov. 14:29, *TLB*).
- "Gentle words cause life and health; griping brings discouragement. . . . Everyone enjoys giving good advice, and how wonderful it is to be able to say the right thing at the right time!" (Prov. 15:4,23, *TLB*).
- "Love forgets mistakes; nagging about them parts the best of friends" (Prov. 17:9, *TLB*).
- "Timely advice is as lovely as golden apples in a silver basket" (Prov. 25:11, *TLB*).
- "A friendly discussion is as stimulating as the sparks that fly when iron strikes iron" (Prov. 27:17, *TLB*).

- "We take our lead from Christ, who is the source of everything we do. He keeps us in step with each other" (Eph. 4:15-16, *THE MESSAGE*).
- "A man who refuses to admit his mistakes can never be successful. But if he confesses and forsakes them, he gets another chance" (Prov. 28:13, *TLB*).
- "Watch the way you talk. Let nothing foul or dirty come out of your mouth. Say only what helps, each word a gift" (Eph. 4:29, *THE MESSAGE*).
- "Let all bitterness and wrath and anger and clamor and slander be put away from you, along with all malice. Be kind to one another, tender-hearted, forgiving each other, just as God in Christ also has forgiven you" (Eph. 4:31-32, *NASB*).
- "For we all stumble in many ways. If anyone does not stumble in what he says, he is a perfect man, able to bridle the whole body as well" (Jas. 3:2, *NASB*).
- "Let him who means to love life and see good days refrain his tongue from evil and his lips from speaking guile" (1 Pet. 3:10, *AMP*, author's paraphrase).

If these behaviors are evident in your marriage, you will be bringing out the best in your wife.

"CHERISH" IS THE WORD

I have one last suggestion, which has not only saved a number of marriages from disaster, but has also taken marriages from a "so-so" level to "this is a great marriage." The principle here in many ways fulfills many of the scriptural guidelines suggested in this book.

Over the years, I have used a pattern for increasing positive behaviors for couples in both counseling and in seminars. I've talked about it and written about it before. It goes by various names, such as "caring behaviors" or "cherishing behaviors." Let me present it in a way so that you can do it for yourself.

Ask each other the question, "What would you like me to do for you to show how much I care for you?" The answer must be positive, specific and something that can be performed daily. The purpose of each action must be to increase positive behavior, not to decrease negative behavior. For example:

- "Please greet me with a hug and a kiss" is positive.
- "Don't ignore me so much" is negative.
- "Please line the children's bikes along the back wall of the garage when you come home" is more specific and thus better than, "please train the children to keep their bikes in the proper place."

Ted would like Sue "to sit next to him on the sofa when they listen to the news after dinner." This is positive and specific. It's better than asking her to "stop being too preoccupied and distant" (a negative and overly general request).

Sue would like Ted "to kiss her good-bye when they part in the morning." This is positive and specific, which is different from "stop being so distant and cold" (a negative and overly general response).

GROUND RULES FOR "CHERISH" REQUESTS

Avoid making vague comments by writing down beforehand your answers to the question, "What would you like me to do for you to show how much I care for you?"

The small, cherishing behaviors *must not concern past conflicts*. Your requests must not be old demands. That is, the requests must not concern any subject over which you have quarreled. The behaviors must be those that can be done on an everyday basis. The behaviors must also be minor ones—those that can be done easily.

These requests should, as much as possible, be something only your wife can fulfill. If they're things that a hired hand could perform, they may create problems. For example, if they're mostly task-oriented, like "wash the car," "take out the trash," "clean out the camper," "have the dishes and house all cleaned up by the time I get home," and so on, they don't reflect intimacy and the building of your personal relationship. Some better responses would be, "Ask me what excites me about my new job," or "Turn out the lights and let's sit holding hands without talking," or "Rub my back for five minutes."

Each list can include 15 to 18 items. Listing as many as 18 creates more interest and makes it easier to follow through with requests. When you give your lists to each other, the only discussion you may carry on about the list is to ask for clarification if it is needed.

Your commitment is to do at least two items on your wife's caring list each day, whether or not she is doing any positive behaviors on your list. I know it sounds unfair, but you can do it.

Here are some suggestions for the "caring" lists:

1. Say "hello" to me and kiss me in the morning when we wake up.
2. Say "goodnight" to me.
3. Sometimes bring me home a pretty flower or leaf.

4. Call me during the day and ask, "How's it going?"
5. Put a candle on the dinner table and turn off the light.
6. Hold me when we're watching TV.
7. Leave me a surprise note.
8. Take a shower or bath with me when the kids are gone.
9. Kiss or touch me when you leave for work.
10. Tell me about your best experience during the day.
11. Hold my hand in public.
12. Tell me I'm nice to be around.
13. Praise me in front of the kids.
14. Ask me how you can pray for me.

Many of the cherishing behaviors you request of your wife may seem unimportant or even trivial. Some may be a bit embarrassing because at first they may seem artificial. That's all right. These small behaviors can set the tone of your relationship. They are the primary building blocks for a fulfilling marriage. They establish an environment of positive expectations and change a negative mindset. I don't know any couple that doesn't want that.

When the lists are completed, exchange them with each other. Discuss the cherishing behaviors you have requested. Don't be hesitant about telling your wife how you would like to have the cherishing behaviors done for you.

For example: "Remember the way you used to bring me a flower when we were first married? You presented it to me when you met me at the door—after you had kissed me. It made me feel really loved."

During the discussion it is likely that both of you will think of a few more cherishing behaviors that you would enjoy receiving. Add them to the lists. The more behaviors on the lists the better. But make sure the lists are approximately equal in length.

The basic principle behind this approach is this: If you will increase your positive actions toward each other, they'll eventually crowd out and eliminate the negative. In addition, behaving in a loving, caring way will generate the habit of responding more positively and can build feelings of love.

DISCOVER THE ENCOURAGER IN YOU

1. What is more typical of you when your wife is talking—to tell her to get to the point, or encourage her to use you as a sounding board? What new insight did you learn in this chapter about a woman's style of communication?

2. When was the last time (if ever) that your wife thanked you for listening to her entire story without interrupting or trying to "fix" any concern she shared?

3. Think back to conversations that have made a difference in your relationship with your wife, for better or for worse. What specific words or phrases came up repeatedly when you spoke to your wife in a negative way; what words or phrases came up when you spoke to her in a positive way?

4. Review the 13 bulleted Scripture passages that are guidelines for communicating with others. Which verse or

verses speak most strongly to you? What words, phrases or behaviors do you need to ask God to help you give up?

5. What requests of your wife would you write on your "Cherish List"?

The Power of a
Praying Man

A **YOUNG WIFE IN MY OFFICE WAS ANIMATED BUT NOT UPSET.** "I never dreamed that what has happened in our marriage during the past year was possible," she said. "We've gone along for years just sort of ho-hum. Nothing bad, nothing spectacular—just steady. I guess we were in a rut. It was comfortable, and I guess we felt, or I did, that this was the way it would always be. But Jim came home from that men's conference and made all kinds of changes. Even though they were mostly positive, it took me awhile to adjust.

"The first thing he did was come up to me and apologize for not telling me that he prayed for me every day and had for years. How would I have ever known? In fact, that's what I started to say, but I caught myself and thanked him for telling me. A week later, he 'casually' asked me how I would feel about praying together and reading from the Bible occasionally. I have to laugh now because it's like he wanted me to but wasn't sure how I would respond. So we did.

"I can't explain why or what happened, but there is this incredible sense of bonding or closeness now that we never had before. We pray, we read, we share. Sometimes I call him and pray a sentence prayer for him over the phone. Others have seen our relationship change. And when they ask, we tell them. I guess we're finally experiencing what the Bible says about cleaving, in the full sense of the word."

What happened to this couple?

We could call it spiritual bonding, spiritual intimacy or spiritual closeness. Whatever it is, it really brought out the best.

What if I asked you, "How close are you spiritually as a couple?" What would you say? Usually there are two responses: (1) "We're not spiritually close" or "We're not as close as we could be"; or (2) "I think we'd like to be." Many couples, when they finally talk about it, discover they would like to be closer spiritually, but they were uncomfortable dealing with it. It was difficult, so it was never discussed. Has that been your experience?

I often hear couples say, "We need to; we want to." What keeps you from developing this area of spiritual togetherness that can bring an even greater depth to the other dimensions of intimacy?

Some say, "We really don't know any couples who do this, and we're not exactly sure how to go about it." Perhaps there is a lack of role models to follow because we don't ask others what they do. We would be embarrassed if asked, so we feel others would be as well. And we avoid putting them on the spot.

Still others say, "We just don't have time. With our schedules we hardly have enough time to say hello to each other, let alone have devotions together."

To relate together spiritually means creatively meshing your schedules. And yet, we have the greatest time-saving gadgets. I'm going to be blunt here: When someone says they don't have time to develop spiritual intimacy in their marriage, I say, "I don't agree. I've never met anyone who couldn't work out the time. It may take some creative juggling, but it's a choice—like so much of the rest of life. You have to be flexible, committed and have realistic expectations for what you want to have happen in the relationship."

Others have said, "We're not at the same place spiritually in order to share this together." Perhaps praying or reading the Bible together would help you become more unified spiritually.

Some husbands have simply asked, "Why? Why develop this? Why do this? I'm not sure of the benefits." If a man says this to me, I won't even debate the issue with him or try to convince him. But I can say this: "I don't know if anyone could really explain why or convince you. Perhaps the best way to discover the benefits of what I'm saying is to try it for a week. Then evaluate the process to see if it does anything for you. Anyone can give one week of his or her life for an experiment such as this."

I know that a man can have a strong personal relationship with the Lord, but never invite his partner into his life to experience the spiritual journey together. When one partner wants this and the other resists overtly or just drags his or her feet, it can have a damaging effect on the relationship.

A friend of mine shared his experience before he and his wife decided to develop this dimension in their relationship:

> When it came to the day-to-day sharing of our own spiritual journeys (the real test of spiritual maturity), it wasn't there.
>
> Jan would want us to read something together, and I would be too busy. She would want us to pray, and I would be too tired. She would share something deeply personal, but I would not respond. I would listen intently, but my sympathetic stares were met with deafening silence. On the rare occasions when I did respond, it was only with a summarization of

what she had said, an acknowledgment, but never a personal reflection.

To Jan, my avoidant behavior communicated that I was not interested in spiritual matters and, to some extent, that I did not care about her needs. Gradually, my excuses and my silence took their toll, and she tired of her efforts. The requests for my involvement, the statements of her need, the times of her own personal sharing—all tapered off. Jan seemed to resign herself to the fact that it just was not going to happen. For whatever reason, we were not going to be spiritually intimate. Our sharing would be limited to crises.

With Jan's resignation came some resentment. This was not a seething caldron type of problem, but on occasion it would become clear that "resignation" had not brought "resolution." Jan still desired the closeness that was missing, and the disappointment was frustrating.[1]

This story is so typical. Many of us avoid this area. Why? It's uncomfortable. We don't feel competent or capable. We'd rather be private about our spiritual life. Sometimes we may feel that our wife prays better than we do.

Many a couple feels close to their partner in every way except spiritually. In that area they feel isolated. But often this isolation can't be kept in check, and it may creep into other areas of a couple's life and impact those areas too. The more one person wants to be close spiritually, and the other resists, the more resentment will build.

Many couples find themselves in this bind, but it can be overcome.

What Is Intimacy?

Intimacy suggests a very strong personal relationship, a special emotional closeness that includes understanding and being understood by someone who is very special.

Intimacy means taking the risk to be close to someone and allowing that someone to step inside your personal boundaries. Sometimes intimacy can hurt. As you lower your defenses to let your wife close, you reveal the real, intimate, secret you to her, which includes your weaknesses and faults. With the real you exposed, you become vulnerable to possible ridicule from her. The risk of pain is there, but the rewards of intimacy greatly overshadow the risk. Believe me, I know.

Although intimacy means vulnerability, it also means security. Openness can be scary, but the acceptance each of you offers in the midst of vulnerability provides a wonderful sense of security. Intimate couples can feel safe and accepted—fully exposed perhaps, yet fully accepted.

It's impossible for a meaningful marriage to exist without intimacy. If you don't know how your wife thinks and feels about various issues or concerns, she is somewhat of a stranger to you.

It's often assumed that intimacy automatically occurs between married partners. But I've seen far too many "married strangers." I've talked to too many husbands and wives who feel isolated from their spouses and lonely, even after many years of marriage. I've heard statements like:

"We share the same house, the same table, and the same bed, but we might as well be strangers."

"We've lived together for 23 years, and yet I don't know my spouse any better now than when we married."

"What really hurts is that we can spend a weekend together and I still feel lonely. I think I married someone who would have preferred being a hermit in some ways."

No, intimacy is not automatic. Actually, there are several dimensions of intimacy. It's not limited to one area of marriage, such as sex. Several elements are involved in creating an intimate relationship. Many marriages have gaps in them for one reason or another. You may be close in two or three areas but distant in others. If you think you have a close, intimate relationship, but you're distant in a couple of them or in each, there's work to be done. Let's consider the various dimensions before looking at the spiritual aspect, because they all relate.

Emotional intimacy is the foundation for relating in a couple's relationship. This isn't easy for most men. There's a sense of closeness when this exists. You share everything in the emotional arena, including your hurts and your joys. You understand each other and you're attentive to your wife's feelings. But this takes work for most men.

Social intimacy involves having friends in common rather than always socializing separately. Having mutual friends to play with, talk with, pray with and give reciprocal support to is reflective of this important dimension.

Sexual intimacy is taken for granted in marriage. Many couples have sex but no sexual intimacy. Performing a physical act is one thing, but communicating about it is another. Sexual intimacy involves satisfaction with what occurs. But it also means you talk about it, endeavor to meet your wife's needs and keep it from becoming routine. There's an understanding of each other's unique gender needs, and flexibility in meeting them.

There is even the dimension of *intellectual intimacy*—the sharing of ideas and the stimulation of each other's level of knowledge and understanding. You are each different, and you have grown because of what your partner has shared with you.

Joyce and I became much more involved in this way in the last 20 years of our marriage. We shared or pointed out some idea or saved something we learned in an article, book, newscast or TV program. We valued each other's opinion. But for this dimension to exist, you need mutual respect. You can't be threatened by the sharing, but must value what's given.

Recreational intimacy means you share and enjoy the same interests and activities. You just like to play together, and it doesn't have to be competitive. You have fun together, and it draws you closer together.

Then we come to *spiritual intimacy*. To keep everything in balance, and to be complete, you also need the other kinds of intimacy. I've seen some couples who have spiritual intimacy but lack social and recreational. That's out of balance.[2]

CREATING SPIRITUAL INTIMACY

I know couples who worship regularly together, but there is no spiritual intimacy. I know couples who regularly read the Scriptures together but have no spiritual intimacy. I know couples who pray and share together but are lacking in spiritual intimacy. I know some couples who don't pray and share, yet they have spiritual intimacy.

What makes the difference? It seems to be their attitudes. Spiritual intimacy is a heart's desire to be close to God and submit to His direction for your lives. It is the willingness to seek His guidance together, to allow the teaching of His Word in your everyday life. It's a willingness to allow God to help you overcome your sense of discomfort over sharing spiritually and learn to see your marriage together as a spiritual adventure. It's a willingness to put Jesus Christ as Lord of your lives and to look to Him for direction in your decisions, such as which house to buy, where to go on vacations or which school is best for the children. He will direct both of you and change your hearts to be in agreement rather than speak just through one of you.

Spiritual intimacy in marriage requires both partners to submit to the leadership and lordship of Christ, instead of competing for control. One author wrote:

We can gather all the facts needed in making a decision. We can thresh out our differences as to the shape and direction our decision should take. We can put off the decision while we allow the relevant information to simmer in our minds. Even then, however, we may be uneasy: we still don't know what is best to do, and the right decisions just won't come.

When we turn to the Lord Jesus Christ and open our consciences to His Spirit's leading, some new events, remembrances and forgotten facts will come to us. A whole new pattern will emerge. We can then move with abandon in a whole new direction that we had not previously considered. Looking back, we may conclude that God's providence delivered us from what would have been the worst possible decision. Jesus as Lord made the difference between deliverance and destruction.[3]

When Jesus is Lord of your marriage, it relieves you of the problem of experiencing a power struggle. Jesus expressed something interesting to His disciples when He said, "You know that those who are regarded as rulers of the Gentiles lord it over them, and their high officials exercise authority over them. Not so with you. Instead, whoever wants to become great among you must be your servant" (Mark 10:42-43).

I've seen marriages in which one member dictates the spiritual dimension by selecting the church to attend, the meetings attended, what magazines and books are allowed, as well as which Bible version is the accepted one! It's difficult to see how this reflects Paul's words: "Outdo one another in showing honor" (Rom. 12:10, *RSV*) to each other.

Even in a spiritually intimate marriage, faith differences may surface occasionally, but that's normal. With tolerance for diversity, couples can have a shared faith relationship that includes his faith, her faith and their faith.

Some couples seem to be able to develop spiritual intimacy, but others never do. What makes the difference? Spiritual intimacy has the opportunity to grow in a relationship that has a degree of stability. When the two of you experience trust, honesty, open communication and dependability, you are more willing to risk being vulnerable spiritually. Creating this dimension will increase the stability factor as well.

For you to have spiritual intimacy, you need shared beliefs as to who Jesus is and the basic tenets of your Christian faith. You may have different beliefs about the Second Coming of Christ, or whether all the spiritual gifts are for today or not. One of you may enjoy an informal church service while the other likes a high church formal service, or one of you may be Charismatic and the other not. It's important that your beliefs are important to you. You've made them something personal and significant for your life. There can still be spiritual intimacy within this diversity.

We hear about mismatched couples when one is a Christian and the other isn't. You can also have a mismatch when both are believers but one wants to grow and is growing, and the other doesn't and isn't![4]

A great way to encourage spiritual intimacy is to share the history of your spiritual life. Many couples know where their spouses are currently, but very little of how they came to that place. You could use the following questions to discover more about your partner's faith:

1. What did your parents believe about God, Jesus, church, prayer, the Bible?
2. What was your definition of being spiritually alive?
3. Which parent did you see as being spiritually alive?
4. What specifically did each teach you directly and indirectly about spiritual matters?
5. Where did you first learn about God? About Jesus? About the Holy Spirit? At what age?
6. What was your best experience in church as a child? As a teen?
7. What was your worst experience in church as a child? As a teen?
8. Describe your conversion experience. When? Who was involved? Where?
9. If possible, describe your baptism. What did it mean to you?
10. Which Sunday School teacher influenced you the most? In what way?
11. Which minister influenced you the most? In what way?
12. What questions did you have as a child/teen about your faith? Who gave you any answers?

13. Was there any camp or special meeting that affected you spiritually?
14. Did you read the Bible as a teen?
15. Did you memorize any Scripture as a child or teen? Do you remember any of that Scripture now?
16. As a child, if you could have asked God any questions, what would they have been?
17. As a teen, if you could have asked God any questions, what would they have been?
18. If you could ask God any questions now, what would they be?
19. What would have helped you more spiritually when you were growing up?
20. Did anyone disappoint you spiritually as a child? If so, how has that impacted you as an adult?
21. When you went through difficult times as a child or teen, how did that affect your faith?
22. What has been the greatest spiritual experience of your life?

Probably the most important question is, How important is prayer together for you as a couple? On a scale of 0 to 10, it's got to be a 10. No other way to put it! Rather than thinking of prayer together as a couple as a duty, a drudgery or a negative mandate, think of it as the gift from God that it is.

Over the years, I've collected statements or quotes from others whose words have encouraged and challenged me in my own marriage. Think about the following statements about prayer:

Prayer is an awareness of the presence of a holy and loving God in one's life, and an awareness of God's relations to one's husband or wife. Prayer is listening to God, a valuable lesson in learning to listen to one another.

It is only when a husband and wife pray together before God that they find the secret of true harmony; that the difference in their temperaments, their ideas and their tastes enriches their home instead of endangering it.

Lines open to God are invariably open to one another, for a person cannot be genuinely open to God and closed to his mate. Praying together especially reduces the sense of competiveness in marriage, at the same time enhancing the sense of completeness.

Scripture also tells us to pray:

As for me, far be it from me that I should sin against the Lord by ending my prayers for you; and I will continue to teach you those things which are good and right (1 Sam. 12:23, *TLB*).

You haven't tried this before, [but begin now]. Ask, using my name, and you will receive, and your cup of joy will overflow (John 16:24, *TLB*).

Don't worry about anything; instead, pray about everything; tell God your needs and don't forget to thank him for his answers (Phil. 4:6, *TLB*).

Always keep on praying (1 Thess. 5:17, *TLB*).

Admit your faults to one another and pray for each other so that you may be healed. The earnest prayer of a righteous man has great power and wonderful results (Jas. 5:16, *TLB*).

GUIDELINES FOR PRAYING TOGETHER

How do you start praying together as a couple? Why not begin by praying by yourself for your partner? Ask God to bless and to lead your spouse. I know couples that call one another during the day to tell them they're praying for each other. Other couples ask each other before they part for the day, "How can I pray for you today?" At the conclusion of the day, it gives you something to discuss. When I was on a trip, I found notes in my clothes from Joyce, stating that she was praying for me.

The easiest way to begin praying together is to take the time and set a time to do it. I've heard so many say that with their schedules it's almost impossible. I disagree. Creativity and flexibility can make it happen. You can put your arms around each other for 30 seconds and pray before you leave for the day, or after dinner. Couples can pray together over the phone when they're apart. Creative couples write their prayers and send them to each other via email. With cellular phones couples can pray while driving (hopefully with their eyes open) and make contact in this way. You can text your prayers to one another.

When you start praying together at home, perhaps it's best just to share some requests and then pray silently together. There is no threat in this.

Praying aloud is something you grow into. It may take awhile to develop a comfort level. Communication doesn't always have to be vocal. We're bombarded with noise all the time. Sometimes couples struggle with audible prayer, because they don't communicate very much with each other or anyone else. Or one spouse feels that the other is much more articulate and fluent. It could be true, but this is not a time for comparison or competitive endeavor. It's time for learning to accept who you are. I always felt that my wife's prayers were much more detailed and in-depth than mine. But that never hindered me from praying aloud.

I like the journey that Charles and Martha Shedd experienced in learning to pray together.

We would take turns telling each other things we'd like to pray about. Then holding hands, we would pray each in our own way, silently.

This was the beginning of praying together that lasted. Naturally, through the years we've learned to pray in everyday language. Seldom with "thee." We laugh, we argue, we enjoy. We hurt together, cry together, wonder together. Together we tune our friendship to the Friend of friends.

Do we still pray silently together? Often. Some groanings of the spirit go better in the silence.

"I've been feeling anxious lately and I don't know why. Will you listen while I tell you what I can? Then let's pray about the known and unknown in silence."

"This is one of my super days. So good. Yet somehow I can't find words to tell you. Let's thank the Lord together in quiet."

Negatives, positives, woes, celebrations, shadowy things—all these, all kinds of things we share in prayer. Aloud we share what we can. Without the vocals we share those things not ready yet for words.

Why would this approach have the feel of the real? Almost from the first we knew we'd discovered an authentic new dimension.

In becoming best friends with each other, we are becoming best friends with the Lord.

And the more we sought his friendship, the more we were becoming best friends with each other.[5]

One of the other reasons for praying silently has to do with the unique way God has created us in both our gender and personality differences. Most of us men prefer to put things on the back burner and think about them for a while. If we have the opportunity to reflect on what we want to pray about, we're eventually more open to praying. Extroverts find it easier to pray aloud because they think aloud; whereas, introverts need to think things through silently in their minds before sharing. Silent prayer is less threatening. Some prefer reflecting for a while first and writing out their prayer. There's nothing wrong with this.

THE RESULTS OF PRAYING TOGETHER

There are benefits to praying together. When a man and woman marry, they no longer think and act as a single person. It's no longer "I" but "we." All life is lived in connection with another person. Everything you do affects this significant person. You're a team of two, and when both of you participate, you function better. When you confront problems and crises in your life (and you will), it's a source of comfort and support to know that here's another person who will pray for you and with you. When you're struggling financially, or with problems at work;

when you have tough decisions to make, or a medical crisis; to be able to share the burden with your spouse lightens the load.

Couples need to pray together for the health of their marriage. When you married, you entered into a high-risk adventure. The vows you took at your wedding will be attacked on all sides. Praying together will make your marriage stronger as well as help to protect you from reacting sinfully toward your spouse.

Scripture's promise about the effectiveness of prayer includes the prayers of married couples. Jesus said, "Again, I tell you that if two of you on earth agree about anything you ask for, it will be done for you by my Father in heaven. For where two or three come together in my name, there am I with them" (Matt. 18:19-20).

Couples who have prayer lists and see the results of answered prayers will be encouraged as they see how God works in their lives.

When couples pray together, it has an impact on disagreements, conflicts and anger expressed toward each other. When you see your spouse as a child of God, valuable and precious in His sight, someone He sent His Son to die for, wouldn't that have an effect on how you pray for him or her? In the book *If Two Shall Agree* by Carey Moore and Pamela Roswell Moore, Carey put it plainly:

> To place Christ at the center of our homes means, of course, to tell Him, "You are our God," not just at prayer time but all day long. I cannot be careless or insensitive in what I say to Pam and then pray with her. Nor can either of us treat anyone else rudely or engage in gossip and criticism or allow conceit and pride to rule in our

relations with others, and expect God to hear our prayers at the end of the day.[6]

Have you ever felt like this when it comes to prayer? "I just don't know what to say when I pray. Sometimes I'm at a loss for words."

If you've ever felt this way, you're not alone. We've all felt like this at some point. Often it's when we attempt to pray that we become very conscious of a spiritual struggle in our life. As we sit down to pray, our minds wander. Every few minutes we sneak a look at the clock to see if we've prayed enough. Has that happened to you when you pray alone? It has to me. But it's interesting that when couples pray together, it happens less often.

The Holy Spirit is God's answer when we don't know how to pray. You and I cannot pray as we ought to pray. We are often crippled in our prayer lives. That's where the work of the Holy Spirit really comes into play. He helps us in our prayer lives by showing us what we should pray for and how we ought to pray. That's quite a promise!

J.B. Phillips translates Romans 8:26-27 in this manner:

The Spirit also helps us in our present limitations. For example, we do not know how to pray worthy as sons of God, but his Spirit within us is actually praying for us in those agonizing longings which never find words. And God who knows the heart's secrets understands, of course, the Spirit's intention as he prays for those who love God.

One of your callings in marriage is to assist your partner when he or she needs help. You are always to be listening for a call for assistance. Similarly, there is someone looking out for us when we need help in our prayer lives: the Holy Spirit. There are several specific ways that He helps us.

First, *the Spirit intercedes for you* when you are oppressed by problems in life or when you feel down on yourself. He brings you to the place where you can pray. Your ability to begin praying is prompted and produced by the working of the Holy Spirit within you. There may be times when all you can do is sigh or sob inwardly. Even this kind of prayer is the result of the Spirit's work.

Second, *the Spirit reveals to your mind what you should pray for.* He makes you conscious of such things as your needs, your lack of faith, your fears, your need to be obedient, and so on. He helps you identify your spiritual needs and bring them into the presence of God. He helps you by diminishing your fears, increasing your faith and strengthening your hope. If you're at a loss to know what you need to pray for about your partner or even what to pray for together, ask the Holy Spirit to intercede for you.

Third, *the Spirit guides you by directing your thoughts* to the promises of God's Word that are best suited to your needs. He helps you realize the truth of God's promises. The discernment you lack is supplied to you by the Spirit. Perhaps you're looking for a verse to apply to your marriage. Again, help is available through the Spirit.

Finally, *the Spirit helps you pray in the right way.* He helps you sift through your prayers and bring them into conformity with the purpose of prayer.

When you experience a crisis, it may be difficult for you to talk. But you and your spouse can hold each other and quietly allow the Holy Spirit to pray for you. This is called the silent prayer of the heart.

When you are having difficulty praying, remember that you have someone to draw on for strength in developing your prayer life.

When is the best time for a couple to pray? You decide for yourself. It may vary or it may be set. There will be all kinds of interferences from the phone and TV, and child interruptions and exhaustion. But a commitment to be faithful in prayer can override excuses. James Dobson shares a situation he and his wife, Shirley, experienced:

> I'll never forget the time a few years ago when our daughter had just learned to drive. . . . It was during this era that Shirley and I covenanted between us to pray for our son and daughter at the close of every day. Not only were we concerned about the risk of an automobile accident, but we were also aware of so many other dangers that lurk out there in a city like Los Angeles. . . . That's one reason we found ourselves on our knees each evening, asking for divine protection for the teenagers whom we love so much.
>
> One night we were particularly tired and collapsed into bed without our benedictory prayer. We were almost asleep before Shirley's voice pierced the night. "Jim," she said, "we haven't prayed for our kids yet today."
>
> I admit it was very difficult for me to pull my 6′ 2″ frame out of the warm bed that night. Nevertheless, we got on our knees and offered a prayer for our children's safety, placing them in the hands of the Father once more.
>
> Later we learned that (our daughter) Danae and a girlfriend had gone to a fast-food establishment and

bought hamburgers and Cokes. They drove up the road a few miles and were sitting in the car eating the meal when a policeman drove by, shining his spotlight in all directions, obviously looking for someone.

In a few minutes, Danae and her friend heard a "clunk" from under the car. They looked at one another nervously and felt another sharp bump. Then a man crawled out from under the car. He was unshaven and looked like he had been on the street for weeks. He tugged at the door attempting to open it. Thank God, it was locked. Danae quickly started the car and drove off . . . no doubt at record speed.

Later when we checked the timing of this incident, we realized that Shirley and I had been on our knees at the precise moment of danger. Our prayers were answered. Our daughter and her friend were safe![7]

We keep appointments with others and make sure we're always available for certain TV shows. Similarly, when you establish a specific time or pattern for prayer, and keep to it consistently, it becomes a regular part of your life. Some couples pray in their kitchen, family room, bedroom, car or on walks. Work out what's best for you.

Sometimes it helps to read prayers out loud that others have written. For years (ever since college!) off and on I've used a book of daily prayers by John Baillie called *A Diary of Private Prayer*. Reading the psalms aloud can be a prayer. You can pray about everything, and I mean everything.

Recently, I found a fascinating resource that personalizes passages of Scripture into prayers for a husband and wife. It is called *Praying God's Will for My Marriage* by Lee Roberts. It simply takes passages of Scripture and rewords them. By reading these aloud for a while, any couple could learn to do this for themselves. Here is a sampling:

> I pray that my spouse and I will be swift to hear, slow to speak, slow to wrath, for the wrath of man does not produce the righteousness of God (James 1:19-20).

> I pray that my spouse and I will always love the Lord our God with all our heart, with all our soul, with all our mind, and with all our strength and that we love our neighbor as ourselves (Mark 12:30-31).

> I pray that when my spouse and I face an obstacle we always remember that God has said, "Not by might nor by power, but by my Spirit" (Zechariah 4:6).

> I pray that if my spouse and I lack wisdom, we ask it of You, God, who gives to all liberally and without reproach and that it will be given to us (James 1:5).

> I pray that because freely my spouse and I have received, freely we will give (Matthew 10:8).

> I pray, O God, that You have comforted my spouse and me and will have mercy on our afflictions (Isaiah 49:13).

> I pray that my spouse and I will bless You, the Lord, at all times; and that your praise continually be in our mouths (Psalm 34:1).

I pray to You, God, that my spouse and I will present our bodies a living sacrifice, holy and acceptable to God, which is our reasonable service. I pray also that we will not be conformed to this work, but transformed by the renewing of our minds, that we may prove what is good and acceptable and the perfect will of God (Romans 12:1-2).[8]

Prayer is one of the best ways to experience closeness. When your wife is discouraged, go up to her and hug her, and pray a one-line prayer of support. You can do this with your eyes open and looking her in the face. When she is upset or stressed, you could touch her on the arm and pray, "Lord, give strength and peace; lift the pressure and show me how to support my loved one." This in itself can be supportive.

What has prayer done for couples? Listen to what some have said:

"We both feel that communication with God deepens . . . the spiritual and emotional intimacy we share with one another," one couple wrote, "Prayer is the means by which we build upon the Lord's love for us as the foundation of our marriage, and the medium by which we achieve spiritual agreement (Amos 3:3). The goal of our prayer life is spiritual unity, emotional oneness and marital harmony."

"Sharing our spiritual lives," said Joel and Maria Shuler, "is one of the ways we work at being truly intimate. We believe that God wants us to be one, to be united in every way possible. Our total couple intimacy is enhanced by our couple prayer. With God, we are at our most vulnerable. It is a gift we give to each other, a special time." This is from a couple who found praying together "awkward" at first.

Joel and Maria are Catholics and have been committed to prayer together since Joel's conversion from Judaism some 10 years ago. "At first," they recall, "we had to pray mostly traditional prayers" from a book, but Maria knew them so well she would run ahead of Joel. At one point their inability to pray at the same pace struck them as very funny. "We laughed so hard we couldn't continue with the prayer, but the experience freed us up to be more comfortable and natural before the Lord," Maria says.

"We believe that God wants us to be united in mind, heart and body. We work toward unity in every area of our lives, and have much to glean when we share our faith and spirituality with each other. We see how we complement and learn from each other, and thank God for bringing us together. God, Joel and I are like a three-ply cord that is woven and intertwined."[9]

If you want to bring out the best in your wife, be the spiritual leader.

If you want to bring out the best in your wife, pray for her.

If you want to bring out the best in your wife, pray together.

DISCOVER THE ENCOURAGER IN YOU

1. Do you pray on a regular basis for your wife, and with your wife? Do you read God's Word together as well? If you do not, why not?

2. How have you defined "intimacy" to this point in your life? Has your definition changed based on what you have read?

3. Why is spiritual intimacy in marriage so important to the health of your total relationship?

4. Can you imagine the effect on your marriage relationship when you use God's Word as your prayers? Why not try it for a one-month experiment, and then note the difference it has made in your marriage.

5. Prayer is such an encouraging way to experience God's work in your life. So what better way to apply all that you have learned about how to bring out the best in your wife than to ask God to guide your steps as you cultivate your home environment? Today, ask God to help you find new ways to encourage your wife.

Prayer of Commitment

Father, I want to encourage my wife, but in so many ways I don't know how. However, I do know that Your Holy Spirit can instruct me and guide me in my efforts to build up my relationship with my wife and to be the leader that You've called me to be. Help me to get past any ingrained habits of reacting and any wrong attitudes. I specifically ask You to help me with [list any specific issues]. Amen.

Some **Concluding Thoughts**

THIS IS NOT AN EASY BOOK TO WRITE FOR ONE SIMPLE REASON:
I am no longer married. I was for 48 years. I wanted it to continue, for it was a good and fulfilling marriage. Joyce was a loving, gracious woman who deeply cared for her Lord and others. Instead of living longer and perhaps experiencing 50 or even 60 years, God had other plans. On September 15, 2007, He called Joyce home. So after all these years of living "with," I've had to learn to live "without." During my months of intense grief, I journaled. My thoughts and feelings became a book, *Reflections of a Grieving Spouse.*

There was one section that I believe fits into the conclusion of this book. This is part of my own personal journey. I hope it generates some thinking on your part about what you can do with the years you have left with your wife.

NEVER ENOUGH

In life, the phrase "never enough" resides in most of us. Some would admit to it, whereas others would deny its presence. Who wouldn't want more of whatever brings satisfaction or delight to our lives. For some it's a constant nagging sense of dissatisfaction, which diminishes the benefit of what they have received, while for others it's because what they experienced was so wonderful they want it to continue if possible.

Parents are heard to tell their children, "You are never satisfied."

Spouses are heard to tell their spouses, "You are never satisfied."

The "never enough" desire can create greed or generosity, selfishness or compassion.

We're admonished to have this feeling by what others have said to us. "You could have studied (practiced, worked out, listened, paid attention) more" and we incorporate their admonition into our own belief system.

Sometimes we wonder if we couldn't have done more, if we really had done enough. I wonder . . .

Saving Private Ryan sent me down this pathway in my mind, and it's come back from time to time over the past few months of my grief over Joyce. In the movie by the same name, a squad of soldiers is deployed to find this man in order to bring him home since his other brothers have already been killed. They eventually find him, but in the battles several of the soldiers are killed, including the captain portrayed by Tom Hanks. As the captain lies dying on a bridge, and the battle has been won, he whispers to Private Ryan, "Earn this . . . earn this," and so Ryan goes through his life with those words ringing forever in the back of his mind: "Men died for you. Live up to their sacrifice for you. Don't let your life be wasted, for it was bought by the blood of others."

How similar to our own spiritual redemption—purchased by the blood of another. At the conclusion of this film, Private Ryan is elderly and takes his family to Europe to visit the gravesite of his captain. His face reflects his memories as well as his feelings, and his unspoken question of wonderment is, "Did I earn this? Did I do enough? Could I have done more?"

As his wife walks up to join him, with a sad, painful expression on his face, he turns to her and says, "Tell me I've led a good life. Tell me I'm a good man." Perhaps these were thoughts that haunted him over the past decades. He could have asked himself these questions thousands of times, like many of us do. But now he voiced them, for he wanted to hear the affirmation, "You are," which he did.

Don't we all have questions of wonderment about ourselves—who we are, who we could be, what we could have done, or what we will be able to do?

When a loved one dies, there will be questions. Was I a good husband to this woman? What could I have done differently? More of or less of? Sometimes these questions reflect just that— a question. In some cases, they're evidence of regret or a wish that something could have been more or less or could have occurred or didn't occur.

I've heard some say, "I have no regrets." Well, perhaps; but deep within us, no matter how much we gave or did, or who we were, is really that sense of satisfaction. A conviction that *it was* enough. Or could we, along with the belief "I really did all that I could or wanted to give," also have that feeling "Did I really do enough? Could I have done more?"

I do. I wonder about many things. It may have been enough for us, but was it enough for the others? For that's what really counts. Was it enough for Joyce? Was it sufficient? Could I have done more or less in some areas? I wish I knew. I don't and won't know.

Like Private Ryan, we live with wonder and unanswered questions.

And it's not just questions that arise about the last months of being together, but over the 48 years of togetherness.

And so I struggle with the same questions: Did I do enough? Could I have done more? Some say these are futile questions, for how can anyone formulate an answer that is factual rather than emotional? But perhaps that's why the question needs to be voiced, to be asked—to give words to the emotion.

The benefit is probably not in any answer but in the introspective process leading to the question. And so I ask, What more could I have done, as Private Ryan asked . . .

- Was I attentive enough?
- Did I listen to you enough?
- How could I have helped and supported you more in your times of confusion?
- Did I walk with you enough during the "terrible" days?
- Did I pray with you enough? No, definitely not.
- Did I turn the radio up enough in the darkness of night so you could hear the music you loved? Oh, how you loved the Word expressed in music!
- Did I encourage you enough in your uniqueness as a person?
- Did I encourage you enough in your art?
- How could I have helped you more with Matthew?[1]

Endnotes

Book 1: Bringing Out the Best in Your Husband

Chapter 1: You Are Called to Be an Encourager

1. Alan Loy McGinnis, *The Friendship Factor* (Minneapolis, MN: Augsburg Publishing House, 1979), pp. 101-102.
2. Robert Sherman, Paul Oresky and Yvonne Rountree, *Solving Problems in Couples and Family Therapy* (New York: Bruner Mazel, 1991), pp. 27-28.
3. Lee Blaine, *The Power Principle* (New York: Simon & Schuster, 1997), pp. 161-162.
4. Dennis and Barbara Rainey, *Building Your Mate's Self-Esteem* (Nashville, TN: Thomas Nelson Publishers, 1993), p. 23.
5. John C. Maxwell, *Be a People Person* (Wheaton, IL: Victor Books, 1994), p. 137.
6. Ibid., pp. 134-135.
7. Blaine, *The Power Principle,* pp. 125-126.
8. Ruth Harms Calkins, *Lord, Could You Hurry a Little* (Wheaton, IL: Tyndale House, 1984), p. 102.
9. Don Dinkmeyer and Lewis Lasney, *The Encouragement Book* (Englewood Cliffs, NJ: Prentice Hall, 1980), pp. 50-83, adapted.
10. H. Norman Wright and Gary J. Oliver, *How to Bring Out the Best in Your Spouse* (Ann Arbor, MI: Servant Publications, 1995), pp. 240-247, adapted.
11. Dr. Richard Matteson and Janis Long Harris, *What If I Married the Wrong Person?* (Minneapolis, MN: 1996), pp. 116-117.

Chapter 2: The Discouraged Husband (He's Not a Pretty Sight)

1. Lewis E. Losaney, *Turning People On—How to Be an Encouraging Person* (England Cliffs, NJ: Prentice Hall, Inc., 1977), pp. 9-31.
2. H. Norman Wright, *The Power of a Parent's Words* (Ventura, CA: Regal Books, 1991), pp. 102-103.
3. Clifford Notarius and Howard Markman, *We Can Work It Out* (New York: G.P. Putnam & Sons, 1939), p. 28.
4. Ibid., pp. 123-124.
5. H. Norman Wright, *Secrets of a Lasting Marriage* (Ventura, CA: Regal Books, 1995), pp. 53-57.
6. Willard R. Harley, Jr., *His Needs, Her Needs* (Grand Rapids, MI: Fleming H. Revell, 1986), p. 12.
7. H. Norman Wright, *What Men Want* (Ventura, CA: Regal Books, 1996), pp. 118-119.
8. Dr. David Ferguson, Dr. Teresa Ferguson and Holly Thurman, *The Pursuit of Intimacy* (Nashville, TN: Thomas Nelson Publishers, 1993), pp. 45-56.

Chapter 3: To Encourage Him, You Have to Understand Him

1. Dennis and Barbara Rainey, *Building Your Mate's Self-Esteem* (Nashville, TN: Thomas Nelson Publishers, 1993), p. 223.
2. H. Norman Wright, *Communication: Key to Your Marriage* (Ventura, CA: Regal, 2000), pp. 118-119.

3. Michael Gurian, *The Wonder of Boys* (New York: Putnam Books, 1996), pp. 20-24.
4. Stephen Arterburn and Dr. David Stoop, *The Angry Man* (Dallas, TX: Word Publishers, 1991), pp. 58-59.
5. Gary B. Lundberg and Joy Saunders Lundberg, *I Don't Have to Make Everything Better* (Las Vegas, NV: Riverpark Publishing Co., 1995), pp. 18-19.
6. Carolyn N. Bushing, *Seven Dumbest Relationship Mistakes Smart People Make* (New York: Villard Publishers, 1997), pp. 86-87.
7. H. Norman Wright, *Understanding the Man in Your Life* (Dallas, TX: Word Publishers, 1989), pp. 27-31.
8. Ibid., pp. 27-31.
9. H. Norman Wright and Gary J. Oliver, *How to Bring Out the Best in Your Spouse* (Ann Arbor, MI: Servant Publications, 1995), pp. 69-71.
10. H. Norman Wright, *Secrets of a Lasting Marriage* (Ventura, CA: Regal Books, 1996), pp. 122-125.
11. Ibid., pp. 167-168.

Chapter 4: Husbands Speak Out
1. Daniel Levinson, *Seasons of a Man's Life* (New York: Ballantine Books, 1978), pp. 332-333.
2. Robert Lewis and William Hendricks, *Rocking the Roles* (Colorado Springs, CO: NavPress, 1991), p. 12.
3. Bill Hendricks and Doug Sherman, *Your Work Matters to God* (Colorado Springs, CO: NavPress, 1987), p. 87.
4. John Gray, *Men Are from Mars, Women Are from Venus* (New York: HarperCollins, 1992), p. 27.
5. Ibid., pp. 20-21,81.
6. John Gray, *Mars and Venus Together Forever* (New York: Harper Perennial, 1994), pp. 106-148, adapted.
7. H. Norman Wright, *What Men Want* (Ventura, CA: Regal Books, 1996), pp. 112-122, adapted.
8. Lucy Sana, *How to Romance the Man You Love* (Rocklin, CA: Prima Publishers, 1966), p. 168.
9. Wright, *What Men Want*, pp. 86-90.
10. Author Unknown.

Chapter 5: What Not to Do (or The Worst Mistakes You Could Make)
1. Nancy Groom, *Married Without Masks* (Colorado Springs, CO: NavPress, 1989), p. 91.
2. Janet Congo, *Free to Be God's Woman* (Ventura, CA: Regal Books, 1985), pp. 47-70, adapted.
3. Ibid., pp. 70-71.
4. Carolyn Bushang, *Seven Dumbest Relationships Mistakes Smart People Make* (New York: Villard Publishers, 1997), pp. 154-168, adapted.
5. Barbara DeAngelis, Ph.D., *Secrets About Men Every Woman Should Know* (New York: Delacorte Press, 1990), pp. 23-32, adapted.
6. James Walker, *Husbands Who Won't Lead and Wives Who Won't Follow* (Minneapolis, MN: Bethany House Publishers, 1989), pp. 100-101. Used by permission.
7. Ibid., pp. 74-75. Used by permission.
8. DeAngelis, *Secrets About Men Every Woman Should Know*, pp. 46-50, adapted.

Chapter 6: Sex and Romance—Yes! It Does Bring Out the Best
1. Archibald Hart, *The Sexual Man* (Dallas, TX: Word Publishing, 1994), p. 5.
2. Ibid., p. 61.
3. Ibid., pp. 78-81, adapted.
4. H. Norman Wright, *Holding On to Romance* (Ventura, CA: Regal Books, 1987), p. 130.
5. Ibid., pp. 134-136, adapted.
6. Ibid., pp. 180-181.
7. Clifford Penner ad Joyce Penner, *Men and Sex* (Nashville, TN: Thomas Nelson Publishers, 1997), pp. 155-156.
8. Wright, *Holding On to Romance,* pp. 200-202.
9. Penner and Penner, *Men and Sex,* pp. 158-181, adapted.

Chapter 7: Women Who Encourage Their Husbands Speak Out
1. Howard and Jeanne Hendricks, general editors with LaVonne Neff, *Husbands and Wives* (Wheaton, IL: Victor Books, 1988), p. 277.

Chapter 9: The Power of a Praying Woman
1. Stormie Omartian, *The Power of a Praying Parent* (Eugene, OR: Harvest House, 1995), pp 18-19.
2. Ibid., p. 17.
3. Carole Mayhall, "The Stale Mate," *Today's Christian Woman,* May/June 1991, p. 39.
4. Quin Sherrer, *How to Pray for Your Family and Friends* (Ventura, CA: Regal Books, 1990), pp. 43-44.
5. Lee Roberts, *Praying God's Will for My Marriage* (Nashville, TN: Thomas Nelson Publishers, 1994), pp. 1,9,19,28,115,102,227,267.

Book 2: Bringing Out the Best in Your Wife

Chapter 1: Believe in Your Wife
1. Lysa Jenkinson, *Capture Her Heart* (Chicago, IL: Moody Press, 2002), p. 93.
2. Alan Loy McGinnis, *The Friendship Factor* (Minneapolis, MN: Augsburg Publishing House, 1979), pp. 101-102.
3. Lee Blaine, *The Power Principle* (New York: Simon & Schuster, 1997), pp. 161-162.
4. John C. Maxwell, *Be a People Person* (Wheaton, IL: Victor Books, 1994), p. 137.
5. Ibid., pp. 134-135.
6. Blaine, *The Power Principle,* pp. 125-126.
7. Don Dinkmeyer and Lewis Lasney, *The Encouragement Book* (Englewood Cliffs, NJ: Prentice Hall, 1980), pp. 50-83, adapted.
8. Dr. Richard Matteson and Janis Long Harris, *What if I Married the Wrong Person?* (Minneapolis, MN: 1996), pp. 116-117.

Chapter 3: Wives Speak Out
1. One Hundred Women with Dan True, *What Do Women Want from Men?* (Grass Valley, CA: Blue Dolphin Publishing, 1994), pp. 42-43.
2. Ibid., p. 129.
3. Clifford I. Notorius and Howard J. Markman, *We Can Work It Out: How to Solve Conflicts, Save Your Marriage, and Strengthen Your Love for Each Other* (New York: GP Putnam's Sons, 1993), pp. 20-21.

4. Ibid., pp. 123-124, adapted.

5. Gregory Papcak, MSW, *The Exceptional Seven Percent* (New York: Citadel Press, 2000), pp. 164-167.

6. True, *What Do Women Want from Men?* pp. 209-211.

Chapter 4: Understand Your Wife

1. Barbara Rosberg, *Connecting with Your Wife* (Wheaton, IL: Tyndale House, 2003), pp. xvii-xviii.

2. Phillip C. McGraw, Ph.D., *Relationship Rescue* (New York: Hyperion, 2000), p. 221.

3. Scott Halzman, M.D., with Theresa Fox, *The Secrets of Happily Married Men* (New York: Jossey-Bass, 2006), adapted, pp. 81-86.

4. Ibid., pp. 87-88.

5. Rosberg, *Connecting with Your Wife*, p. 58.

6. Lillian Glass, Ph.D., *Complete Idiot's Guide to Understanding Men and Women* (Indianapolis, IN: Alpha Books, 2000), adapted, p. 33.

7. Halzman, *The Secrets of Happily Married Men*, adapted, pp. 172-176.

8. John Gray, Ph.D., *Mars and Venus Together Forever* (New York: Harper & Row, 1996), pp. 148-149.

9. Willard F. Harley, Jr., *His Needs, Her Needs* (Grand Rapids, MI: Zondervan, 1986), pp. 77-78.

10. David L. Leucke, *The Relationship Manual* (Columbia, MD: The Relationship Institute, 1981), adapted, p. 25.

Chapter 5: Romancing Your Wife

1. *Webster's New Collegiate Dictionary*, p. 996

2. Lucy Sanna and Kathy Miller, *How to Romance the Woman You Love—The Way She Wants You To!* (Rocklin, CA: Prima Publishing, 1995), p. xvii.

3. Ibid., pp. 184-185.

4. Ibid., adapted, p. 158.

5. Ibid., pp. 158-159.

6. Joseph Dillow, *Solomon on Sex* (Nashville, TN: Thomas Nelson, 1977).

7. Willard F. Harley, Jr., *His Needs, Her Needs* (Grand Rapids, MI: Zondervan, 1986), p. 38.

8. Ibid., p. 47.

9. Leo F. Buscaglia, *Loving Each Other* (New York: Random House, Inc. Faucett Columbine, 1984), adapted, pp. 135-146.

10. Original source unknown.

11. David Luecke, *The Relationship Manual* (Columbia, MD: The Relationship Institute, 1981), adapted, p 74.

Chapter 6: God's Plan for Husbands

1. Gary Thomas, *Sacred Marriage* (Grand Rapids, MI: Zondervan, 2000), p. 33

2. Ed Young, *The Ten Commandments of Marriage* (Chicago: Moody Press, 2003), p. 11.

3. Stormie Omartian, *The Power of a Praying Husband* (Eugene, OR: Harvest House Publishers, 2007), p. 23.

4. Bryan Chapell, *Each for the Other* (Grand Rapids, MI: Baker Books, 1988), adapted, pp. 47-50.

5. Ibid., p. 51.

6. Ibid., p. 52.

7. Omartian, *The Power of a Praying Husband*, p. 33.

8. Ibid., pp. 35-41.
9. H. Norman Wright, *One Marriage Under God* (Portland, OR: Multnomah Publishers, 2005), adapted, pp. 19-36.

Chapter 7: Questions Men Ask
1. Georgie Witkin-Lanoil, *The Male Stress Syndrome* (New York: New Market Press, 1986), p. 129.
2. James G. T. Fairfield, *When You Don't Agree* (Scottsdale, PA: Herald Press, 1977).
3. Jeanette Lauer and Robert Lauer, *Til Death Do We Part* (New York: Routledge, 1986), adapted, p. 158.
4. Ed and Carol Neuenschwander, *Two Friends in Love* (Portland, OR: Multnomah Press, 1986), p. 108.
5. Norm Wright, *Communication: Key to Your Marriage* (Ventura, CA: Regal, 2000), pp. 118-119.
6. Michael McGill, *The McGill Report on Male Intimacy* (San Francisco: Harper & Row, 1985), p. 74.
7. Bill and Pam Ferrel, *Men Are Like Waffles—Women Are Like Spaghetti* (Eugene, OR: Harvest House, 2001), pp. 28-30.

Chapter 8: The Power of a Praying Man
1. Donald R. Harvey, *The Spiritually Intimate Marriage* (Grand Rapids, MI: Fleming H. Revell, 1991), p. 24.
2. Ibid., p. 24.
3. Howard and Jeanne Hendricks, general editors, with LaVonne Neff, *Husbands and Wives* (Wheaton, IL: Victor Books, 1988), p. 158.
4. Harvey, *The Spiritually Intimate Marriage,* adapted, pp. 54-56.
5. From "How to Start and Keep It Going," by Charlie and Martha Shedd, cited by Fritz Ridenour in "Praying Together," *The Marriage Collection* (Grand Rapids, MI: Zondervan Publishers, 1989), pp. 442-443.
6. Carey Moore and Pamela Roswell Moore, *If Two Shall Agree* (Grand Rapids, MI: Chosen Books, Baker Book House, 1992).
7. James C. Dobson, *Love for a Lifetime* (Portland, OR: Multnomah Press, 1987), pp. 51-52.
8. Lee Roberts, *Praying God's Will for My Marriage* (Nashville: Thomas Nelson, 1994), pp. 1,9,19,28,115,162,227,267.
9. Moore and Roswell Moore, *If Two Shall Agree,* pp. 194-195.

Chapter 9: Some Concluding Thoughts
1. H. Norman Wright, *Reflections of a Grieving Spouse* (Eugene, OR: Harvest House, 2009).

23117355R00253

Printed in Great Britain
by Amazon